Edward Alfred Pollard

The Virginia Tourist

Sketches of the Springs and Mountains of Virginia

Edward Alfred Pollard

The Virginia Tourist
Sketches of the Springs and Mountains of Virginia

ISBN/EAN: 9783337190514

Printed in Europe, USA, Canada, Australia, Japan

Cover: Foto ©ninafisch / pixelio.de

More available books at **www.hansebooks.com**

THE

VIRGINIA TOURIST.

SKETCHES OF THE

SPRINGS AND MOUNTAINS OF VIRGINIA:

CONTAINING

AN EXPOSITION OF FIELDS FOR THE TOURIST IN VIRGINIA; NATURAL
BEAUTIES AND WONDERS OF THE STATE; ALSO ACCOUNTS OF
ITS MINERAL SPRINGS; AND A MEDICAL GUIDE TO
THE USE OF THE WATERS, ETC., ETC.

BY

EDWARD A. POLLARD,

AUTHOR OF "THE BLACK DIAMONDS," "THE LOST CAUSE," ETC. ETC.

ILLUSTRATED BY ENGRAVINGS FROM ACTUAL SKETCHES.

PHILADELPHIA
J. B. LIPPINCOTT & CO.
1870.

Entered according to Act of Congress, in the year 1870, by

J. B. LIPPINCOTT & CO.,

In the Clerk's Office of the District Court of the United States for the Eastern District of Pennsylvania.

LIPPINCOTT'S PRESS,
PHILADELPHIA.

ANNOUNCEMENT.

THE Author comes before the public, this time, humbly bearing what may be described to many readers in America as the discoveries or revelations of a *New World!*

So little known, even among his own countrymen, is Transmontane Virginia; not now referring to its undeveloped industrial resources, but to its unappreciated wealth of natural scenery, its unknown rivers and its unexplored mountains; the beauties and wonders which designate this region as the richest field, the most abundant area of adventure and discovery, yet remaining for the American Tourist; and, added to these gifts, the curious and magnificent dowry that Nature has bestowed in the distribution here of Mineral Springs unequaled in the world.

It is believed that the many interests contained in this work will embrace many classes of readers. In brief, it is designed to be a Traveller's or Tourist's Guide, a Medical Guide, a Sketch Book and an Artist's Portfolio of the Great Mountain Belt of Virginia; a region in which is displayed a Scenery that, positively, when known, will admit no rivals on this continent, and in which is provided the additional and illimitable attraction of the great *Sanitarium* of America.

The author has told the unaffected story of a real tour, but he has attempted something more than a slight or a temporary work. He has designed, not without some pride in the undertaking, a great patriotic contribution to the State of Virginia, developing a source of prosperity as fruitful and real as that of her fields and mines; and he has aimed to lay a worthy literary offering on those high altars of worship which he has found in some of the grandest scenes of Nature.

Among the few persons he has to thank for any favors the author would testify here his gratitude to his artist friend, Warren C. White, Esq., whose assistance in sketching some of the scenes of the work not only deserves acknowledgment, but whose affectionate companionship on the journey is remembered in another sense and with a tenderer gratitude.

The author has but little else to be thankful for in the way of encouragement of his work. However, he is accustomed to submit his writings on their merit alone; and he is proud to say that, however the envy of criticism may have interposed and expostulated, the favors of the reading public have never yet failed to give him signal rewards.

EDWARD A. POLLARD.

HOME IN VIRGINIA.

CONTENTS.

CHAPTER I.

INTRODUCTORY.

                                                PAGE

Neglect of the Natural Scenery of Virginia—A Glance over its Beauties and Wonders—THE NATURAL STRUCTURE OF VIRGINIA—Design of our Work—" Old " Virginia—Natural Divisions of the State—Piedmont Virginia—The Valley of Virginia—Husbandmen of the Valley—South-west Virginia—Picture Galleries constituted by the Mountains—Three Notable Pictures—Virginia as a Recent *Discovery*—THE SPRINGS REGION OF VIRGINIA—THE SANITARIUM OF AMERICA—The Boundaries of this Region—Its Relation to the Mississippi Valley—Hotel Accommodations at the Springs—Their Defects—Investments in Springs' Property—GUIDE TO THE VIRGINIA TOURIST—The Angle which measures the Springs Region—How it may be Traversed—Stage Routes over the Mountains—TABLE OF ROUTES IN AND ABOUT THE SPRINGS REGION—A Topographical *Coup d'Œil* of a Tour in Virginia.................................. 13

CHAPTER II.

LYNCHBURG AND ITS SURROUNDINGS.

Lynchburg recommended as a Starting-point of a Tour in Virginia—Superior Attractions of South-west Virginia for the Tourist—Obscurities of this Part of the State—Description of "the Hill City"—Mountain Scenery around Lynchburg—A Royal Peculiarity of the Blue Ridge—Ancient Memories of Lynchburg—The James River and Kanawha Canal—

George Washington's Vision—THE GREAT WATER LINE OF VIRGINIA—A Vision of Romance as well as of Empire—The Boast of New River—An Heraldic Ensign for " New " Virginia.. 37

CHAPTER III.

FROM LYNCHBURG TO THE NATURAL BRIDGE.

Recent Neglect of the Natural Bridge by Sight-Seers—Directions of Route to it—On the Banks of the James—Balcony Falls—Views from the Stage Road—Scenery on North River—THE NATURAL BRIDGE—First Sight of it—Curious Proportions of Art in its Structure—The Angle of Ascent—View from the Creek below—A Strange Imagination—Gates of Hell—The Natural Bridge compared with Niagara Falls—Two Illustrations of the Sublime in our American Schools of Æsthetics—CLIMBING THE NATURAL BRIDGE—Testimony of an Eye-witness... 48

CHAPTER IV.

THE PEAKS OF OTTER.

Journey to the Peaks—Experiences by the Wayside—Panoramic Views—Picture of a Feudal Proprietorship—Grape-growing in the Mountains—Toilsome Ascent—On the Peak—Standing up in the great Hollowness of the Sky—Peculiar Sublimity of the Peaks of Otter—A Religious Reflection on the Scene—Bird of the Mountain—The Sublime Effect of a Striking Contrast—The Little Earth and the Great Heavens.. 60

CHAPTER V.

ALLEGHANY SPRINGS AND SURROUNDINGS.

Route to the Alleghany Springs—At the Heart of the Mountains of Virginia—Access to the Springs North and South—The Water *sui generis*, and the most elaborate in the World—Analysis of the Water—Medical Guide to its Uses—Wonderful Effects of the Water—The Scenery around the Springs the most Remarkable in Virginia—PUNCHEON RUN FALLS—Romance of its Discovery—Climbing the Mountain—A Rough Journey—Sublimity of the Falls—Descent Two Thousand Feet—Scenes on Puncheon Run—" Purgatory"—The Deserters' Fortress—FISHER'S VIEW—Looking from the Mountain's Top—Characteristics of Mountain Views—Sublime Effect of a View of and beyond the Alleghany...... 70

CHAPTER VI.

A WEEK IN SOUTH-WEST VIRGINIA.

Going to the Natural Tunnel—A SEAT OF EMPIRE—Bristol and its Surroundings—A RIDE THROUGH TWO STATES—The White Ships of the Mountains—Estillville—A Glance at the Mineral Wealth of the Country—" Boone's Trace"—Indian Relics and Traditions—THE NATURAL TUNNEL—First View of the Tunnel—Its Dimensions—Frightful Passage through it—Sublime View from the Lower Entrance—Speculations as to the Cause of this great Natural Wonder—The Tunnel seen by Sunrise—Sublime and Picturesque Effects—Association of an Indian Story—The Tragedy of Masoa—The Adventure of Dodson—A Battle with an Eagle—THE CAVE OF THE UNKNOWN—Almost Lost—A Cavernous Country—BLOOMING ROCKS—A Poetical Countryman—THE HOLSTON SPRINGS—Analysis of the "Hot Spring"—Attractions of the Place.................................. 91

CHAPTER VII.

THE MONTGOMERY WHITE SULPHUR SPRINGS, AND THE YELLOW SULPHUR SPRINGS.

Locality of the Montgomery White Sulphur Springs—Beauties and Attractions of the Place—Medical Description of the Water—Reputation of the Springs for Social Gayeties—A Criticism on Southern Society—A GALA DAY AT THE MONTGOMERY WHITE SULPHUR—Description of a "Grand" Tournament—"Gander-pulling"—A Knightly Defence of the Tournament—A Beautiful Illumination in the Mountains—A Night Picture—THE YELLOW SULPHUR SPRINGS—Analysis and Virtues of the Water—Within Sixty Feet of the Alleghany Summit.. 119

CHAPTER VIII.

A TRIP TO NEW RIVER, SALT POND, BALD KNOB AND LITTLE STONY CREEK.

Plan of a Trip into Giles County—Crossing the Mountain—A Ride through a Night-storm—The Adventure of a Lost Hat—Benighted in the Woods—Singular Experience with a Mountaineer—One of "Nature's Noblemen"—EGGLESTON'S WHITE SULPHUR SPRINGS—SCENERY OF NEW RIVER—"Pompey's Pillar" and "Cæsar's Arch"—"The Narrows"—"Hawk's Nest"—New River compared with the Rhine—LITTLE STONY FALLS—Terrific Leap of the Water—SALT POND—A Lake of Fresh Water suspended among the Clouds—A Submerged Forest—Part of the Lake Unfathomable—An Old Lady's Theory—An Emigrant Company of East Tennesseeans—Talks with Them—A Picture of Solitude—BALD KNOB—Looking into Five States—Effects as compared with the View from the Peaks of Otter—Cloud-ships—A Fog-ocean—A Hospitable Rest..... 130

CHAPTER IX.

TAZEWELL COUNTY THE SWITZERLAND OF VIRGINIA.

How to go to Tazewell County—Description of the Route—Saltville—The Alps of Virginia—"THE PEAK"—An Indian Battle-Field—Dial Rock—Climbing the Cliffs—VALLEY OF THE CLINCH RIVER—View of it on a Summer's Evening—Burke's Garden—Abb's Valley—The Flora of South-west Virginia—The Tazewell Historical Society—Was Tazewell County ancient Xuala?—Social and Literary Culture in the Mountains—Romance on Horseback—A RIDE THROUGH THE MOUNTAINS—HOMES OF THE MOUNTAINEERS—Comparison of the Mountaineer and the Lowland Rustic—Dialect of the Mountains—Traditions of the Early Commerce of South-west Virginia—" Uncle Billy "—Isolation of the Mountaineer's Home—An Observation of Mr. Horace Greeley—Simplicity of a Primitive Society—A COMEDY IN THE MOUNTAINS—" Sal's" Courtship—The " beatingest " Dog—A Lock of Hair—Reflections on the Mountain Maid —A Vision of Beauty.......... 154

CHAPTER X.

LEXINGTON AND THE VALLEY OF VIRGINIA.

From South-west Virginia to Lexington—COYNER'S SPRINGS—Reputation of the Water—LEXINGTON AND ITS SURROUNDINGS—" The Athens of Virginia "—Its Educational Institutions—General Lee's Professorship—THE GRAVE OF STONEWALL JACKSON—A curious letter from a former Governor of Virginia—THE ROCKBRIDGE BATHS—A Buoyant Water—THE ROCKBRIDGE ALUM SPRINGS—Mountain Views—A Remarkable Advantage of the Watering-Places of Virginia—Testimony of Dr. Cartwright—THE VALLEY OF VIRGINIA—Its Physical Geography—Peculiarity of Minor Formations—The Luray Valley—View from Thornton's Gap—A Recollection of the War—Mineral Springs on the Flanks of the Alleghany—The Valley of Virginia, as a Fancy and as a Reality.......... 180

CHAPTER XI.

A ROMANCE OF THE VALLEY OF VIRGINIA.

Geographical Fables of the early Virginia Colonists—Mr. Jefferson's belief in the Mastodon—A Curious Indian Myth—The Barrier of the Blue Ridge—Influx of Pennsylvania Germans into the Valley of Virginia—The Adventures of John Salling—The Lewis Family—Remarkable Result of a Buffalo Hunt—Burden's Grant—Andrew Lewis' Explorations on Greenbrier River—The Shawnees—Death of Cornstalk—Relations of the Germans and of the Scotch-Irish in the Valley—Characteristics of the Scotch-Irish—

Their Churches and Schools—Three Generations in the Valley—The Progress of America in Miniature............... 198

CHAPTER XII.

THE GREENBRIER WHITE SULPHUR SPRINGS.

The Railroad through the Mountains—Site of the White Sulphur Springs—Pleasing Scenery—The Springs in 1772—Hotel Improvements—The Grounds—Analysis of the White Sulphur Water—Remarks on the Use of Mineral Waters—Popular Errors on the Subject—Debauchery in Mineral Waters—A Guide to the Use of the White Sulphur Water—The Theory of *Fresh vs. Stale*—The Bathing Establishment—Life at the Springs—"Jenkins" in Virginia—A Ball-room Conversation—A Southern Editor on Society and Comfort at the Springs—Why Virginians "can't keep Hotels"—An Anecdote of Boniface—The White Sulphur Hotel a Superior one.. 222

CHAPTER XIII.

THE SPRINGS OF MONROE AND BATH COUNTIES.

The Springs Region described from the White Sulphur as a Centre—Surrounding Scenery—View from Dry Creek—THE OLD SWEET SPRINGS—A Ride through the Rain—An Aristocratic Resort—Medical Description of the Old Sweet Water—THE SALT SULPHUR SPRINGS—Observations of Dr. Mütter—THE RED SULPHUR SPRINGS—Reported cures of Consumption—THE BLUE SULPHUR SPRINGS—Analysis of the Water—Routes from the Greenbrier White Sulphur Springs into Bath County—THE CASCADE OF THE FALLING SPRINGS—Views through a New Atmosphere—THE BLOWING CAVE—Thomas Jefferson's Description Incorrect—THE WARM SPRINGS MOUNTAIN—Looking from "Flag Rock"—THE HOT SPRINGS—Virtues of the Thermal Baths—THE WARM SPRINGS—An Indian Tradition—THE HEALING SPRINGS—Beauties of Scenery—Pleasures of Trout-fishing—Dr. Burke on these Springs

CONTENTS.

—The Bath Alum Springs—Effects of the Water—Painful Aspects of Invalidism at the Springs............ 239

CHAPTER XIV.

FROM STAUNTON TO WEYER'S CAVE.

The Chesapeake and Ohio Railroad—Looking to the Occident—A Wilderness of Riches—The Town of Staunton—A Glance at its History—Views of the Surrounding Country—The Virginian "Apology" for Roads—Weyer's Cave—A Subterranean Diorama—"Formations" and Curiosities—Peculiarities of Subterranean Nomenclature—"Washington's Hall"—A Flight of Fancies—Dimensions of the Cave—Estimate of it as a Natural Wonder—Age of the Stalactites—The Sublimity of Nature as a Workman......... 260

Practical Hints to the Virginia Tourist............... 273

LIST OF ILLUSTRATIONS.

	PAGE
MAP OF SPRINGS REGION	FRONTISPIECE.
SCENE ON NORTH RIVER	50
PUNCHEON RUN FALLS	77
"PURGATORY"—VIEW ON PUNCHEON RUN	85
FISHER'S VIEW—THE ALLEGHANY SPRINGS	89
THE NATURAL TUNNEL—THE INTERIOR	103
" " " —LOOKING OUT	106
LITTLE STONY FALLS	143
VIEW FROM THORNTON'S GAP—THE LURAY VALLEY	195
VIEW ON DRY CREEK	240
TROUT POOL	256

THE VIRGINIA TOURIST.

CHAPTER I.

INTRODUCTORY.

Neglect of the Natural Scenery of Virginia—A Glance over its Beauties and Wonders—THE NATURAL STRUCTURE OF VIRGINIA—Design of our Work—"Old" Virginia—Natural Divisions of the State—Piedmont Virginia—The Valley of Virginia—Husbandmen of the Valley—South-west Virginia—Picture Galleries constituted by the Mountains—Three Notable Pictures—Virginia as a Recent *Discovery*—THE SPRINGS REGION OF VIRGINIA—THE SANITARIUM OF AMERICA—The Boundaries of this Region—Its Relation to the Mississippi Valley—Hotel Accommodations at the Springs—Their Defects—Investments in Springs' Property—GUIDE TO THE VIRGINIA TOURIST—The Angle which measures the Springs Region—How it may be Traversed—Stage Routes over the Mountains—TABLE OF ROUTES IN AND ABOUT THE SPRINGS REGION—A Topographical *Coup d'Œil* of a Tour in Virginia.

T is a subject of complaint, and a sore reflection with Virginians, that the natural scenery of their State, which they claim excels in interest any equal area of the Union, and surpasses that of Europe in the breadth of its panoramas and in many other effects, has been so long neglected, obtaining hitherto so small a patronage of the traveler and the artist. Certainly no other State in the Union can make the same number of exhibitions of the sublime and curious in works of the wonder and cunning of Nature. Yet these are but little known north of the Potomac, and a population unskilled in advertising the attractions of their neighborhood see them neglected, while inferior scenes and resorts in the North are attended every convenient season by tens of thousands of visitors, are displayed in illustrated papers, written of, ostentatiously described, and made objects of curiosity and of interest to the whole world. The writer was recently shown a book entitled *Summer Resorts of America*, in which not a single place attractive to travelers for health or pleasure was noted south of Cape May. Yet here, in this wonderful State of Virginia, we have a well-defined belt of territory containing more than twenty mineral springs, in the variety and efficacy of their waters certainly unequaled in the whole world, and offering the remarkable double attraction that these fountains of health and pleasure are set in a scenery unsurpassed, and wherein stand numerous wonders of Nature, which have been sometimes esteemed by the few foreign travelers who have penetrated to our mountain lands as, indeed, the greatest sights of the American continent.

In years before the war these scenes were visited from abroad to some extent. This awakening interest must have been cut short by the war, or, for some other reason, curiosity has resiled from the mountains of Virginia; for it is certain that scenes among them, once referred to as wonderful and interesting, have fallen into comparative obscurity, and have for years since the war failed to make their appearance, even in the advertisement columns of the newspapers. Yet what beauties and wonders may be swept by a glance of the eye across less than half the breadth of the State!

Take the Natural Bridge in Rockbridge county, its arch fifty-five feet higher than Niagara Falls, its mystic rocks rising with the decision of a wall.

The Peaks of Otter (Bedford county), 5307 feet above the sea-level, where John Randolph, once witnessing the sun rise over the majestic scene, turned to his servant, having no other to whom he could express his thoughts, and charged him "never, from that time, to believe any one who told him there was no God!"

Hawk's Nest, or Marshall's Pillar (Fayette county), the latter name in honor of Chief Justice Marshall, who, as one of the State commissioners, stood upon its fearful brink, the entire spot not affording standing-room for half a dozen persons, and sounded its exact depth to the river margin, which exceeds one thousand feet.

The Natural Tunnel (Scott county), passing one hundred and fifty yards through the solid rock, making a huge subterraneous cavern or grotto, whose vaulted roof rises seventy to eighty feet above its floor, and facing the entrance to which is an amphitheatre of rude and frightful precipices, looking like the deserted thrones of the genii of the mountain.

Weyer's Cave (Augusta county), which has been compared to the celebrated Grotto of Antiparos, traversing in length more than sixteen hundred feet, its innumerable apartments filled with snowy-white concretions of a thousand various forms, among which stands "the Nation's Hero," a concretion having the form and drapery of a gigantic statue.

A mountain scenery, of a portion of which an English traveler, passing through the Kanawha country to the White Sulphur Springs, has written: "For one hundred and sixty miles you pass through a gallery of pictures most exquisite, most varied, most beautiful—one that will not suffer in comparison with a row along the finest portions of the Rhine."

Again, on the very waters of "the Rhine of Virginia," beautiful, wonderful New River, cutting with its steel-blue blade into the very rock, and, even at the base of its cliffs, passing one hundred and fifty feet deep through glittering banks of the mineral wealth of the State.

The Bald Knob, with nothing but a broken crown of rock on its scarred summit, from which we may look as far as eye can reach, and watch the passenger clouds into five States.

The Salt Pond, the mysterious lake hanging among the clouds on the side of Bald Knob, *unfathomable*, or measured in places only by the submerged forest which we see as if cast in bronze in the depths of the emerald waters.

A little farther away "a new Switzerland," compassed in Tazewell county, where "Burke's Garden" smiles in the shadow of "the Peak," and the swift streams dash like arrows through the mountain sides.

And lastly—that the freshness of a recent discovery may adorn the catalogue—the Puncheon Run Falls, discovered near the Alleghany Springs, the water, hurled from the brow of the mountain, descending at an angle near the perpendicular eighteen hundred or two thousand feet—a scene, in its union of the picturesque and grand, unexcelled, yet which had never been noticed until the summer of 1869, but by the rude and stoical mountaineers, who had never thought of advertising it to the world.

But this is only an enumeration of scenes at random. There is a remarkable system of distribution in the natural scenery of Virginia. There is an order in the exhibition—a dioramic order in which its scenes pass before our eyes; a succession of galleries constituted by its rivers and mountains.

This by way of prefatory remark. In affording the reader an introduction to the scenery loosely enumerated above, and to other interests of our work, it will be convenient here to lay the foundation of the tour we propose in some general remarks, and to indicate our plan under some different heads.

THE NATURAL STRUCTURE OF VIRGINIA.

We are not going to write of the physical geography of the State, its geology, or its agriculture. It is not the design of our work to descant on the "resources" of Virginia, to uncover her robes of field and forest, or to throw curious and scientific glances into her beauteous bosom. The author is simply a tourist; he is traveling for pleasure; and he cannot pause to observe what there is of scientific or commercial interest in the country he traverses, unless such as falls obviously under the attention of the ordinary traveler. Such "incidental mentionings" may be not without value or interest. But the main purpose of the author is simply to record the impressions of a real journey from the stand-points of pleasure and recreation. He is a tourist, not a scientific explorer, or even a "commercial traveler;" he is to tell what there is of the beautiful and the enjoyable in "the grand old State"—and the task is plentiful enough. It is distinct enough, too, though it may sometimes fall into reflections on "resources" of the State as seen from the wayside, and mingle something slight of "the material" with the æsthetic and luxurious.

The Natural Structure of Virginia constitutes those remarkable divisions of scenery to which we have already referred. They are divisions which have grown up on differences of topography and soil, and to which the steps are geographical. The common impressions of Virginia which the larger mass of travelers passing hurriedly through it obtain are those of the Atlantic slope, and they are impressions by no means prepossessing. Passing from the Potomac through a series of dreary country towns to the unclean city of Richmond, or floated there from Norfolk on the tidewater of the James, or going even for many miles on the railroads leading from the capital of the State, the traveler on the ordinary routes has but a sorry sight of "old" Virginia, in her galled hills and old fields, worn to exhaustion by the plough and hoe in the culture of tobacco and corn. It is a level and barren picture. The old field pines, the broom sedge and the persimmons are the memorials of "improvement" under the past system of slavery. The traveler from the North thinks of his own populous landscapes, he compares what he sees along the low, scanty banks of the historic rivers of Virginia with the valleys of the Hudson, the Mohawk and the Susquehanna, and, having seen the decays of *Eastern* Virginia, he carries home the impression that there is but little worth seeing in the State, except for those "prospecting" for cheap farms and speculating in impoverished lands.

But never were impressions more partial or unjust. He has traversed but the decayed framework of the beauties of Virginia scenery and the bounties of her soil. He has not yet seen through the blue-gilded mists of the mountains, which his eye has caught only desultorily and in the distance. Let him approach those distant heights, of which he has seen only the faint outline from the windows of the railroad car, and in the picturesque landscape there rise up in perspective the Blue Ridge, the Peaks of

Otter and Monticello, overlooking the grand dome of the University of Virginia.

He is now in Piedmont Virginia. The character of the agriculture is changed. There is a mixed system of farming, planting and grazing. He goes beyond the blue mountains—that mysteriously and beautifully robed boundary which Nature has lifted up into the sky, in the *Blue* Ridge, the barrier for a century against the early enterprise of the Virginia colonist—and new scenes unfold. He has struck the rich soils of clay, loam and limestone—the grand, rock-ribbed belt that girds the mountains from the Potomac to Tennessee and Kentucky, and widens and embraces the beautiful Valley of Virginia. He is in a country where every view is of wonder, and admiration, and thankfulness. The fields are dressed with the green grass and the blue grass; the hills and the mountains and the valleys smile with verdure; there are the golden harvests, and fruits of summer and autumn, and the wealth of flowers; the year is crowned with goodness; the pure "encasing air" is as an invisible garment of inspiration; the pastures are clothed with flocks and herds, which are led into green pastures and lie down by still waters. There are the cattle upon a thousand hills. There are the husbandmen of the Valley, a simple and prosperous race; there are real Arcadians; there Plenty smiles in the sunburnt face; there, in the sweet and fruitful fields, men send up the incense of grateful hearts, and invoke the blessing of Him who "visits the earth and waters it," upon the fruits of honest toil.

Upon these mountain shelves Nature has placed the great stores of her fertilizers, to renovate the worn and barren lands which decline to the sea. Along its entire northern border, throughout the whole extent of the Valley and South-west Virginia, lie buried, deep down in the earth, beds of limestone, cropping out upon the surface everywhere, and inviting capital and enterprise to burn and market millions of tons of it, and to spread it upon the clay and sand soils of all Eastern Virginia. There are no sour growths here; the sorrel, the pines, and the broom sedge have been exchanged for the vigorous cereals and all the healthful blooms of domesticated vegetation.

The topography, the frame of the earth here, is worthy of its garniture. The most remarkable topographical feature of Virginia is the grand gallery constituted by its mountain ranges, the Blue Ridge and the Alleghany, and a distribution of rivers which we shall elsewhere notice; and it is a gallery where are not only piled up the deposits of its wealth and the displays of its bounty, but where the loveliest and the grandest pictures succeed wherever the eye roves. Here are the mountains—that wonderful feature of Nature which is the universal expression of the sublime, the types of the highest mystery; for it is on the mountains where the religions of all men have, by curious universal instinct, placed the oracles of God and the altars of sacrifice. Here are the valleys, the abode of the beautiful; that which the universal spirit of poetry has chosen as its favorite part of earth; here the variegated display, the walk of meditation, the home of the thankful laborer, the loveliness of Nature with the usefulness of man; no longer the severity of the mountain robe of solitude, but the warm colors of human life o the landscape. We are in the Garden of Virginia, a its boundaries are the mountains that stand out as lan marks on the vast and shoreless sea of the azure heavel

Let the traveler now pass out of the Valley of Virginia, crossing the range of the Alleghany where it declines to the south-west—its altitudes sunken and broken—and he is in another division of the State. He passes through a shattered side of a natural gallery, a picturesque confusion, where the great Appalachian system apparently loses its unity and is tossed into a sea of mountains. He passes by the salt wells, that remarkable source of the supply of brine which the wants of six millions of people in a four years' war did not sensibly diminish; a never-failing fountain of waters welling up perennially in the deep, beautiful basin of the richest land in the State. He is now in South-west Virginia. He is in a country richer in mineral resources than California, and more beautiful and various in its natural scenery than any equal area in America. The modern El Dorado boasts only of gold; but here are not only salt, plaster, limestone and marble, but in the same belt, in an area twenty miles in width by sixty in length, are clustered iron, lead, copper, zinc, baryta and numerous other minerals, discovered but not developed. Gold is no longer the measure of mineral wealth. The lead mines of South-west Virginia supplied the Confederacy with shot during the war. The iron alone hid in its mountains is said by Pennsylvania iron men to be worth, if developed, more than the gold mines of California. And just beyond this richly-jeweled belt, toward the Cumberland range and the Ohio, is a vast coal field, richer, more extensive, than the coal field of Pennsylvania—the "black diamonds" more indispensable for the crown of Modern Commerce than the gems of Golconda.

Here, too, the natural scenery of Virginia has its last, and, perhaps, supremest development. It is a region almost unknown to tourists. The wild and rugged scenery at Harper's Ferry, where the mad rush of the mingled waters of the Shenandoah and the Potomac bursts the mountain barrier, has been rendered famous by the pen of Thomas Jefferson; the grandeur and beauty of "Balcony Falls," where the James river makes its passage through the Blue Ridge, glancing and murmuring through the rock-ribbed bosom of the everlasting hills, is a common spectacle to the traveler; but the third grand picture of the same peculiar sort, constituted by the river and its barrier, and fitted in the Mountain Gallery of Virginia—"the Breaks of the Sandy," where the Cumberland range is riven asunder by the accumulated forces of the headwaters of Big Sandy, the mountain rent from apex to base by the rushing and resistless surge—is comparatively unvisited and unknown. There is an order in these three notable pictures of the savage sublimity of mountain and river—a system founded in the relations of the two elements of natural scenery in Virginia; but of these kindred scenes that of the Sandy is undoubtedly the surpassing one. Here is the colossal and ruined "Chimney," standing four hundred feet, in the deep, blue sky, above the other gigantic rocks, the fallen walls and shattered arches of antediluvian architecture. The scene from the bed of the stream has been thus described by one who, like ourselves—and even beyond those routes which we have considered accessible to the ordinary traveler, and which, therefore, limit this work—has sought out the beauties of Virginia scenery: "Bald and perpendicular walls of sandstone rise in naked majesty hundreds of feet above, whilst the waters which chafe and madden at their base are filled and choked by the shattered fragments which have been riven from their summits. Here and there the hand of Nature, the great Restorer, has softened the asperities of the scene, and clothed in verdure and beauty both beetling cliff and precipitous ravine. Here the spruce towers in sombre majesty, or the laurel and ivy throw their dark mantle over the spectral rocks; and there the bramble and the muscadine mingle their foliage and their fruit in wild and graceful beauty, crowning with tender tendrils and purple berries some tempest-riven or lightning-blasted trunk. For three or four miles this wild and savage scene stretches in unbroken continuity."

. . . Yet of the Virginia we have thus described, beyond the dead and uninteresting levels of the East—of Piedmont Virginia, of the Valley of Virginia, of South-west Virginia— how little is known! A Southern writer has ingeniously remarked: "A Northern editor recently visited Virginia, and on his return wrote just such a descriptive account of the people and the country as we should expect from an explorer into an unknown region: Indeed, one of the most noticeable things of the civil war was the *discovery* of Virginia and the Southern States by the Yankees."

While capital and emigrants stand gazing into this *terra incognita*, we may disclose aspects of it to yet another class of adventure and of travel. Fortunately, at the time of this writing, the attention of the country has been powerfully drawn upon Virginia, in the interest of its wonderful industrial resources and of a system of internal improvements that has risen to national importance. It is reasonable that such a vivid and searching regard of the State must, in the end, suggest and develop all the elements of interest which it contains; that the natural scenery which envelopes its resources will not be much longer slighted by the world; that the tourist will follow in the track of adventurers in other pursuits, bringing a novel and important element of travel into the State, and discovering a new world of beauty, as well as new kingdoms of commerce and industry. It is, as seizing this rising interest in Virginia, to reveal to it, along with other aspects, the peculiar objects to which our book is devoted, that we consider our work well designed, and aided by time and opportunity in its claim upon the attention of the country.

But even within the limits of our design we have so far directed the reader but to one of its topics—viz., the natural scenery of Virginia. We have yet to show another curious element of interest, which has so far appeared only in the title or announcement of our work, and which we have delayed in these introductory pages, beyond a bare reference in the first paragraph, for a separate treatment becoming its importance. Associated with the scenes we have rather mapped out than described are the various *Mineral Springs* of Virginia. Here, bound in a natural scenery unsurpassed, fenced by the mountains, is that wonderful sanitary enclosu- Virginia *Medicatrix*—an invitation for health to ' world. It is an invitation which we propose to we out at some length.

THE SPRINGS REGION OF VIRGINIA: THE SANITARIU
AMERICA.

THE territory in which the most famous of the m nd springs of Virginia are sought may be rudely desc*he as a belt or crescent, averaging in width a doubl lar of counties, commencing at the Alleghany Spring et Montgomery county, running north through the co ir of Monroe, Greenbrier, embracing Rockbridge and ts gusta, and having its northern termination or horn at

INTRODUCTORY.

the thick group of springs in Bath county. This description will answer our purposes here: it will be enlarged, of course, in the progress of our work; but it occurs to us here to say that, within these boundaries, with an occasional excursion, the traveler may derive most of the interest to be found in the mountain region of Virginia.

The boundaries desultorily sketched above, we repeat, contain by no means the entire Springs Region of Virginia. Beyond these there are outlying mineral waters of value, to which the traveler may have ready access from the great routes of travel through the State. Indeed, the true extent of the Springs Region of Virginia is from near North Carolina, along the Alleghanies and their spurs, quite to the Potomac. The development of mineral springs along the line of the great Appalachian chain, and among its upheavings, extending from the various mineral waters of comparatively recent discovery in Southwest Virginia to the valuable waters of Capon and Berkley in the north; late explorations in the interest of such discoveries; evidences already obtained of the general geological character of this entire range of country, all point to an extension of the Springs Region to embrace the entire eastern and western bases of the Alleghany.

But for the present, and for the purposes of this work, have selected as the Springs Region that where the mountains of mineral water *abound*—where there is, so to speak, a *continuity* of these springs. It is a collection within limits on both sides of the Alleghany mountains, a comparatively small body of territory, but one so rich and various in mineral waters that it may claim the designation, *par excellence*, of the Springs Region of Virginia, and the merit of being a sufficient *sanitarium* for all America.

Within the area described there is every variety of mineral water, a fountain for almost every conceivable disease. It is a body of country to which there is easy access from every portion of the Union. The North and the South, the East and the West, may meet here in the common pursuit of health, or at common resorts of pleasure. But what is most remarkable of the Virginia springs is their peculiar accommodation as a summer retreat from those vast malarious districts which extend through the richest portions of the South and lie in the Valley of the Mississippi. The fertile regions of the Mississippi are liable to fevers (the *calentures* of the Spaniards' time), and will always be so: wherever vegetation is prolific and exuberant—precisely in the richest portions of the South— the wealth which Nature has bestowed is counterbalanced by chills and fevers. The escape from these malarious influences, and from the diseases which abound in summer along all the tributaries of the Mississippi, is naturally to the springs and mountains of Virginia—that area of high land crowned with health-giving waters and beautified by the finest natural scenery of America. It is when the tide of the class of visitors we have described is fully turned into the Springs Region of Virginia that this portion of the State will be developed in its peculiar element of prosperity, creating sources of wealth as real as those to be found in any of the producing industries of the Commonwealth. The springs of Virginia have a future before them that can scarcely be measured. It will be realized when those tides of summer travel from the South which were previously extended to tours in the North, and were distributed from Saratoga and Cape May, are collected, and obtain their true direction to the mineral waters and mountain scenes of Virginia. The extent and peculiarities of the vast populations of the South naturally turned to these as a summer retreat; the numbers, the wealth, the munificent habits of a class of visitors coming from the richest portions of the cotton and sugar regions of the South, will constitute the future prosperity of the springs of Virginia, and be the only limits to what are already the just expectations of the thoughtful and the enterprising.

The only difficulty will be as to the comforts and accommodations of these places. This difficulty is already apparent. The hotel accommodations of the springs of Virginia are generally insufficient or imperfect or unattractive. People traveling for health or for pleasure—especially the latter, persons accustomed to the luxuries of cities—will not visit places, however blessed and adorned by Nature, where there is only a dreary hotel of whitewashed boards, and some thin cottages uniformed with wooden washstands, bare floors and cheap, crying bedsteads. Nor will they be satisfied where the untraveled proprietor, in his coarse estimate of human needs, thinks that only certain quantities of food have to be put into the stomachs of his guests, insensible of the truth that the human stomach of the civilization outside of his mountains needs a delicate chemistry, and that the *cuisine* is really an *art*—not contemptible, as some vulgar satirists have supposed, but one belonging to the dignity of man.

But even where the accommodations are finer and irreproachable, the hotel establishments of the Virginia springs may be said generally to be conducted on false and defective principles. They are usually conducted on the narrow methods of short and exclusive leases; or there is a monopoly of proprietorship that excludes from the grounds everything but its own ideas and fancies. The North builds at all its watering-places *competitive* hotels; it sets up shops and competes for every want of its visitors; and the entire hotel system at such places is conducted on the principle of adaptation to different classes of visitors—comfortable accommodations and necessaries for all, and luxuries for those who wish them, and are able to pay for them. The hotel establishment of the Virginia spring is generally a single caravansary, with *uniformity* of accommodations throughout—the narrow, one-price system of the single hotel, and its stiff rows of cottages as alike as the barracks of a regiment, even to the pine furniture and the huckaback towels. The hotel proprietor of the Northern watering-place calculates that the man who is able and willing to spend his six dollars a day shall find occasion for it; while at the same time he does not neglect the privileges of another who does not want luxuries, who is not able to pay for a private parlor or a special chamber, and who does not demand a degree of accommodation beyond the average guest. The hotel proprietor of the Virginia springs, on the contrary, has but one price and one accommodation. There are no degrees of comfort, or, what is more, degrees of privacy, such as are found in the hotel life of the North; none of its wonderful resources; in short, too much of the old country tavern as it existed before the modern hotel became one of the phenomena of our civilization, an "institution," an empire and a study.

The defective hotel establishment (generally speaking) of the Virginia springs is, doubtless, a check on the prosperity of those places. Happily, however, it is a check that may be readily removed; and the present disposition, shown at the time of this writing, to improve and develop springs property, argues the commencement of an expansion of prosperity that will not be the least among the great elements of wealth in the State. The argument is simply this: There is no disposition now among the people of the Cotton States to go to the Northern cities or watering-places, they greatly prefer the Virginia springs; only *give them, and advertise to them, the accommodations*, and they will come. It is said that in the summer of 1869 there were two thousand visitors at one of these springs. There might as well have been ten thousand there from the great stock of summer custom—persons not only from the South, but from every part of the Union, who should find at these favored spots of Nature the comforts of home and the pleasures of gay society, and who would delight to linger there for at least four months of the year.

Enterprise and better management are yet to be more fully learned by the proprietors of these places. In the lesson of the latter is the art of advertising. It is the custom of the Virginia springs to advertise in a few local papers—the lowest appreciation of advertising, a system of waste, since it addresses only those best calculated to know otherwise of subjects in their neighborhood, neglecting those who are removed from sources of information other than comes to them by the skill and enterprise of the advertiser. Such skill and enterprise are yet to carry a knowledge of the Springs Region of Virginia beyond the contracted borders of special localities and to all parts of the country—the knowledge that here, accessible to the traveler from North, South, East and West, is a region more healthful than the fabled islands and more beautiful than Dreamland—a region where Nature has intermingled the fountains of health with the feasts of the eye—where she presses to the lips of the invalid the living waters in the garnished and jeweled urns of mountain rock, and spreads before the eyes scenes lovelier and grander than those which imagination with remote and wandering steps pursues beyond seas and deserts.

It is a striking knowledge: it cannot fail of effects. When the invalids who sigh in every corner of the country shall know the true value of the mineral waters of Virginia; when the æsthetic man of the North, the artist and the tourist shall learn that there is a natural scenery in Virginia which in the richness and variety of its expression is so admirable, unsurpassed perhaps in its whole effects in any equal spaces of the world; when the guide-book of Virginia is admitted into the current literature of our times as freely and commonly as the pretentious and more intricate *vade mecum* of Northern and European tours,—we may justly then expect that a bulk of travel and of wealth will be poured through this region not much less than that which has built up Long Branches and Saratogas, or that which, each summer, crosses the Atlantic to dissipate its curiosity and its money in foreign lands. The future of the Virginia springs is a magnificent speculation, and there are great prizes bound up in it.

At present we are firmly persuaded that there is no field of investment in Virginia that presents such opportunities as does the already awakened improvement of springs property. Nor do we regard this matter only in the light of benefits to a class of property-holders; nor even exclusively in the interest of the numbers resorting to these places for health and pleasure. It is a real element of public prosperity—part of the economy of the resources of Virginia, and pertaining to the interests of the whole Commonwealth. The aggregate r whole State of the development of the Springs Region is no mean consideration. It is an interest not only to the philanthropist concerned with the ills of humanity, not only to men of sentiment and pleasure, but an interest to be cultivated in our public economy, our legislation, our system of internal improvements, our press, our literature, and to be shared by all who truly and in all respects desire the prosperity of Virginia.

GUIDE TO THE VIRGINIA TOURIST.

THE two principal points of departure to the Springs Region of Virginia, and to the Natural Scenery interlocked by these springs or adjacent to them—to that Field of the Tourist which we propose to traverse—are *Staunton* and *Lynchburg*. With these two points held in his mind, the reader may have a clear and comprehensive view of the Springs Region, and of the area of those places which may be most recommended to the attention of the tourist. If we look at the map, we find that the two points, Staunton and Lynchburg, are extremities of a fork of railroads, the Chesapeake and Ohio and the Orange and Alexandria, dividing from the main stem of travel at *Charlottesville;* the real point of junction, however, being twenty-one miles farther east, at Gordonsville, the cars of the Orange and Alexandria and the Chesapeake and Ohio roads running on a double track from Gordonsville to Charlottesville. The geographical angle, however, is at Charlottesville; and it is this angle, one line running through Staunton toward the Ohio, the other through Lynchburg to Tennessee, which measures the Springs Region and that section of the great Mountain Belt of Virginia most interesting in its displays of scenery.

We shall see now how we may penetrate the breadth of this country, and what are its remarkable divisions with reference to the distribution of its mineral waters and natural scenery.

The access to Staunton from the North is by the great route of travel coming down the Orange and Alexandria road from Washington, Baltimore, Philadelphia, New York, etc. The access to Lynchburg from the South and South-west is by the great routes of travel leading up to the Virginia and Tennessee Railroad from Knoxville, Chattanooga, Memphis, New Orleans, Montgomery, Mobile, etc. There is no difficulty in tracing out these broad and common routes on any ordinary map.

The Springs Region of Virginia, which we have elsewhere roughly described, has its upper portion adjacent to Staunton and penetrated by the Chesapeake and Ohio Railroad, while its lower portion rests on the Virginia and Tennessee Railroad. Staunton and Lynchburg are thus the great converging and diverging points of the travel of this region. From Staunton we penetrate that part of this region most thickly populated with springs; the most famous of these resorts being congregated within a limited space of which the Chesapeake and Ohio railroad furnishes all the points of *détour*. From Lynchburg we traverse the south-western tier of springs, less numerous than those which cluster in the upper region, but having the advantage of a more striking diorama of natural scenery; the two elements of attraction being associated and both parallel to the Virginia and Tennessee road.

Let us pass our finger along the lines of these two roads, and we shall enumerate the principal objects of interest the tourist has in either direction.

From Staunton we may go by stages to Augusta Springs

and Weyer's Cave. From Goshen, a little farther on the Chesapeake and Ohio road, by stages to Rockbridge Alum Springs, Rockbridge Baths and Cold Sulphur Springs. From Millboro', by stages, to Bath Alum and Warm Springs. From Covington, by stages, to Hot Springs and Healing Springs. From Alleghany, by stages, to Old Sweet and Red Sweet Springs. *From the Greenbrier White Sulphur Springs*, by stages, to Salt Sulphur Springs, etc., and, indeed, to almost every point within the diagram of the Springs Region.

From Lynchburg, on the Virginia and Tennessee road, we have in succession the Alum Springs at New London, Coyner's, the Alleghany, the Montgomery White Sulphur and the Yellow Sulphur (counting, as in the preceding paragraph, only those springs which are well known). All these are immediately on the rail or within a few miles of it. But we have something more than this tier of mineral waters. In the same direction, or within parallels of convenient travel, we have the Peaks of Otter, the Natural Bridge, the Salt Pond, Bald Knob, Puncheon Run Falls, Burke's Garden, the Natural Tunnel, etc.— a succession of scenes and curiosities adjacent to that of the springs of the South-west, and all having their points of détour from the Virginia and Tennessee road.

We have thus generally described the area of a practicable tour in Virginia and the field of our present work. The natural division into two departments of the Springs Region contained in the angle of the railroads referred to is designed only as an element of simplicity in the geographical description; for the intercommunication of these departments is direct and easy. The intercommunication is by a system of *stage*-routes which cross the angle at various points, and make the whole country contained in it practicable for the traveler. Thus he may cross the angle from the region of the Alleghany Springs or from that of the Montgomery White, both near *Christiansburg*,* to the Greenbrier White Sulphur Springs, and the watering-places yet north of it, by stages all the way, taking Salt Pond and Bald Knob in the route, and passing by the Sweet and Red Sweet Springs; or he may cross lower down, from *Salem*, on the Virginia and Tennessee road; or yet lower down, from *Bonsack's* (Coyner's Springs), taking in succession such objects of interest as the Natural Bridge, Lexington, Rockbridge Baths, etc., to Goshen, or any other point in the northern tier of springs. The details of these routes will be given hereafter as they occur in our journey. For the present, the subjoined table of routes may serve for general reference within the limits of the diagram we have marked out:

TABLE OF ROUTES IN AND ABOUT THE SPRINGS REGION.

From	To	Conveyance.	Miles.
Staunton	Augusta Springs	Stages	12
Staunton	Weyer's Cave	Stages	17
Staunton	Goshen	Ches. and Ohio R. R.	32
Goshen	Cold Sulphur Springs	Stages	1
Goshen	Rockbridge Alum Springs	Stages	8
Goshen	Rockbridge Baths	Stages	9

* The *angle* of the Springs Region is yet more conveniently (in point of distance) crossed by travelers coming *from the South-west* at Newbern, where they may leave the railroad (Virginia and Tennessee) and proceed directly to the Red Sulphur or Salt Sulphur Springs in Monroe county, and thence to the whole northern range of mineral waters commanded by the Greenbrier White Sulphur. But this route leaves out the lower or south-western portion of the Springs Region, neglecting the valuable waters of the Alleghany and the Montgomery White, and is indicated only in cases where a traveler from points south of the Ohio river desires the nearest in miles, to points within what we have designated as the more northern division of Virginia watering-places.

INTRODUCTORY.

From	To	Conveyance.	Miles.
Goshen	Lexington	Stages	21
Goshen	Natural Bridge	Stages	35
Goshen	Millboro'	Ches. and Ohio R.R.	8
Millboro'	Bath Alum	Stages	10
Millboro'	Warm Springs	Stages	15
Millboro'	Covington	Ches. and Ohio R.R.	29
Covington	Hot Springs	Stages	18
Covington	Healing Springs	Stages	15
Covington	Alleghany Station	Ches. and Ohio R.R.	16
Alleghany	Old Sweet	Stages	9
Alleghany	Red Sweet	Stages	8
Alleghany	White Sulphur Springs	Ches. and Ohio R.R.	6
White Sulphur Springs	Blue Sulphur	Stages	22
White Sulphur	Salt Sulphur	Stages	25
White Sulphur	Red Sulphur	Stages	40
White Sulphur	Red Sweet	Stages	16
White Sulphur	Old Sweet	Stages	17
White Sulphur	Hot Springs	Stages	37
White Sulphur	Healing Springs	Stages	40
White Sulphur	Warm Springs	Stages	42
White Sulphur	Bath Alum	Stages	47
White Sulphur	Rockbridge Alum	Stages	62
Lynchburg	Natural Bridge	Canal-boat	36
Lynchburg	Lexington	Canal-boat	40
Lexington	Natural Bridge	Stages	14
Lynchburg	Forrest Depôt	Va. and Tenn. R.R.	11
Forrest Depôt	New London and Alum Springs	Stages	4
Forrest Depôt	Liberty	Va. and Tenn. R.R.	14
Liberty	Peaks of Otter	Country road	12
Liberty	Bonsack's (Coyner's Springs)	Va. and Tenn. R.R.	22
Bonsack's	Natural Bridge	Stages	30
Bonsack's	Lexington	Stages	42
Bonsack's	Sweet Springs*	Stages	47
Bonsack's	White Sulphur, etc. etc.	Stages	64
Bonsack's	Salem	Va. and Tenn. R.R.	13
Salem	Sweet Springs	Stages	36
Salem	White Sulphur, etc. etc.	Stages	53
Salem	Shawsville	Va. and Tenn. R.R.	17
Shawsville	Alleghany Springs	Stages	4
Alleghany Springs	Puncheon Run Falls	Country road	8
Shawsville	Montgomery Wh. Sulphur Station	Va. and Tenn. R.R.	6
Montgomery White	Christiansburg	Va. and Tenn. R.R.	3
Christiansburg	Yellow Sulphur	Stages	4
Christiansburg	New River White Sulphur	Stages	24
Christiansburg	Salt Pond	Stages	32
Christiansburg	Bald Knob	Stages	32
Christiansburg	Salt Sulphur	Stages	40

* Old Sweet and the Red Sweet are but one mile apart.

From	To	Conveyance.	Miles.
Christiansburg	Sweet Springs	Stages	48
Christiansburg	White Sulphur	Stages	65
Christiansburg	Newbern	Va. and Tenn. R.R.	19
Newbern	Red Sulphur	Stages	35
Newbern	Salt Sulphur	Stages	52
Newbern	White Sulphur	Stages	77
Newbern	Glade Springs Station	Va. and Tenn. R.R.	70
Glade Springs Station	Saltville	Branch railroad	8
Saltville	Jeffersonville	Country road	18
Saltville	Burke's Garden	Country road	26
Glade Springs Station	Bristol	Va. and Tenn. R.R.	28
Bristol	Natural Tunnel	Country road	42
Bristol	Holston Springs	Country road	28

The reader may easily trace out on the map the routes noted above as the exigencies of his journey may require. In this place—one of introduction—we design only to give a topographical *coup d'œil* of the country we propose to traverse on a pursuit of pleasure and in the garb of the tourist.

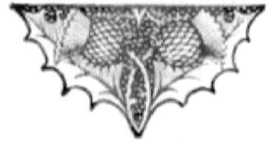

CHAPTER II.

LYNCHBURG AND ITS SURROUNDINGS.

Lynchburg recommended as a Starting-point of a Tour in Virginia—Superior Attractions of South-west Virginia for the Tourist—Obscurities of this Part of the State—Description of "the Hill City"—Mountain Scenery around Lynchburg—A Royal Peculiarity of the Blue Ridge—Ancient Memories of Lynchburg—The James River and Kanawha Canal—George Washington's Vision—THE GREAT WATER LINE OF VIRGINIA—A Vision of Romance as well as of Empire—The Boast of New River—An Heraldic Ensign for "New" Virginia.

YNCHBURG is not made the starting-point of our tour in Virginia by accident. We have made it so by a well-considered design. It is true that the Virginia and Tennessee Railroad leading out of this town does not command as large a number of the springs as does the Chesapeake and Ohio Railroad (a comparison of the *value* of the waters is not made in this place), but it has the advantage, and offers to the tourist the additional compensation, of a scenery lying about its summer resorts unequaled in the State. As our work is in both interests—that of the springs and that of the mountains and other natural wonders—our explorations are then commenced at Lynchburg, and the reader may imagine himself put down in sight of the blue mountains, and close to the most abundant fields for the tourist in our "many-sided" Virginia.

Of all the divisions of the State, South-west Virginia, we repeat, is undoubtedly that most interesting to the tourist, and it, therefore, occupies an indisputable prominence in our work. It is comparatively but little known; it has been neglected in most of the histories of the State; and there is to this day a lingering popular notion in the comfortable homes of Eastern Virginia of a wild, *impracticable* country, and an unkempt people classed under the vague and harsh names of "mountains" and "mountaineers." We may find on the map a well-defined trans-Alleghany district, composed of the southwestern portion of Virginia, eastern portions of Kentucky and Tennessee, and the north-western portion of North Carolina, having remarkable similitudes of population, soil and climate, its inhabitants sympathizing in the common complaint that they have been neglected by their respective State governments. They are called contemptuously "corner men;" the systems of internal improvements in the States named have seldom reached to them; they are to a great extent practically isolated, and they are yet remarkable for a curious primitive life. Of this country South-west Virginia is the imperial portion—a land of incalculable wealth in minerals, and one, as we shall soon discover, containing a natural scenery to which the most famous tourist routes in Switzerland and Germany, combined, could scarcely furnish the parallel. And yet what must be the surprise of the traveler when, penetrating this beautiful and wonderful country, he finds it not only unadvertised to the world (his experience already being that at such an outpost as Lynchburg he could scarcely get directions for his journey away from the railroad), but that even among its own people it is almost unknown beyond the circles of their neighborhoods; that persons residing within a few hours' ride of scenes which he had come hundreds of miles to see are ignorant of them, or can give nothing more than that laconic information which he hears so often in the mountains, that they had "*hear'n tell*" of such places. A gentleman of Tazewell county, writing a local history of it, testifies: "There is in all South-west Virginia scarcely a schoolboy who is not better acquainted with the history and geography of New York or Massachusetts than those of his own beautiful State of mountains and hills and valleys and streams!"

The truth is, the neglect of their scenery lies at the doors of the Virginians themselves. If the obscurity of a country, however, is an invitation to the explorer and tourist, it should avail for South-west Virginia. Discoveries of the artist, as well as of other adventurers, are already in progress there, and are opening up a country as grand in its scenic effects as it is wonderfully rich in the products of its fields and mines. Its mountain views, its waterfalls, its natural curiosities, its stupendous wonders of rock-work, the revelation of the scenery of New river, is a combination that the sight-seer can find nowhere else in the world.

The author is not mistaken in filling so large a portion of his work with such a country. He returns to Lynchburg, repeating his designation of it as the point of departure to the most interesting tour in Virginia. And now, with such method or order of treatment as the nature of his work will admit, he proposes not only to attempt descriptions of scenes visited, but, with less of literary ambition, to mingle with his sketches observations and guides useful to those who may come after him.

The following general directions may avail the traveler. Persons from all points north of Baltimore may take the train which leaves New York city in the evening, reaching Washington City about 6 A. M. This train makes close connection with the Orange and Alexandria train, which arrives in Lynchburg at 4.20 P. M. The traveler may also come by the Bay route to Norfolk, and thence to Lynchburg over the Norfolk and Petersburg and Southside Railroads, without change of cars. There is only one passenger train daily over each of these roads.

The town of Lynchburg is not without its interest—even such as is admissible in these pages—and it should not be hurriedly passed. From "the Hill City," as the burg is supremely spoken of by its people, the peaks of the Blue Ridge are already plainly visible, and the scenery that surrounds this really most delightful town—which boasts, with reason, the reputation of containing the best remnant of the old-fashioned and hospitable society of Virginia—invites the eye, and with its fine healthy airs would constitute itself a pleasing summer resort to one habituated to cities. There are some views around the town which might well repay the tourist a day's saunter on its hills, and which, perhaps, might be more highly esteemed if they were not quite so accessible. On College Hill, across which runs the south-western boundary of the city, we may obtain a fine view of the Peaks of Otter in the distance, faint, but as well defined as a cloud redoubt; while the lesser humped mountains to the north, their buttresses on the horizon, look like a caravan of camels scattered and reposing at evening on the dim outline of a desert.

A peculiarity of the Blue Ridge may be noticed here, and it is a royal one. It is the change of its robes, and especially of those gorgeous ones which it puts on at evening. All mountains seen afar are *blue*—distance lends this enchantment to the view—but this particular range of mountains in Virginia has a depth, a variety and a wealth of different shades of blue that are strikingly peculiar, and so much so that the color has given them their name. It is a blue of infinite richness, of a strange misty depth that baffles analysis, and as variable as the sunset sky that joins with it. Now mist-gilded, again light as the heaven's arch, again purplish, again indescribable as a mixture of blue and red, and all these phenomena taking place, perhaps, in half an hour's span of the sun, the garments of the mountain changed, swift as the weaver's shuttle that makes them in the light woven of earth and sky. The writer has repeatedly, while traveling near these mountains and struck by effects of color, found himself reflecting that if these effects were transferred to canvas, how art-critics would exclaim that they were fictitious and impossible! So *strange* is nature—a strangeness so little recognized in our schools of criticism. Here where we stand on College Hill, just on the confines of Lynchburg, we were never more struck by this shading and shifting of colors as they appear under the sky of a May evening. The sun is sinking, and the two peaks of Otter, towering far over all around them, appear as pillars in the sky, while the clouds gathered at the gate of Evening are slowly passing into the infinite fields beyond. There are ranks of color in the scene from the foot-hills of the Blue Ridge to the horizon's verge. The near mountains are gray and mottled, for we see the soil and can count their ribs of rock; next is a broken rank of haggard mountains, a pale, indescribable blue; then, where it touches the sky, an outline of blue and gold and purple all around, fit hem of garment for the beautiful and majestic world!

We leave College Hill, wondering that this view of a summer evening has not drawn out a single person, besides our small party, to a walk more beautiful than in any park of Northern city, and to a scene more glorious than what people sometimes travel or toil many miles to see. In another direction there is yet another view to reward us. About a mile and a half east of the city, where a little white-painted country church—Tyreeanna Chapel—stands by the grass-covered fortifications of the late war, there is a view which some might think finer than that just described. For besides the mountains is a piece of water scenery; the island-dotted James, no longer broad-breasted and strong as when making its way through mountain passes, but lingering around its green islands, or lying careless and indolent in the peaceful landscape.

These views are ornaments to Lynchburg, quite in contrast to the mud-defiled and decayed town having its Rip Van Winkle sleep under the hills, and seeing which only, the traveler carries away the impression of a sloppy and uninteresting place, from which he has been glad to get away.

It is a town of some ancient memories. It was established in 1786 by an Irish emigrant of the name of Lynch. *En passant*, the term "Lynch law" was derived from his brother, a hot-tempered Irishman, who was a colonel in the Revolutionary war, and who was in the habit of dealing summarily with the Tories and desperadoes who infested this part of the country. Despite the uncertainty of the traditional origin of most popular appellations, the reader may be satisfied of the authenticity of this bit of philological information. Mr. Wirt, in his *Life of Henry*, says: "In 1792, there were many suits on the south side of James river for inflicting Lynch's law." Almost exclusively from the immense tobacco trade of Virginia and North Carolina the town derived its growth, being raised from the lowliness and poverty of Lynch's Ferry to the wealth and dignity of a city—from an insignificant James river warehouse to a position which commanded respect both in this country and Europe, as one of the best tobacco markets in the world. But besides its tobacco interests, Lynchburg has but little trade or prosperity at present—although, as other Virginia towns, it is "great in possibilities."

The natural adaptation of the site of Lynchburg to ample water-power indicates especially the possibility of its importance as a manufacturing town. But this gift of Nature is as yet undeveloped, and is found to have been strangely abused, chiefly through the mistake in not locating the James River and Kanawha Canal sufficiently high to secure the water-power. At the highest point of the city the water is brought up by double forcing pumps at the elevation of 253 feet above the level of the river, and these works, constructed in 1828, were then celebrated in a local paper as "unprecedented in this country." The mistake in the location of the canal (which was opened to navigation in 1841) on the river level it has been attempted to remedy by raising the dams which afford the supply of water; but this work was left unfinished at the breaking out of the war, and, owing to the financial distress of the Canal company, has not been since resumed.

There is no doubt that the management of this great water-artery and the project of its extension to the Ohio have been embarrassed and delayed by the prospect of selling it out to French capitalists. Since the dissipation of this prospect, some disposition has been shown by the Canal company to repair their finances, and to resume the enterprise of past years. An attempt is now being made to fund their debt, under an act of the Legislature authorizing the mortgage of works to the extent of seven hundred and fifty thousand dollars; but the progress is slow, and the local trade has so fallen off that it is scarcely adequate to pay the current expenses and the interest on the funded debt. It is obvious that while the work is local, all its operations and benefits must be to a great extent local; and to complete its original design, which was to connect the Eastern and Western waters, and thus realize the full benefits which were predicated on the consummation of the work, it is equally clear that Virginia must look to capital from abroad, and to the interest which distant and opulent States of the Union have in an enterprise so large and far-reaching. Indeed, this canal is perhaps the most important unfinished improvement in Virginia waiting upon that tide of capital which is expected to flow into the State upon the assurance of her political reconstruction, already so much advanced by the late elections. Efforts have been recently noticed to revive interest in a work which has floated so long in imagination, and which repeats the idea of Washington of joining the waters of the continent

THE GREAT WATER LINE OF VIRGINIA.

Even a traveler of ordinary views cannot help having his attention arrested by the visions of commercial empire which cling to the banks of the James and its tributaries. The Water Line of Virginia, in its conceptions, is one of those large works of the industrial enterprise of the age, which rises above the boundaries of statistical and commercial details to the dignity of a monument or a poem. The unsightly thread of water coursing along the James binds up a romance of modern commerce. Now the narrow canal extending from tidewater to Buchanan is an almost deserted thoroughfare. The boat-horn is now but seldom heard along its banks, and its waters are disturbed only by some small barges doing the droning and desultory trade of a few neighborhoods. But in this infant canal grown to a water-route, with a capacity as great as the waterfall and the feeders of its tributaries can supply, extended to the Kanawha river, and reaching by its silver arm to the great system of Western waters, is destined to pour a mighty stream of commerce, contributed from the very heart of the agricultural empire of America.

It is then that the State of Virginia itself will obtain its fullest development—when the coal and minerals of the State are brought together; then that the hydrographic basins of the Mississippi and the Missouri shall be drained into the long-neglected waters of the Chesapeake, and its riches float into its heretofore stagnant harbors; then that we shall behold a water-route in connection with, or rather supplemented by, the South-western system of railroads in Virginia, "bringing in connection with the Chesapeake bay sixteen thousand miles of navigable rivers in the Mississippi Valley, and twenty-one thousand miles of railroad already in operation there" (see Professor Maury); bringing Norfolk two hundred and ninety-three miles nearer than New York is by present routes to all places on the Mississippi river that are situated above the mouth of the Illinois river; bringing the cities on the Ohio one thousand to fifteen hundred miles nearer to New York, *via* Norfolk, than they are either *via* the Gulf or the Lakes; giving the North-west a water-route through Virginia to the seaboard shorter and more practicable than the one by the Lakes and the Erie Canal to New York, or the other by the Mississippi river to New Orleans, with transhipment to New York, Liverpool and other parts; in short, making Virginia the highway of the granary of America, and solving, at once, the greatest problem of the political economy of our country, and a most difficult question of sectional estrangement and national polity.

The future of the James River and Kanawha Canal is even a romance outside of its commercial aspects. It is not to be studied in a statistical closet; it is not to be immured in dry figures. We have felt that we might admit it even to the interest of these pages as an element of beauty and of order springing out of the geographical position and physical relations of Virginia, that fall obviously under the eyes of the traveler. The Water Line of Virginia solves a question of the age scarcely less great than the Pacific Railroad. It will be a monument in the country. It will realize a vision that has been traditional in Virginia, which more than a hundred years ago prophesied that "whoever shall be master of the Ohio and the Lakes, shall become sole and absolute lord of North America." And as a last romantic interest is the curious system of design by which Nature has invited and pointed out the work.

"It," as Mr. Sheffey says, in a recent speech to an agricultural society in Virginia, "would solve the mystery what that grand, rugged, limpid stream, New river and Kanawha, with its successive falls, was made for. Without capacity for navigation or fish, it has been pronounced the most useless stream of its size in the world. And so it is unimproved; but improved, it has no superior in power and value. It intersects and cuts down to their bases every mountain barrier in the old State, from its source in the south-west to its mouth in the north-west. Falling over successive steeps, it is the great waterfall of Virginia, and affords sites for a hundred Lowells. I hesitate not to say that the stream has more water-power from its source to its mouth than all the other rivers in the State combined. I assert, further, that it intersects more mineral wealth, more copper, lead, iron, zinc, salt and coal, than all the other rivers of the State together."

But we close the page on a vision of wealth, in which there is yet as much of poetry as in the loveliest and grandest scenes that adorn the banks of those two rivers with which Nature has blessed Virginia—the James and the Kanawha. They are the two arms of the State—one laid on the mane of Ocean; the other beckoning in the distance to smiling and not unwilling fields to bring their treasures to the crouching wave.

CHAPTER III.

FROM LYNCHBURG TO THE NATURAL BRIDGE.

Recent Neglect of the Natural Bridge by Sight-Seers—Directions of Route to it—On the Banks of the James—Balcony Falls—Views from the Stage Road—Scenery on North River—THE NATURAL BRIDGE—First Sight of it—Curious Proportions of Art in its Structure—The Angle of Ascent—View from the Creek below—A Strange Imagination—Gates of Hell—The Natural Bridge compared with Niagara Falls—Two Illustrations of the Sublime in our American Schools of Æsthetics—CLIMBING THE NATURAL BRIDGE—Testimony of an Eye-witness.

THERE was a time when the Natural Bridge was esteemed among the greatest wonders of this continent. Of late years it has languished in obscurity and neglect, visited only by stray travelers from the Virginia springs, or, as we may judge, by frugal picnic parties from the near town of Lexington and the neighborhood—a conclusion drawn from a notice extraordinary posted at the hotel, that unless visitors patronized its larder they would be charged fifty cents a head for the privilege of looking at the Bridge! The neglect of this sublime spectacle in the mountains of Virginia, once so attractive to the multitude of sight-seers, is difficult to be explained when we consider the easy access to it—an access improved, too, by all that a beautiful and various natural scenery can bestow upon the traveler's route.

The common route is by way of Lynchburg, thence

thirty-eight miles on the James river and Kanawha Canal. The canal divides immediately at the foot of the Blue Ridge, a section being extended up the North River to the town of Lexington, and the other pursuing the banks of the James to Buchanan, short of which you can stop at the mouth of Cedar creek, within two miles of the Natural Bridge. From a few miles above Lynchburg the route by canal is adorned with mountain scenery of the richest and most various description, and the traveler passes slowly, going scarcely more than three miles an hour, through an almost continuous gallery of pictures. The writer on his trip had the advantage of a moonlit night and of the company of some musical ladies. As the boat moves slowly and so easily that you can imagine it at rest, unless for passing objects, you see a horizon broken and pierced with mountain spurs; at one time under the shadow of great cliffs, again passing along silver-clad willows where the James flows placidly through meadows with the trophy of shivered moonbeams on its bosom; in the distance by mountains with twinkling fires on them, or the red glare of burning woods kindled by stray fires during the drought; and so, in this dioramic procession, with the music of sweet voices on the air and the melancholy wail of the boatman's horn occasionally intruding, we travel on to the rugged backbone of the Blue Ridge.

Here, where the James river emerges from the mountains on the line of Amherst and Rockbridge counties, the scene is surpassingly picturesque. Overlooking Balcony Falls, the pyramid-shaped mountain throws in the night its pointed shadow in the mingled waters of the James and North rivers like a great spear-head to divide them. Where it terminates in the water it falls in a precipitous cliff, the rocky face of which looked at once grand and weird as we saw it in the moonlight. A branch of the canal proceeds up the North river to Lexington, while that along the banks of the James, which we pursue to our destination, passes into a wilder scene.

The accompanying views were taken by the writer at another time in daylight, and on a trip preferable to that of the canal-boat, in the circumstance of its being performed by day. The stage-road, coincident here with the canal—either conveyance being at the choice of the traveler—affords a succession of views by daylight of the most picturesque and romantic effect. As the traveler enters the gap of the Blue Ridge from the east, the winding courses of the stage-coach carry him up the mountain's side until he has gained an elevation of hundreds of feet above the James river, over the waters of which the zigzag and rotten road hangs fearfully. On every side are gigantic mountains hemming him in; there are black ravines in the great prison-house; and the lengthened arms of the winds smite the strained ear with the sounds of the rapids below. While he looks at the distance, a mountain rivulet, slight and glittering from amid the primeval forest, dashes across his path, and, leaping from rock to rock, goes joyously on its way.

On the North river the scenes are quieter. Emerging here, the traveler sees a beautiful and fertile country opening before him, while still westward the blue outlines of distant mountains in Rockbridge bound his vision. The water landscape is beautiful. Lovely valleys debouch upon the stream; there are peaceful shadows in the steel-blue waters, and on the broad shoulders of the cattle on the banks we see the drapery of the shadows of the trees beneath which they rest. The fisherman

SCENE ON NORTH RIVER.

Page 50.

standing leg-deep in the water can see his face as in a mirror.

But at present our way does not lie through these scenes. The canal-boat is taking us along the James in the moonlit night, and by the time the day has broken we are within two miles of the Natural Bridge. A rickety team awaits us at the lock-house where we disembark. Through an air filled with golden vapor, and with the mists of the morning yet hanging in the trees by the wayside, we proceed on our journey. The old stage-coach lumbers along under the thick, overhanging boughs of the forest pines, which ever and anon scrape its top or strike in through the windows, scattering the dew-drops in the very faces of the passengers, or perhaps smiting their cheeks with their sharp-pointed leaves.

THE NATURAL BRIDGE.

THE first view of the Bridge is obtained half a mile from it at a turn on the stage-road. It is revealed with the suddenness of an apparition. Raised a hundred feet above the highest trees of the forest, and relieved against the purple side of a distant mountain, a whitish-gray arch is seen, in the effect of distance as perfect and clean-cut an arch as its Egyptian inventor could have defined. The tops of trees are waving in the interval, the upper half of which we only see, and the stupendous arch that spans the upper air is relieved from the first impression that it is man's masonry, the work of art, by the fifteen or twenty feet of soil that it supports, in which trees and shrubbery are firmly imbedded—the verdant crown and testimony of Nature's great work. And here we are divested of an imagination which we believe is popular, that the Bridge is merely a huge slab of rock thrown across a chasm, or some such hasty and violent arrangement. It is no such thing. The arch and whole interval are contained in one solid rock; the average width of that which makes the Bridge is eighty feet, and beyond this the rock extends for a hundred feet or so in mural precipices, divided by only a single fissure, that makes a natural pier on the upper side of the Bridge, and up which climb the hardy firs, ascending step by step on the noble rock-work till they overshadow you.

This mighty rock, a single mass sunk in the earth's side, of which even what appears is stupendous, is of the same geological character—of limestone covered to the depth of from four to six feet with alluvial and clayey earth. The span of the arch runs from forty-five to sixty feet wide, and its height to the under line is one hundred and ninety-six feet, and to the head two hundred and fifteen feet. The form of the arch approaches to the elliptical; the stage-road which passes over the Bridge runs from north to south, with an acclivity of thirty-five degrees, and the arch is carried over on a diagonal line—the very line of all others the most difficult for the architect to realize, and the one best calculated for picturesque effects. It is the proportions of Art in this wild, strange work of Nature, its adjustment in the very perfection of mechanical skill, its apparently deliberate purpose, that create an interest the most curious and thoughtful. The deep ravine over which it sweeps, and through which traverses the beautiful Cedar creek, is not otherwise easily passed for several miles, either above or below the Bridge. It is needful to the spot, and yet so little likely to have survived the great fracture, the evidences of which are visible around, and which has made a fissure of about ninety feet through the breadth of a rock-ribbed hill, that we are at first disposed to reflect upon it as the work of man. It is only when we contemplate its full measure of grandeur that we are assured it is the work of God. We have the pier, the arch, the studied angle of ascent; and that nothing might be wanted in the evidences of design, the Bridge is guarded by a parapet of rocks, so covered with fine shrubs and trees that a person traveling the stage-road running over it would, if not informed of the curiosity, pass it unnoticed.

But let him approach through the foliage to the side. More than two hundred feet below is the creek, apparently motionless, except where it flashes with light as it breaks on an obstruction in the channel; there are trees, attaining to grander heights as they ascend the face of the pier; and far below this bed of verdure the majestic rock rises with the decision of a wall, and the spectator shrinks from contemplating the grand but cruel depths, and turns away with dizzy sensations. But the most effective view is from the base of the Bridge, where you descend by a circuitous and romantic path. Even to escape from the hot sun into these verdant and cool bottoms is of itself a luxury, and it prepares you for the deliberate enjoyment of the scene. Everything reposes in the most delightful shade, set off by the streaming rays of the sun, which shoot across the head of the picture far above you, and sweeten with softer touches the solitude below. Standing by the rippling, gushing waters of the creek, and raising your eyes to the arch, massive and yet light and beautiful from its height, its elevation apparently increased by the narrowness of its piers and by its projection on the blue sky, you gaze on the great work of Nature in wonder and astonishment. Yet a hundred beauties beckon you from the severe emotion of the sublime. When you have sustained this view of the arch raised against the sky, its black patches here and there shaped by imagination into grand and weird figures—among them the eagle, the lion's head, and the heroic countenance of Washington; when you have taken in the proportions and circumstances of this elevated and wide span of rock—so wide that the skies seem to slope from it to the horizon—you are called to investigate other parts of the scene which strain the emotions less, and are distributed around in almost endless variety. Looking through the arch, the eye is engaged with a various vista. Just beyond rises the frayed, unseamed wall of rock; the purple mountains stand out in the background; beneath them is a rank of hills and matted woods enclosing the dell below, while the creek coursing away from them appears to have been fed in their recesses. A few feet above the bridge the stream deflects, and invites to a point of view of the most curious effect. Taking a few steps backward, moving diagonally on the course of the stream, we see the interval of sky between the great abutments gradually shut out; thus apparently joined or lapped over, they give the effect of the face of a rock, with a straight seam running down it, and the imagination seizes the picture as of mighty gates closed upon us. We are shut in a wild and perturbed scene by these gates of hell; behind and around us is the contracted and high boundary of mountains and hills, and in this close and vexed scene we are for a moment prisoners. Now let us move across, step by step, to a position fronting where these gates apparently close. Slowly they seem to swing open on unseen and noiseless hinges; wider and wider grows the happy interval of sky, until at last wide open stands the gateway raised above the forest, resting as it were on the brow of heaven—a world lying beyond it, its rivers and its hills expanding themselves to the light and splendor of the unshadowed day.

To an observer of both places a comparison is naturally suggested between the Natural Bridge and Niagara Falls in respect of the sublime and the beautiful; and, indeed, as in this respect the two greatest works of Nature on this continent, they may well be used as illustrations in our American schools of æsthetics. The first is unique in its aspects of Nature like Art; it is Nature with the proportions of Art. In its expressions of power, in its concentration of emotion, as when we look at it *distinct* or *complete*, it is truly sublime; and its effect is alleviated (for it is a maxim in æsthetics that the sublime cannot be long sustained) by the picturesque scenery which surrounds it. It is a greater natural curiosity and more wonderful than Niagara, although it lacks the elements of sublimity which the other has in sound, and of the visible, actual struggle in which it displays the powers of Nature. Niagara is a living thing, while the Natural Bridge is *monumental*. The first represents the sublime as allied to the terrific—in contemplating it we are overwhelmed with a sense of our insignificance; while the Natural Bridge associates the sublime with the pleasing and curious, and, not transporting us as violently as Niagara, entertains us more equably, and dismisses us, we think, with more distinct and fruitful perceptions of the grandeur and beneficence and variety of Nature which have been distributed in the picture.

CLIMBING THE NATURAL BRIDGE—BY THE ONLY SURVIVING WITNESS OF THAT EXTRAORDINARY FEAT.*

I THINK it was in the summer of 1818 that James H. Piper, William Reveley, William Wallace and myself, being then students of Washington College, Virginia, determined to make a jaunt to the Natural Bridge, fourteen miles off. Having obtained permission of the president, we proceeded on our way rejoicing. When we arrived at the Bridge, nearly all of us commenced climbing up the precipitous sides in order to immortalize our names, as usual.

We had not been long thus employed before we were joined by Robert Penn, of Amherst, then a pupil of the Rev. Samuel Houston's grammar-school, in the immediate neighborhood of the Bridge. Mr. Piper, the hero of the occasion, commenced climbing on the opposite side of the creek from the one by which the pathway ascends the ravine. He began down on the banks of the brook so far that we did not know where he had gone, and were only apprised of his whereabouts by his shouting above our heads. When we looked up, he was standing apparently right under the arch, I suppose a hundred feet from the bottom, and that on the smooth side, which is generally considered inaccessible without a ladder. He was standing far above the spot where General Washington is said to have inscribed his name when a youth. The ledge of the rock by which he ascended to this perilous height does not appear from below to be three inches wide, and runs almost at right angles to the abutment of the bridge; of course, its termination is far down the cliff on that

* The narrative is from the pen of William A. Caruthers, and was originally published in the New York *Knickerbocker*.

side. Many of the written and traditional accounts state this to be the side of the bridge up which he climbed. I believe Miss Martineau so states; but it is altogether a mistake, as any one may see by casting an eye up the precipice on that side. The story, no doubt, originated from this preliminary exploit.

The ledge of rock on which he was standing appeared so narrow to us below, as to make us believe his position a very perilous one, and we earnestly entreated him to come down. He answered us with loud shouts of derision. At this stage of the business Mr. Penn and servant left us. He would not have done so, I suppose, had he known what was to follow, but up to this time not one of us had the slightest suspicion that Mr. Piper intended the daring exploit which he afterward accomplished. He soon after descended from that side, crossed the brook, and commenced climbing on the side by which all visitors ascend the ravine. He first mounted the rocks on this side, as he had done on the other, far down the abutment, but not so far as on the opposite side. The projecting ledge may be distinctly seen by any visitor. It commences four or five feet from the pathway on the lower side, and winds round, gradually ascending, until it meets the cleft of rock over which the celebrated cedar stump hangs. Following this ledge to its termination, it brought him thirty or forty feet from the ground, and placed him between two deep fissures, one on each side of the gigantic column of rock on which the aforementioned cedar stump stands. This column stands out from the bridge, as separate and distinct as if placed there by Nature on purpose for an observatory to the wonderful arch and ravine which it overlooks. A huge crack or fissure extends from its base to the summit; indeed, it is cracked on both sides, but much more perceptibly on one side than the other. Both of these fissures are thickly overgrown with bushes, and numerous roots project into them from trees growing on the precipice. It was between these that the aforementioned ledge conducted him. Here he stopped, pulled off his coat and shoes and threw them down to me. And this, in my opinion, is a sufficient refutation of the story so often told, that he went up to inscribe his name, and ascended so high that he found it more difficult to return than to go forward. He could have returned easily from the point where he disencumbered himself, but the fact that he did thus prepare so early, and so near the ground, and after he had ascended more than double that height on the other side, is clear proof that to inscribe his name was not, and to climb the bridge was, his object. He had already inscribed his name above Washington himself more than fifty feet.

Around the face of this huge column, and between the clefts, he now moved backward and forward, still ascending as he found convenient foothold. When he had ascended about one hundred and seventy feet from the earth, and had reached the point where the pillar overhangs the ravine, his heart seemed to fail him. He stopped, and seemed to us to be balancing midway between heaven and earth. We were in dread suspense, expecting every moment to see him dashed in atoms at our feet. We had already exhausted our powers of entreaty in persuading him to return, but all to no purpose. Now it was perilous even to speak to him, and very difficult to carry on conversation at all, from the immense height to which he had ascended, and the noise made by the bubbling of the little brook as it tumbled in tiny cascades over its rocky bed at our feet. At length he seemed to discover that one of the clefts before mentioned retreated backward from the overhanging position of the pillar. Into this he sprang at once, and was soon out of sight and out of danger.

There is not a word of truth in all that story about our hauling him up with ropes, and his fainting away so soon as he landed on the summit. Those acquainted with the localities will at once perceive its absurdity; for we were beneath the arch, and it is half a mile round to the top, and for the most part up a ragged mountain. Instead of fainting away, Mr. Piper proceeded down the hill to meet us and obtain his hat and shoes. We met about halfway, and then he lay down for a few moments to recover himself of his fatigue.

CHAPTER IV.

THE PEAKS OF OTTER.

Journey to the Peaks—Experiences by the Wayside—Panoramic Views—Picture of a Feudal Proprietorship—Grape-growing in the Mountains—Toilsome Ascent—On the Peak—Standing up in the great Hollowness of the Sky—Peculiar Sublimity of the Peaks of Otter—A Religious Reflection on the Scene—Bird of the Mountain—The Sublime Effect of a Striking Contrast—The Little Earth and the Great Heavens.

THE Peaks of Otter are situated in Bedford county, Virginia, rising from the Blue Ridge, which here runs to the right and left across the horizon for many miles. They take their name from Otter creek, which courses near them. They are the highest peaks of the Blue Ridge, and are generally accounted—although recently there has been some question of their comparative elevation—the highest mountains in Virginia. The estimated height of the northern Peak, which is the more elevated, is forty-two hundred feet above the plain, and fifty-three hundred and seven feet above the level of the sea. The more sharply-pointed Peak to the south is, however, more commanding and more romantic, and is the one usually visited.

From the town of Liberty, twenty-five miles on the Virginia and Tennessee Railroad from Lynchburg, the turnpike to Buchanan leads through a gap high up on the side of the mountain we have described, and a country road deflects to the summit of the Peak. The distance is good fourteen miles. And here we may give an admonition to the traveler that should avail him in all the Mountain Region of Virginia: it is, never to lose time or temper by asking distances of the country-people. If he does so he will be driven out of his wits by the inconsistencies and absurdities of the answers given; and it is not only ignorant people who will innocently misinform and annoy him, but it is remarkable that the most intelligent persons residing in this country blunder most unaccountably as to distances, and that on roads familiar to them. "Just over the mountain" is generally ten miles; and "a piece further" may be half a mile or five miles. When at Liberty I mounted for the Peak, I was told by the nimble barkeeper at the hotel that it was ten miles away: the fat proprietor, who shuffled in slippers, said fifteen. I had ridden a mile out of town when I met a wagoner and asked the distance to the Peak. "It's nigh onto nine mile." I had traveled five miles farther when I accosted a man on horseback: "How far to the top of the mountain?" "It is eleven miles," he said, solemnly. I was halfway up the mountain when I discovered a sleek negro at the door of a cabin, to whom I repeated the incessant question. "Yes, sir," with an air of importance—then throwing up his eyes to the sun as if making an astronomical calculation—"yes, sir: it's just exactly about *twenty-five miles!*" I answered nothing and rode on. I have no commentary to make, except the assurance that each answer was given me precisely as recorded, and that I have related an actual experience.

But the road, however variously described as to distances, and although for three or four miles it appeared to be in the bed of a mountain torrent, was never wearisome or dull for a moment. From the time I rode out of the village of Liberty the grand Peak was constantly visible just before me, and it was a curious and vivid interest to notice how at each stage of the journey the mountain changed its envelope. It was constantly presenting new vestures and aspects and dyes as mile by mile I approached it. I could see the blue surface lifted up before me become brown as I rode toward it; then it ripened into rock and shrub; until at last yet closer I could see the naked scars and the wrinkled soil of its sides. On each side of my bridle, as I rode over the warm plain to the foot of the mountain, magnificent scenes stretched away. Broad fields palpitated under the sun; on the foot-hills were bands of young tall oaks standing as firm and even as regiments of infantry; while on the mountain slopes and far up to their summits, shadows of clouds swept and broke upon the unmoving ranks of the forest. It was a scene full of animation; Nature had bestowed everything upon it, and a beautiful day had filled it with the images of fancy.

At last I am ascending the mountain through a succession of panoramic views. The road at one time seems going away from the Peak; now it bends back with new determination; now it flattens out on an observatory, where I pause with involuntary exclamations as I see the country below rolled out, and far beneath me the red stripe of road by which I have come. It is a wild and desolate country immediately around me. I ride for miles with no sign of human life by the roadside but what some hut contains; some dogs bark at the horse's heels, and an old, half-nude negro glares at the traveler with savage curiosity, ceasing his work in a half-scratched field of withered corn. Suddenly, and as if by a magical translation, the road that has hesitated in such scenes, comes out upon a broad shoulder of the mountain, in sight of a pleasing mansion, and where are noticed, with infinite surprise, all the evidences of the broad and garnished farm of a wealthy planter.

It was indeed a surprising revelation to find displayed here something like a vision of feudal proprietorship. I had got to the "gap" of the Peak before I was aware. Fenced in by hills, it affords no view of the country below, and thus gives no idea of its elevation save by comparison with the yet unscaled top of the mountain; and I had thus insensibly ridden from an almost savage surrounding into a scene of broad acres and cultivated rural life. Mr. H———, a well-known gentleman of Virginia, owns three thousand acres here, and has a numerous tenantry. It was a picture of the old plantation life of Virginia hid away in the niche of a mountain; the romantic home of a modern feodary suspended in the clouds. The hospitality of the proprietor detained me; and it was indeed as refreshing as it was unexpected to dismount at a house which would have been of no mean pretensions even among our lowland gentry, crossing a cultivated lawn to it, and noting evidences around of a thrifty industry as well as of a refined taste. The name of the place is "Bellevue." But there is no view, so concealed is the place in the mountain gap, except the Peak, which stares into the sky and throws a shadow down sharp as a spearhead at evening. The neck of land which constitutes the farm is well cultivated, tobacco being the staple production. There were no workmen in the fields; and their absence there was painfully explained to me when a few minutes later there passed the house a funeral procession of negroes, in their decentest attire, following a short pine coffin placed in a rude wagon, that drove slowly to a grave dug in the obscure side of the mountain that perhaps had bounded all that the dead one ever knew of the life of this world.

Mr. H——, a representative of the best of the intelligent large land-proprietors of Virginia, instructed and interested me greatly in descriptions of resources of the mountain region which he so eminently occupied. I found that the people were developing a new industry here in the raising of fruit, and especially in the culture of the grape. Mr. H—— had just sold for fourteen hundred dollars the apples he had gathered from trees scattered about in the fields, and hitherto grown without the least attention. He was now about to make a large experiment in the production of wine from the Joplin grape. The description of the country about the Peaks of Otter answers, in respect of the grape, for nearly the whole length of the Blue Ridge in Virginia. On the sunny slopes of these mountains there is said to be precisely the conditions needed for the growing of wine-making grapes. The air is dry, the warmth entirely sufficient, the soil suitable; so that there would be no mildew, the fruit would ripen at the proper time, and the crop would be abundant. These were the conditions indispensable to the production of the juicy wine-grape. The want of proper geniality and warmth in the climate of the North disables that country from producing the wine-grape, while it succeeds well in producing the solid table-grape. On the other hand, south of Virginia, there is danger of mildew from the dews and fogs. Mildew is the great enemy of the grape, and it cannot flourish where the causes of the disease prevail. On the sunny slopes of the Blue Ridge there is no danger of this evil; and I was assured that there the wine-grape could be produced to perfection, and to an extent that would soon make a new feature of industry and a new resource of wealth in the State. But a truce to speculations induced by the wayside; although here, as elsewhere on a tour devoted to scenery, the writer has yet dismounted to pluck some chance new blossom of the wealth of Virginia.

Refreshed by some glasses of home-made wine, we soon returned to the main object of our journey. From the portico of Mr. H———'s house could be plainly seen the top of the mountain we had come to explore, projected into the sky, garnished with a cap of dark, rusty rock that ran up to a point and nodded over the precipice. It was a mile and a half by road and by path to the mountain's top. The writer had been joined at Mr. H———'s by a young physician of the neighborhood, and by a student from the University of Virginia, who were as anxious as himself to climb to the narrow and perilous summit. Our horses struggled a mile up the mountain side; we had then to hitch them and complete the ascent, half a mile farther, by a path so steep and so badly graded that we had to assist our uncertain foothold by grasping the boughs of trees within reach. It was hard work under a July sun. There was nothing to repay us in intermediate views; we might mark our elevation by imperfect glimpses of some red hills below, but the foliage was too thick to afford any extent of view, and before us was nothing but the rugged inclined plane, the rotten ascent up which we were toiling. It was interesting, however, to notice the steady diminution of the trees as we ascended; we had ridden through stately trees a little while before, now we were among stunted pines and dwarfed oaks, the limbs of the latter crooked and twisted by storms that for years had tortured and deformed them.

In this narrow scene we toiled up to the great overhanging rocks of the mountains, realizing nothing of the view that awaited us. The path here is yet obscure; it winds up under a shelf of rock; it is overhung and shut up to the very last moment; and then a single step, as it were, a single curve, and the whole scene *bursts* upon us, an infinite apparition!

It is the suddenness of the grand and limitless revelation that first seizes and alarms the soul. There was a loose slanting board, a remnant of an old walk, at the last turn of the path, crouching on which I had to climb to a huge boulder. There, yet on all-fours, faint, dizzy, trembling, I clung to the slippery summit, finding suddenly that it was all that was left me beneath the skies! I felt suspended under the dome of the heavens. I could not rise to my feet, I could not survey the scene around me; prostrate and almost breathless, I clung to the small space on the crown of rock on which I had been lifted up as on a pinnacle into the limitless air. It was only after the suggestion of one of my companions that I should not look into the awful chasm below, but should relieve the eye by resting it on the milder ascent up which I had come, that I regained command of myself, and was able to rise to my feet and survey what was around me.

It is the exceeding keenness of the summit of the Peaks of Otter that gives an effect of sublimity perhaps unequaled by any mountain view in the world. There are many mountains higher than where we stood; there are others, it may be, with more merit or interest in the surroundings; but none, we imagine, which produce so terribly sublime an emotion of suspension in the sky. There is a rude, circular arrangement of immense rocks on the top of the mountain, suggesting the crater of an extinct volcano, and there are no less than three points that thrust up, on any one of which we may stand with no more room beneath the great blue heavens than that on which the feet are planted. The traveler stands up in the great hollowness of the sky, alone, naked in the dead air. It is not the common intoxication of a pinnacle; it is the awful sublimity of an insecure suspension, the steps to which, looking from a summit that nods on one side over the world below, his imagination does not retrace and his eyes do not see.

I had to get accustomed to the narrow and impending observatory before I could take in or enjoy the scene it commanded. It was a scene whose grand boundaries were even with the sky. Here was Bedford county at our feet, a patchwork of farms, tufted and tasseled with beautiful forests. Here were mountains all around us; some near, gashed into red clay, their bare, macerated sides plain to the vision; on others we could see the mottled soil and plumes of the forest; others, clothed with the hues of distance, gave only smooth surfaces to the eye as they joined the sky. There were mountains of all imaginable shapes—flat-top mountains, peaked mountains, every form of the cone and the pyramid, perfect, broken, or truncated. There was the curiously-shaped "House Mountain" near Lexington, then far to the south-west, a grotesque, misshapen pyramid, a broken fang on the pearly crust of sky. Out of all this confusion ran away steadily the great ranges of the Alleghany and Blue Ridge, giving order and disposition to the wild scene, and tracing out of it the mountain system of Virginia.

No wonder that John Randolph's infidelity was shaken in such a scene. There were the prints of the Great Creator's hands on the earth. A world was at our feet to display design; the strong sun was hung up in the infinite air; a thousand beauties were kindled around us; world and sky were in the garments of a new creation—the aurora of a new and sublime significance;

> "And luminous beyond the golden mist,
> Something that looked to my young eyes like God."

Sounds from the world below traveled up to us with strange distinctness. I could hear the tinkle of a cowbell a mile and a half away. Some buzzards, attracted by the unwonted spectacle of human figures on the Peak, sailed around us, gradually contracting the circle as impelled by curiosity, until they swept almost within pistol shot. I am sure that I abuse neither my own imagination nor the credulity of my readers in saying that I could hear the flapping of their wings in the dead, stagnated air! Wearied by their circuits, continued for half an hour, several of these monstrous birds—than whom, despite their uncleanliness, there are no more graceful travelers of the air, none that move through it with slower and more magnificent stroke—perched on a cliff below us, and yawned at us by an occasional motion of the wings.

There was one reflection in the scene which remains to be indicated, and which will live always in the writer's recollections of it. Looking down upon the map of country below us, the mind is seized with the reflection, How conventional are our ideas of spaces and of magnitudes! The speed of modern travel has no more remarkable fact than the change it has wrought in our ideas of distance—a change in some respects painful and unpoetical, for in it we have lost some of the dearest images, and instead of the "wide, wide world," the tradition of our childhood, we find ourselves reflecting in this age of steam and telegraphs, How small, in what narrow spaces are now held all the habitations of men! The reflection comes to us with additional pangs on this wild platform of Nature's observatory. The great stretch of territory from the remotest ranges of the Alleghany, sweeping down to the North Mountain away down in Shenandoah county, extending to the "backbone" of the mountains separating Eastern and Western Virginia, lies at our feet in miniature—a patch of a map that we might sweep over with a motion of the arm. The zigzag turnpikes along the mountain sides, where the stage-coach winds its way day and night for successive days to reach its destination, are but threads swept by a single glance of the eye; a distant train on the Virginia and Tennessee Railroad appears but a child's toy; the space of a whole day's journey seems but a few strides. The poetry of distance is gone; but with the pain of the diminution of the theatre of life and of man's empire of industry at our feet, there was yet a moral usefulness in the scene, and, in the language of another observer, "I was impressively reminded of the extreme littleness with which these things of earth would all appear when the tie of life which binds us here is broken, and we shall be able to look back and down upon them from another world!"

Our eyes involuntarily turn upward. It is the same canopy of blue sky; *that* has not changed, that not diminished; and our idea of magnitude is more than satisfied. We are lost in the sensation of immensity, raised into God's universe, and entranced with the thought that when the earth beneath our feet shall have passed away and the mountains melted down like wax, there shall still remain room, infinite room, for the habitations of man and the excursions of his spirit!

CHAPTER V.

ALLEGHANY SPRINGS AND SURROUNDINGS.

Route to the Alleghany Springs—At the Heart of the Mountains of Virginia—Access to the Springs, North and South—The Water *sui generis*, and the most elaborate in the World—Analysis of the Water—Medical Guide to its Uses—Wonderful Effects of the Water—The Scenery around the Springs the most Remarkable in Virginia—PUNCHEON RUN FALLS—Romance of its Discovery—Climbing the Mountain—A Rough Journey—Sublimity of the Falls—Descent Two Thousand Feet—Scenes on Puncheon Run—"Purgatory"—The Deserters' Fortress—FISHER'S VIEW—Looking from the Mountain's Top—Characteristics of Mountain Views—Sublime Effect of a View of and beyond the Alleghany.

E do not hold ourselves under any obligation to take the objects of our travels in strict geographical succession. We would be but poor tourists to do so. So from the Peaks of Otter, remounting the cars at Liberty and passing objects of interest to which we meditate return, we are rapidly carried fifty miles on the railroad to what is likely to become, on various accounts, the most famous of the summer resorts of Virginia—the Alleghany Springs in Montgomery county. It is not only for the value of its incomparable waters that we thus speak of this resort, but for its fortunate position, holding, as it does, the key to the finest scenery and one of the greatest natural wonders of Virginia.

We leave the railroad at Shawsville,* the springs being three miles distant. Here, at the railroad station, the

* Since named Alleghany Station, in consideration of the springs.

Springs' managers have erected a commodious and pleasant hotel—an outcropping, in fact, of their increased scale of accommodations, keeping pace with increased patronage—it being designed as a convenience for visitors who, leaving the cars in the night-time, may choose to defer the brief remainder of the trip by stage-coach until next morning, or may possibly be detained by the swollen mountain streams. In any circumstances, however, the traveler will not regret staying over night at this hotel, for the scenery through which he is to ride to the springs should be seen by daylight. To traverse the beautiful valley leading up to the springs' hotel, and to see over the mist-fretted tops of the mountains which overhang the way the sun coming up "with all his traveling glories round him," his early rays working into heavenly alchemy the steel-blue mountain streams, is a reward not to be despised, and a fitting preface to pictures which the Alleghany holds yet in reserve for the happy visitor.

"The Mountains of Virginia" is a vague term in the popular geography of the State. Wherever is found a sulphur spring bubbling from a foot-hill, or not even within the skirmish-line of our great mountain ridges, we have advertised in the newspapers a "*mountain* resort," as if this elevation of figure could catch and cheat the imagination of the heat-burdened inhabitants of the lowlands. But the writer is now quite well satisfied that he is really in the mountains of Virginia, at the very heart of them, situated as he is now on the Roanoke river, in the county of Montgomery, at the eastern foot of the Alleghany Mountains—the most elevated region between the Atlantic Ocean and the Rocky Mountains. Here he reposes (for writing is scarcely a labor in such surroundings) in the midst of the numerous and lofty "spurs" of the king of mountains—the hotel of the Alleghany Springs and its picturesque ranges of cottages occupying smooth and undulating hills, which descend to a lawn extending to the banks of the tuneful and trout-inhabited stream that flows far away into the sounds of North Carolina. And yet this place, apparently so remote and intricate, is within three miles of the Virginia and Tennessee Railroad, is accessible by continuous railroad travel from the four points of the compass, and invites its visitors from every city of the Union, not only to see its abounding scenery, but to drink of a water which we shall presently describe as unequaled in any of the cunning of Nature's pharmacy. By the rapid motion of the steam car, the valetudinarian of Boston, escaping from the dark and dense rheumatism-and-consumption-provoking fogs of the North, and the invalid of New Orleans, fleeing from the malaria of the Mississippi swamp, may (starting at the same time) in seventy hours find themselves sociably seated side by side at the foot of the great Appalachian chain of mountains, at an elevation of two thousand feet above the level of their homes, breathing an air more salubrious and bracing than that of Montpelier, and able to shake hands literally across the line of 36° 30', that being the exact latitude of the springs.

The Alleghany Springs is about the extreme of the southern tier of Virginia watering-places scattered along the route of the Virginia and Tennessee Railroad. The water is *sui generis*, peculiar, and the most elaborate mineral water in the world, containing nearly thirty elements, many of them possessing active medical properties. Sulphur water is cheap in Virginia; we have all quantities and varieties—white, red, yellow, salt, cold, etc. The Alleghany water, which is of comparatively recent discovery, is most remarkable for the active salts of lime and magnesia; but an analysis which lies before me (most skillfully made in a Northern laboratory) shows that it exceeds in the number and variety of its elements the famous waters of both the Bedford Springs in Pennsylvania and the Congress Spring at Saratoga. Of metals (which, with the exception of iron, are scarcely ever found in the mineral waters of Virginia) there are no less than seven; of the alkalies, three; of the earths, six; and of acids the same number, in intimate chemical combination, many of them forming salts of known medicinal virtues. Indeed, it is not a curious reasoning, but one drawn strictly from analogy, that Nature, which never does anything in vain, and which no doubt has a design in its pharmacy as in its other workshops, has, in elaborating a compound containing so many elements, many of them known to possess active medical properties, furnished a potent remedial agent for the uses of afflicted and unhealthy man. Experience has already taught the uses of the water for those commonest afflictions of human flesh, the diseases of the stomach and liver, and it is already famous for its specific conquest, its "sovereign cure," of that Protean monster, dyspepsia—our "American disease." But it is yet only in the infancy of its fame: there are other encouraging inferences as to its therapeutic qualities, which the writer describes below, after having named the crowning glory of the water as he has experienced it in his own flesh—its specific tonic action upon the various organs concerned in the vital function of digestion.

In the Springs Region of Virginia the *sulphur* waters in their various modifications are common: there are *thermal* waters of temperature ranging from 62° to 106°;

the *chalybeates*, simple and compound, are found in many places; while of the *aluminous* or acidulated aluminous chalybeates there are three or four varieties.

But the Alleghany Springs belong to the rarer class of what are known as *saline* waters, and yet with a variety or elaboration that renders them peculiar.

The annexed analysis of the water was made by Dr. F. A. Genth, of Philadelphia:

ONE GALLON, SEVENTY THOUSAND GRAINS, CONTAINS:

Sulphate of Magnesia..	50.884290 grains.	
Do. Lime	115.294022 "	
Do. Soda	1.717059 "	
Do. Potassa	3.699081 "	
Carbonate of Copper..	0.000359 "	
Do. Lead	0.000569 "	
Do. Zinc	0.001713 "	
Do. Iron	0.157049 "	
Do. Manganese	0.060617 "	
Do. Lime	3.613209 "	
Do. Magnesia..	0.362362 "	
Do. Strontia..	0.060536 "	
Do. Baryta	0.022404 "	
Do. Lithia	0.001679 "	
Nitrate of Magnesia...	3.219362 grains.	
Do. Ammonia...	0.559412 "	
Phosphate of Alumina.	0.025549 "	
Silicate of Alumina....	0.207399 "	
Fluoride of Calcium..	0.022858 "	
Chloride of Sodium..	0.274676 "	
Silicic Acid	0.882782 "	
Crenic Acid	0.001921 "	
Apocrenic Acid	0.000192 "	
Other Organic Matter.	1.939121 "	
Carbonate of Cobalt } Teroxide of Antimony }	Traces.	
	183.068321 "	
Solid ingredients by direct evaporation gave	184.072000 "	
Half-combined carbonic acid	1.885526 "	
Free carbonic acid	5.455726 "	
Hydro-sulphuric acid	0.001339 "	
Total amount of ingredients	190.411912 "	

The effects of the Alleghany water are cathartic, diuretic and tonic. Their main efficacy appears to depend on their laxative and purgative operations, by which the alimentary canal is excited to copious secretions, and the secretory functions of the liver and pancreas are stimulated to pour out their appropriate fluids. The sympathy between the organs upon which they operate primarily gives them a very wide range of value, as in relieving congestion or irritation of distant organs.

When the water is used in small, regulated quantities, best calculated to meet the indications of cure in the large class of diseases in which it seems to have almost a *specific* action, the leading characteristics are *tonic, alterative* and *detergent*. That the two last-named properties of the water, acting on the vascular, capillary and glandular system, purify the blood and other secretions, throwing off dead "peccant matter," is shown by the softness, pliancy and smoothness of the skin, which it never fails to produce (a property which must commend it to the favor of the ladies as the safest and surest cosmetic), the speedy clearing of the complexion in the worst cases of jaundice, and the cure of scrofula—next to cancer, the most intractable glandular affection.

The catalogue of diseases for which the Alleghany water is indicated and recommended is—dyspepsia; obstructions of the abdominal viscera generally; depraved and vitiated biliary secretions; obstinate and habitual costiveness; scrofula and cutaneous exanthemata; jaundice; biliary calculi; sympathetic affection of the lungs, and incipient consumption.

But the crowning virtue of this water, as we have already remarked, is its *specific tonic* action upon the various organs concerned in the vital function of digestion. Its effect in correcting deranged and morbid action in these organs, and restoring them to their healthful strength and tone and vigor, is almost miraculous, and must be witnessed or experienced to be fully appreciated.

Directions in the use of the water are very necessary to their effect; and fortunately the resident physician, Dr. White, is a gentleman who has accumulated a large experience on this subject, and the renown of whose skill has been carried by many a grateful patient to distant parts of the country. It is observed commonly that the water purges mildly or actively according to the quantities taken into the system; but what is most noticed, to the pleased surprise of the invalid, is that he can keep up the action upon his bowels for a number of days without feeling any debilitation, and instead of losing his appetite, as from ordinary purging, always experiencing a positive increase of it. This effect is of the happiest sort. It may be said, in popular language, that the system is cleaned out and built up at the same time, and thus renewed by a process which is all the time exhilarating and agreeable.

It is not necessary to be an invalid to obtain benefits from such a water. It improves even those in average health. The writer recollects the singular observation he made at the Alleghany Springs, that not only were the invalids bettered, as they are more or less at such resorts, but that *all the visitors* were improved; the remark being common, even from the healthy as well as the sick, that they never felt so well before.

Such a testimony points out the Alleghany as a resort for the *entire public*. The man out of health wants to get it; the man in health wants to increase and to secure it; and the Alleghany seems to accommodate in a special manner, and beyond most other springs, each of the two universal desires.

The country around the Alleghany Springs is a succession of wild, strange pictures; and the astonished amphitheatre of the mountains looks down upon the illuminated ball-room and scenes transported from city life. The advantage of these springs—an extraordinary one when added to the surpassing virtue of the water—is the attractions of natural scenery just about them, among these a

PUNCHEON RUN FALLS.

romantic discovery of the *seventh* wonder of Virginia. The writer recollects having been recently shown, in a Northern city, some stereoscopic views of wild watercourses and picturesque cañons in distant parts of the world, but while the exhibitor was waiting for our admiration we could not help exclaiming, "We have seen much finer around the Alleghany Springs in the State of Virginia." From a number of such views, embarrassed, in fact, by the riches of the scenery around us, we have chosen some for description, or rather for an attempt at such performance, where pen and pencil are alike so inadequate.

PUNCHEON RUN FALLS.

Our first task is to give some account of a scene which ranks, we think—and our estimation has been improved by travel—with the most wonderful and grand sights of this continent. It has the freshness and romance of discovery. Within the leafy and untrodden forest of Montgomery county, in the south-western quarter of Virginia, on one of the rocky ribs of the Alleghanies, not more than eight miles from the famous Alleghany Springs, which for years have numbered their visitors by the thousand from all parts of the Union, a gentleman (Dr. Isaac White, the resident physician of the springs), rambling for trout up one of the forks of the Roanoke river, found hid in the green curtains of the woods, and defended by fortress and palisade of rock, what is now known as, or rudely called, the "Puncheon Run Falls," and what is destined (if I can trust my own impressions) to exceed in its attractions those already well-known "sights," such as the Natural Bridge, the Peaks of Otter, Weyer's Cave, etc., which have made Virginia famous for its monuments of the beauty and cunning of Nature. In the midst of what must have been once a grand convulsion of the elements, and where the mountain side appears to have been torn open almost to the primitive rock—a wound from an unknown source, unhealed and kept open and fretted with huge masses of stone—a mountain stream descends, not perpendicularly, nor yet by stages of descent, but at an angle near the perpendicular, in a smooth plait of currents knotted with white cascades, some eighteen hundred or two thousand feet, measuring the length of the water. But the scene and its surroundings are best described from different stand-points of personal observation; and as the journey to secure these is not without interest, the writer proposes to attempt some record of the trip which made for him a day of various and ineffaceable memories.

The first expression of curious inquiry which the visitor at Alleghany Springs makes concerning this grand and even sublime scene, so close to a resort thronged no less by lovers of Nature than by those who come to drink of the most wonderful health-giving waters of this State, is that it should have remained so long undiscovered, or rather unnoticed, to the world. It is wonderful, almost ludicrously so, that a singular class of people, for whom there is no other name here but the general one of "Mountaineers," living close to the Falls, where they scratch the ground for a meagre subsistence, and sometimes visiting the springs, bringing chickens, eggs, fruit, etc., should yet never have mentioned, not even signified by a word casually dropped in conversation, the existence of this wonder of Nature, in the presence or within the sound of which they lived daily, and some of them had been born. There is a "settlement" within a quarter of a mile of the foot of the Falls, and a number of clearings about their summit. The people who inhabit these spaces on the mountains are a singular class of country people; very ignorant of course, but always striking us as possessing much of the silence and stoicism of the red man: but little disposed to converse except with those who have the art to fall in with their manner, jealous or disdainful of "city folks," and in their uncouth life showing much more of a harsh reserve than of mere rustic shyness. These "mountaineers" are not communicative (except in whisky): they are, of course, desperately ignorant, but their singular impassiveness is what most strikes the traveler. Those who lived near the Puncheon Run Falls saw nothing very remarkable in it, and therefore never spoke of it. Not a word, not even an accidental allusion from these people, ever discovered that there was within eight miles of Alleghany Springs what was worth crossing half the breadth of this continent to see. But for the adventurous steps of an enthusiastic sportsman, the ramparts of rocks and the veil of the forest would yet have secured against intrusion this grand and cunning work of Nature, now accessible to the army of tourists and the thousands who pursue in all the ways of travel the genius of natural scenery.

Speaking to a neighboring mountaineer after his first impression from the discovery of these Falls, Doctor White moderately remarked that they were a great curiosity.

"I don't see nothing kewrus about 'em," responded the man, disdainfully. "When the water comes over the top it is bound to run down to the bottom, and der ain't nothing kewrus or *comical*" (a rustic synonym for "strange") "in that. Now"—adding meditatively—"if the water was to *run up*, you see, then I allow it would be a *kewrosity*"—a characteristic expression truly of rustic philosophy.

Only eight miles from the smooth lawns and picturesque cottages and lively clamor of the springs! But an eight miles that I would not like to travel again for a less prize than the spectacle at the end. Half of the distance is over a passable road, with some pleasant stretches along the murmuring waters of the Roanoke river, with entrancing vistas through the forest and visions of lazy cattle by the stream. But now comes the unbroken ascent (possibly on horseback) of a mountain at an unceasing angle near the perpendicular, a mile and a quarter—not a single table-land for rest, and where, if we walk, we must cling to the underbrush while we pause to take breath. On a momentary foothold near the top we look abroad. There is a girdle of mountains, patches of golden grain in the valleys below us, and the squat houses of the mountaineers; and on the limits of vision across from where we stand the scarred, black peaks of the almost leafless Poor Mountain. In amazing contrast, on the summit of this mountain near where we stand, are immense towering trees of the yellow poplar, some of them sixty feet high before the first limb puts out, and in a single one of which cylinders, estimating the cubic feet of timber, there is a possible undeveloped house, awaiting, as the statue in the block of marble, the workmanship of man. Half a mile's ride on the level summit, and under such majestic though spare shade, and we are within a quarter of a mile of the Falls, where we must dismount and commence to go down a mountain side even more precipitous than that we have ascended, where we have no advantage of path, no guide but a low, uncertain sound as from the depth of the earth, confused by the whispering winds which embrace it and bear it away, toying with it through the forest. Through nets of underbrush, over great boulders of rock, cutting gashes in the loose soil with our iron-shod boots, clinging to the ivy bush or to a point of uncertain stone while we get a foothold, we appear to be descending into a great fissure in the earth's surface, for there is nothing opposite to view through the torn or imperfect shade but the rocky face of another mountain patched with stunted growths and dead timber.

The difficulties of the way are not described excessively; but to show what is the resolution of sight-seekers, I may mention that a party of ladies, animated by the adventurous spirit of Miss M., of Louisville, Ky., a young lady just released from boarding-school, as dauntless in every exercise of mountain-life as she is graceful and radiant in the ball-room, and sustained by the matronly though youthful countenance of Mrs. Rosa C., whom every visitor of the springs will recognize whenever there is a kindness to be done for any of the guests or an occasion of pleasure to be dispensed, actually made the descent described, went to the very foot of the Falls, and, what is more, climbed the mountain in returning—all the gentlemen of the party being ordered to the front on this part of the trip. In what plight they emerged, what ravages of dry goods marked the way, the rents and mischances and losses of the adventure, are not for me to report; and Miss M., of the ladies, to all the importunate curiosity which assailed them on their return, happily under cover of night, to the springs, protests that a full relation of the adventure is not to be given until at the approaching masked ball of the season, and then under masks, or literally *sub rosa*.

But to describe my own experience of a journey so difficult. About two-thirds of the way down one of our party called, joyously, "The Falls!" We had for some time heard the sound of it, though on the uncertain shifts of the wind, and now a few steps or scrambles brought me to the view pointed out by our companion. I was disappointed and sullenly silent. There was nothing to be seen but ten or twelve feet span of falling water, and I readily imagined that the whole Fall was composed of such short stages of descent, breaking all effect of a continuity of view. "We must go to the bottom," said Wills, whose long stride and fine eye had constituted him our leader. An aggravated struggle with loosened earth and over the sharp, remorseless rock succeeds, and we are at the bottom of this strange, almost ghastly, fissure, the awful, rock-ribbed residence of Solitude.

Heavens! what a scene opens upon me! What I had taken for an abrupt termination of the cascade proves only to be a deflection out of sight, and a few shifts of position at last give a point of view from which can be seen the sweep of the Fall, but out of a straight line, its white currents writhing close at the top, with their knotted muscles standing out, spreading, uniting, divided for a moment, then joined in loud foaming combat, again on the jut of a rock, again over the perilous edge in locked, fatal embrace, and all descending in one tempestuous roar of conflict into the wild channel of the water that rocks on the attenuated sand at our feet. And still the struggle goes on, for there are yet more falls even after this great descent, more conflicts and writhings of water, and twisted currents and great bowls worn in the rock, in which the foam splashes in feastful music. As far as the eye can reach—for two hundred yards at least from the foot of the great Falls—the stream is white with cascades, and bent and tortured with great masses of stone; some of these huge boulders or loose rocks containing more than a thousand cubic feet, others piled by the side of the water, their great seams like recesses or gaps of Nature's masonry, mysterious openings into the side of earth. It appears, indeed, as if Nature had made all the surroundings of this wonderful scene to secure the greatest effect of wildness and sublimity. The solitude is deep, impenetrable. We are in the green heart of the wood, deep down in a narrow fissure; rocks embroidered with mosses as *black* and as brilliant as French broadcloth are close to the stream, and invite us to repose; the drapery of the forest, the rich foliage of the spruce, starred here and there with the pinkish-white of the abounding laurel, conceals even the outlines of the summit from which we have descended. We are alone; walled in and curtained in from the outer world with Nature's wildest work, the sublime manifestations of an elemental violence piled around us in the channel of a stream cleft and gashed in the mountain side, and riveted in the everlasting rock. There is not a sound of life in the forest; not a lizard disturbs the leaves, not a bird twitters, not a living thing moves. There is nothing but the endless sound of the Falls—not so loud, of course, as that of Niagara, but the same deep, solemn monotone of falling waters. *Unceasing!* Through night, through storm, through sunshine, through all the world's changes, when other sounds are interrupted and changed, or travel or cease, and even the measures of time cease to beat, and the sweet cadences of health are gone and the pulses are still, yet uninterrupted, the same to-day as yesterday—the same when those who saw it then are passed into the ignorance and silence of the grave.

The best effect of the Falls, no doubt, is that derived from the vexed channel through which it descends. If the water fell from such a height over a smooth and unconfined face, it is evident that it would assume a fan-like shape, losing its body and be dissipated into spray. As it is, the interruption from the points of rock in the channel, with here and there larger obstructions—one of the most remarkable, a tall pine grown straight into the air from a cape of soil—separates and divides out the currents to reunite or to unravel in separate strands, making effects picturesque beyond the power of description. The most vivid comparison we can make to realize the spectacle is, a plait of white, glistening currents, at top closely interlaced, now knotted with white lumps of foam, the plaits again and again shaken out, again and again united, and at the last frayed out like a whiplash of silver cords.

The day was singularly propitious for every accumulation of sublimity in the scene. My companions had strolled down the stream in search of trout, and I was left alone in the heart of the great scene. One of those storms so rapid and sublime in this mountainous region was rising, and the solemn rumble of the thunder down the narrow valley, like the distant chariot wheels of the Almighty marshaling the storm, mingled with the deep roar of the Falls, and made a combination of sound in which the very soul of man was mixed with the grand commotion around him.

The scene was inexpressibly sublime, and yet various, when explored to its extremity. For farther down the stream, where the eye could reach, and where my com-

"PURGATORY"—VIEW ON PUNCHEON RUN.

Page 85.

panions had passed out of sight, and where I at last rejoined them, there were gentler passages, and

> "Still waters between walls
> Of shadowy granite in a gleaming pass;
> Music that gentlier on the spirit lies
> Than tired eyelids upon tired eyes; .
> Music that brings sweet sleep down from the blissful skies—
> Here are cool mosses deep,
> And through the moss the ivies creep,
> And in the stream the long-leaved flowers weep.
>
> . . . . My soul was an enchanted boat,
> Which, like a sleeping swan, did float
> Upon the silver waves of her sweet singing."

The most romantic route to the Falls is undoubtedly that up the stream, clinging to its banks or stepping along the rocks piled in its channel. It is perhaps no more difficult than the scrambling down the mountain side which has been described; and if one can work his way through the "purgatory" of broken timber, brush and rock, he will be rewarded on his way with vistas of wonderful beauty. Occasionally he may look to a long distance through the cañon. For miles the stream is contained closely by walls of shrub-covered rock; and in the patch of sky overhead the sun is visible but for two or three hours of the day. An old mountaineer remarked to us that of deer, bear and other wild animals hunted in that vicinity, none had ever been known to attempt the crossing of Puncheon Run until it emerges from the mountain, so wild and violent is the chasm.

But the signal is given for departure, and we are forced to take the return route up the harsh side of the mountain in time to escape the rain. The ascent is made with difficulty and labor; but at every pause of it I am constantly thankful that I have striven to look upon a scene that has stored my heart for ever with images of beauty and grandeur; for it is thus, indeed, that Nature is to us a "*perpetual* field of nectared sweets," and its inspirations a possession for ever. All the difficulties of the travel are immensely repaid; but yet it is pleasant to know that this wondrous scene is in a short while to be laid open to the great host of sight-seers, and made accessible to visitors generally, through the enterprise of Mr. Calhoun, the energetic and popular proprietor of the Alleghany Springs. It is already planned to cut a path down the mountain side, and to overcome the most difficult spaces with ladders, and, besides these aids to the traveler, to open some romantic vistas through the forest, and to cut some timber that obstructs the otherwise easiest views of the Falls. There is no doubt that a scene which one of our company, who had traveled on every continent of the globe, pronounced to be incomparable in its combinations of the picturesque and the grand, is to become famous, especially in its convenient conjunction with the best health-giving waters of Virginia; and it is already contemplated to build another mammoth hotel at the Alleghany Springs, in view of the accumulation of visitors from such double attractions for the health of the invalid and the interest of the tourist.

There are local associations of the Falls of a singularly romantic nature, which are not to be omitted from my narrative, and which appropriately conclude its interest. In the almost inaccessible country near the top of the Falls, where there was a more modern settlement known as Puncheon Camp, there are remains of a noted refuge of deserters in the war of 1812. There are imperfect walls of stone yet visible where they constructed rude abodes and defied pursuit. Farther down the side of the mountain, perched on a steep slope, where a single man might hold in check a thousand pursuers, there is an object of yet greater interest—a house or cabin built of large stones, and so cunningly thatched with mosses that to the distant eye it has the appearance of one large rock on the perilous edge of the precipice. This singular structure is now known as the fortress and abode of a number of deserters from the Confederate army in the late war; and it is reported that as many as forty or fifty of them harbored here, making predatory excursions into the surrounding country for subsistence, and invariably escaping those who pursued them by the ingenuity of their refuge. The place knows them no more; but it yet hangs on the mountain side, its loosened thatches of moss fluttering in the breeze, one of the most interesting relics of a war whose crooked paths of romance are yet untrodden by historical detail, and are yet to be illuminated in story.

FISHER'S VIEW.

About five miles from the Alleghany Springs towers "Fisher's View"—one of the finest and most characteristic mountain views to be found in this region. It is approached by a well-graded road, which will soon be completed to the mountain top, and which is now eked out by a narrow but sound path, along which one may ride safely on horseback. A few dead, dismantled pines project from the mountain comb, which affords a view around half the horizon. A natural platform juts out, a convenient observatory strewed with leaves and dead soil, on which we may luxuriously recline while "taking in" the delicious draughts of beauty in the scene.

We have described the scene as a *characteristic* mountain view. It is emphatically so, and one obtains here a vivid general idea, a typical impression, of the aspects of our mountainous country. There is scarcely a single breadth of landscape in the scene, if we may except the patch of open land on which glimmer the white cottages of the springs, and the imperfect glimpses of a valley of gray fields breaking away toward the Virginia and Tennessee Railroad. It is mountains—mountains all around, mountains interminable. The first element of the scene is the broken, unequal band of mountains that describes the half circle that limits our vision in front; now running in straight ranges with almost mathematical decision, again rising into pyramidal points, again jagged and eaten in by the blue sky. And within this boundary lies rank after rank of lesser mountains, a great expanse of country, dented and worked up as dough or potters' clay—plastic shapes, half regular in groups and rows, as if the hand of some great Power had pinched the loose soil into grotesque shapes, and again as if its fingers had touched here in careless disposition the immature crust of earth.

This is the *mountains*. It is the wild, dented arena, clad with unbroken forests, that is the characteristic feature of the scene, so strange to the lowlander. Homely comparisons seldom miss being graphic. A companion compared the knotted expanse to "tobacco hills." Yet more picturesque was the anecdote of an old lady who had never lived above tidewater, and, having been transported in the night-time on a swift railroad crossing the Blue Ridge, looked in the morning from the windows of

FISHER'S VIEW—THE ALLEGHANY SPRINGS.

the cars, and exclaimed, "Law sakes! what a *bumpy* country!"

The name of the view is taken from Fisher, the artist, who made a picture of it last season, declaring that he had seen nothing in Europe to equal its wild and unkempt variety. It is seldom, indeed, that a mountain scene is so little disturbed by "clearings," the signs of cultivation, or even the habitations of man. Excepting the buildings of the Alleghany Springs, which lie at our feet, there is nothing in the intervening valleys to indicate the presence of man; while, in the distance, the huge mountains, dark, forbidding and sombre, do not relent from their frown until far away the dark blue grows fainter and fainter, and they soften to meet the embraces of the sky and mingle in the same light cerulean hue.

. . . . . Another experience of mountain scenery close to Fisher's View—but a few miles on a road turned to the south from that leading to the springs—occurs to our recollection. We had been riding on horseback for exercise, when, on the road to Franklin Court-house—a little beyond where a rickety sign-post marked twenty-six miles from there—Dr. W. pointed me out a mountain scene equal to that viewed from the Peaks of Otter, except in extent, as it occupied but one-fourth of the horizon. The spot is nameless, yet as a mountain view it has but few superiors in Virginia. For a hundred miles we could see the billows of the Alleghany. But there was a peculiar impression I wished to record—one due to certain atmospheric effects which are sometimes observed in these views of distant mountains, and which a distinguished and traveled Northern gentleman assured me that he had never seen under other skies. It was a faint, whitish band of light on the horizon, the deep blue of the sky melted into a radiant, indescribable hue as it descended to join the outline of the mountains, and there, ending in a streak of something like gray twilight, through which we could look farther and farther as into the immensity of space, the boundless sea of an outlying eternity! The air was slightly misty when this effect was observed. Any description in words is but a poor approximation, and I doubt as well whether human pencil could produce such an irradiation, such a mixture of softened colors and lights, as that in which I looked beyond the Alleghany into a world without trace or measure or post of distance on it, and which I was yet sure was infinite!

CHAPTER VI.

A WEEK IN SOUTH-WEST VIRGINIA.

Going to the Natural Tunnel—A SEAT OF EMPIRE—Bristol and its Surroundings—A RIDE THROUGH TWO STATES—The White Ships of the Mountains—Estillville—A Glance at the Mineral Wealth of the Country—" Boone's Trace "—Indian Relics and Traditions—THE NATURAL TUNNEL—First View of the Tunnel—Its Dimensions—Frightful Passage through It—Sublime View from the Lower Entrance—Speculations as to the Cause of this great Natural Wonder—The Tunnel seen by Sunrise—Sublime and Picturesque Effects—Association of an Indian Story—The Tragedy of Masoa—The Adventure of Dodson—A Battle with an Eagle—THE CAVE OF THE UNKNOWN—Almost Lost—A Cavernous Country—BLOOMING ROCKS—A Poetical Countryman—THE HOLSTON SPRINGS—Analysis of the " Hot Spring "—Attractions of the Place.

HE writer opines that many persons living beyond the limits of Virginia—and he *knows* that even a considerable number of natives of this grand and wonderful State—have never heard of the Natural Tunnel. Whether or not it is one of the greatest wonders of this continent, let the reader determine when he has read our description, rude and insufficient as it may be. Much has been written vaguely (and our own pen is already dipped in the subject) of the natural scenery of Virginia, its supreme claims on the American tourist, and the neglect of those claims; but it is certainly an extraordinary instance of such neglect that there is within our memory no printed account of the Natural Tunnel, and that even the curiosity of the newspaper man has scarcely penetrated its obscurity. It has occurred to us to attempt some account of this greatest curiosity of Vir-

ginia, and to add to it some notes of a tour in a part of this State hitherto but little known to the outside public, yet recently the subject of great and eager interests of the capitalist, and abounding with many new fields and objects for the American traveler and artist.

A SEAT OF EMPIRE.

WE leave the Virginia and Tennessee Railroad at Bristol, the most bustling town of Virginia, and one of the liveliest and most animated for its size south of the Potomac. It has the peculiar appearance of a nascent metropolis; and what this little town, which has accumulated a population of eighteen hundred souls since the Virginia and Tennessee Railroad developed its first importance, and where a few years ago sportsmen hunted wild ducks on what is now the site of the Nickels House, a hotel of metropolitan dimensions, may become, when the system of railroads is completed that will establish it as the halfway house between the Mississippi Valley and the Atlantic seaboard, the doorway of the Central West, standing, in fact, between the centre of production of the West—which Professor Maury now calculates to be in the mouth of the Ohio—and the outlet to the great commercial ocean of the world through Hampton Roads, is one of those subjects of vivid imagination belonging to the grand possibilities of the future progress of our country. Bristol may yet be the radiating-point of a scheme of improvement scarcely less great or brilliant than the Pacific Railroad; of which, if the reader doubts, let him consult Professor Maury's Physical Survey of Virginia— a work whose grand imaginations one may well study in surveying this part of Virginia, which thrusts out as a *cape* across which must come the great highway of the trade of the boundless West. The figure of the State here terminating in the form of a long cape—the thin tongue of land thrust out of the jaws of the great Appalachian chain of mountains, extending through the United States from New Hampshire to Alabama—gives distinctness to the imagination of the commercial importance of that part of Virginia of which Bristol is the emporium; and that without statistics and trade details, which we have no room for in these pages, and which would be misplaced there anyhow, unless incidentally. When the Norfolk and Great Western Railroad is built, and the Virginia and Kentucky also, it is very certain that we shall hear of Bristol again, and that in a much larger sense than a point of debarkation or departure for a tourist (such as the author) to an interesting patch of mountain scenery and natural curiosities in Virginia.

Without exceeding the limits of the design of our present writing, without going into the commercial and industrial resources of the country, which we traverse in another interest, we may yet, standing at Bristol, take that cursory glance which the general traveler may afford in such circumstances. Such a glance, in fact, is irrepressible. Here, at this particular point, a vision of industrial empire bursts on the tourist and mingles with the other interest of his journey, even if his mission be not more serious or more thrifty than to see the natural beauties of the country and to make the ordinary trip of pleasure. He stands where he cannot help seeing the elements of power and of wealth around him. He is in the heart of the richest portion of Virginia. The estimate of it may be made in a single paragraph taken from an intelligent journal:

"The rich and productive counties constituting what is known as South-west Virginia are among the most favored localities on the American continent. Their climate, scenery, mineral productions, their coal, iron, lead, salt, plaster, their splendid valleys watered by never-failing streams, their boundless pastures, their rich mountain sides, capable, in many instances, of cultivation to the very summits, their vast yield of hay, their fine horses, sheep and cattle, and last, but not least, their noble breed of men and women, are destined, by the help of the great Virginia and Tennessee Air-Line and the James River and Kanawha Canal, to be distinguished as the very *crème de la crème* of Virginia. South-west Virginia is often called an empire of herself."

Yet this is but one and the smallest element of the vision that floats around Bristol. We are in one of the greatest gateways of the trade of America. In the times in which we write it remained for the genius of General Mahone to display the value of this portion of the State as holding the thoroughfares of a far-reaching and opulent trade. The eye of such a man sweeps a magnificent scene; a breadth of internal improvement; the thoroughfare of the Norfolk and Great Western road; its neighbor in the Danville road, pushed by a judicious and masterly system of friendly connections into the very heart of the Gulf States; the consolidation of the three lines reaching from Norfolk to Bristol, raised beyond small and fretful local interests into a system of thoroughfares for a continent; and finally and generally, the terminus at Bristol expanded into a great funnel for pouring through the accumulated freights of the South-west, conducting them on to their ultimate markets, then draining the whole region between Bristol and Norfolk of its vast products, distributing its due proportion to each of the cities of Virginia, and throwing the remainder upon its long-neglected seaboard, and laying the foundations there for the elevation of Norfolk to the height of one of the great commercial capitals of the world.

But to return to the immediate aspects of Bristol. It is a town that will repay the curious traveler at least a day's delay in it. It is broadly scattered on some rolling hills, and there is a bit of mountain view in the distance. The common acceptation places the town just astride of the Virginia and Tennessee boundary, the line running from the Nickels House just through the middle of the main street, so that the passenger, by a few steps, may cross from State to State, and may be one moment in Virginia and another in Tennessee. But this boundary, though of legal and traditional effect, dividing the town by almost exact halves in respect both of size and property, is said to be incorrect; and it was reported to the writer that the recent party of government officers that had observed the eclipse of 1869 from Bristol had determined, from astronomical observations, that the town laid several miles within the true limits of Virginia; and, indeed, it is so located in the later and more careful maps of the State. But until a joint commission of the States of Virginia and Tennessee shall determine the true boundary (if it ever does), the citizens of Bristol appear satisfied to live in a double jurisdiction, there being, in fact, two corporations and two sets of municipal officers; and, contrary to what might be expected, we were assured that no case of conflict had occurred of the adjoining authorities, and that perfect peace reigned in the bicephalous town.

Bristol is interesting at present as the depôt of a *wagon-*

trade—that curious and primitive apparition of commerce which we remember in our boyhood in other parts of Virginia, and which we supposed had disappeared since the advent of the steam-car. But it survives in its glory in Bristol. It is a great part of the present prosperity of the place; the busy streets are choked with wagons, some of which have traveled sixty or seventy miles to these markets, bearing the stores of an abundant country. At every step we meet the wagoner, and the streets are garish with the gilt signboards and flame with the immense placards which denote an appeal to the country customer. It is the peculiar display of a thriving country town, and the effects of the gilded letters and the painted pasteboard, though coarse, are brilliant, and, we doubt not, "stunning" to the rustic. The hotel accommodations of the place are fine, and even unexceptionable.

A RIDE THROUGH TWO STATES.

A DAY's journey from Bristol transports us to the Natural Tunnel; but so little is it visited by travelers from a distance, and so imperfectly appreciated is the sublime scene by persons who live near it and have grown familiar with it, that there is some hesitation in giving the directions of the road to it. Yet there is a passably good road to it, and a plain one, too. The traveler goes westerly twenty-eight miles to Estillville, the seat of Scott county, and thence again westerly and slightly to the north for fourteen miles, crossing the Clinch river, and he is at the Natural Tunnel, having made the distance, forty-two miles, on a road the great portion of which is the main thoroughfare to Cumberland Gap, and all of which may be pleasantly traveled either in a vehicle or on horseback.

We chose the latter conveyance. The road to Estillville takes us, in turns, through two States. It is the great thoroughfare of the wagon-trade to Bristol, and it is picturesque with white-covered wagons winding over the hills, separate or in trains, dotting the landscape, several of them being almost constantly visible on the tract of country that the eye sweeps. These are *the white ships of the mountains.* They are freighted with grain and fruit, and the other stores necessary in the distant homes from which they have come. Some of them were emigrant trains traveling westward. The modes of "moving" are interesting. Whole families live for days, and even weeks, in the covered bodies of these wagons, cooking and sleeping under the trees by the wayside; and as the heavy vehicle lumbers on in the day, such of the emigrants as are able to walk trudge by the side of it, while the aged and feeble ride; and it is not uncommon to see the curious eyes of little children, in various begrimed conditions, peeping from the white canvas that covers the moving household.

In one passage of the road we met a close train of five covered wagons—a few men in front with rifles on their shoulders, and some six or seven *barefoot* women in their rear, of all ages, from the old crone in her narrow and dirty dress of linsey-woolsey to the young girl of mountain beauty unadorned, walking slowly and painfully over the stones as their teams labored up the hill.

"Where are you going?" we asked one of the men.

"Gwine to Ar-kan-*sas*," was the reply, with a strong accent on the last syllable.

"You have a long journey before you, my friend."

"Yes, furrer'n five hundred miles, I reckon," was the answer, with a certain air of determination in the bronzed, set face; and slowly, sturdily, the train moved on in that long and weary journey which poverty and disappointment elsewhere had appointed for the emigrants.

We were weary from riding when we got sight of the village of Estillville. Passing through the well-defined Moccasin Gap, after having crossed the North Fork of the Holston river, there suddenly came into view the twenty or thirty houses which compose Estillville, overlooking a beautiful bit of meadow bounded by a line of "river knobs." It is a village that boasts of a half-finished church on the hill-side, and a new court-house with a cupola and gilt ball. Spending the night at a so-called hotel, where the real and unaffected kindness of the lady proprietor made amends for the imperfect accommodations, and more than compensated for the single dollar that was asked for supper, lodging, breakfast for ourselves and stabling for our horse, we were fortunate in making acquaintance with two young gentlemen, who accompanied and helped us in our journey the next day to the Natural Tunnel. One incident of Estillville must not be omitted. It was natural for a traveler, wearied by a long ride, to ask for a glass of spirits, and one whose experience hitherto had been that there was not a cross-roads, much less a village, in Virginia where whisky of some quality might not be procured. But not a drop of liquor of any sort is to be got in Estillville, and the remarkable fact was ascertained that not for fifteen years has there been a license to sell liquor in the county. Here is a record indeed for the temperance cause, and that, too, in a mountain county of Virginia, where the display of so much virtue has been lost to fame. A little observation was convincing enough that there were no hardier, healthier, manlier people to be found in Virginia than those among whom our lot had fallen for a few days; and recollections of their hospitality, their intelligence, their thrifty and honest and innocent lives have been borne away by at least one grateful traveler.

The ride in the fresh air and through the scenes of the next morning was delightful, and we were constantly entertained by information of the country through which we passed. Here, on each side of the road and in every direction, were pointed out the undeveloped resources of one of the richest parts of Virginia. The intelligent conversation of Mr. W——, of Estillville, was constantly directing us to the wonderful mineral resources of this region—the iron of which had already been tested in the workshops of Cincinnati as the best from any quarter of the Union; the copper mines that abounded and were yet unexplored; the wonderful deposits of the lead, so rich that from a bank a mile from Clinch river, where our road lies, the neighbors had cut out plugs and moulded bullets from them in the late war. But all these resources are as yet undeveloped, and while Scott county awaits the marches of enterprise, the people are satisfied to raise grain and fruit—the latter so abundant that in the scarcity of money it has actually furnished a currency, and dollars and cents are counted by peaches and apples.

The incessant question in all the conversations of the people touching the resources of this country is of the railroad that is shortly expected to furnish them an outlet —meaning the Virginia and Kentucky Railroad, which is to extend from Bristol to Cumberland Gap, connecting there with the Kentucky system of railroads, and running away to Louisville, Cincinnati and Cairo, bringing in fact Louisville three hundred miles nearer to the sea— through the Chesapeake Bay—than she is now by rail through the narrows of Sandy Hook. Some work had been done on this road when the war broke out, and its grades are yet visible along the route we are traveling. That it will be built in a few years (when the State of Virginia is able to redeem her pledge of a million and a half dollars toward its construction, or when capitalists have had the great benefits of such an improvement brought fully to their attention) we do not permit ourselves to doubt; for it is in fact a continuance of the Norfolk and Great Western Railroad, a necessary link in that great line of communication at which we have already imperfectly glanced, and which, joining at Bristol with the railroads of Tennessee, and connecting at Cumberland Gap with the Louisville, Harrodsburg and Virginia road, is to bring the most productive regions of the West into commercial connection with the tidewater ports of Virginia. The grades to Cumberland Gap are easy. And curious enough, this important railroad finds a passage through the Natural Tunnel which we are proceeding to visit, and such as the human resources of the engineer might not soon accomplish. The Natural Bridge in Rockbridge county has been remarked for the convenience it furnishes—a stage-road passing over it. And here we have a yet more remarkable instance of the generosity of Nature in furnishing a natural tunnel just where a railroad must seek the passage of an almost impenetrable mountain ridge. It is certainly a singular correspondence of natural gifts, and one, too, of natural wonders.

Riding through the beautiful and remarkable scenery that hedges our way to the Natural Tunnel, our attention soon falls off from railroads and trade, and we are lost in very different meditations. A single remark conjures up all the resources of romance. *We are traveling precisely the same road that Daniel Boone traversed a hundred years ago, when he moved into Kentucky.* It is still the great thoroughfare into Kentucky, opening out from Moccasin Gap, and passing through the different chambers or galleries that run into each other along the lovely waters of the Clinch. It was known for many years as "Boone's Trace," and is yet called so by the emigrant. The whole country around here is rich with Indian traditions, which have been neglected in comparison with those of Eastern Virginia, and which might yet furnish a volume of vivid interest. The country we are traversing, and the surrounding counties, formed properly part of the "Dark and Bloody Ground," which the historian and novelist have too exclusively placed in Kentucky. Five miles from Estillville, and on the road by which we approached it from Bristol, are the ruins of a block-house which protected the early settlers; and a fearful story yet clings to a spring within the limits of the village, where a family of the name of Farris perished under the tomahawks of the savages, their blood dying the waters of the brook Passing on our way a little farther west, we are reminded that we are in the thoroughfare through which the tribes inhabiting the Rockcastle hills, in the wilderness of Kentucky, passed to the old settlements of Virginia. Not far from here, too, was the range of the celebrated Cherokee chief, "Dragon Canoe," worthy to be ranked with Tecumseh or Osceola in courage or skill, and who suffered a defeat fatal to his tribe in 1776, at the battle of the Great Island in the Holston river. What tales of blood yet cling to these mountains! What calamities and trials come fresh in remembrance in the midst of these scenes! They compose a story as yet but scantily written, and one that cannot be written entirely to the advantage and honor of the white man, when we remember that ruthless warfare sometimes made by the settlers, and call to mind a message from Mr. Jefferson, when governor of Virginia (1781), congratulating the success of an expedition against the Cherokees already mentioned as inhabiting this region, "it having destroyed fourteen Indian towns, and burnt fifty thousand bushels of corn!" It is a history, perhaps, not in the interest of the present day to revive; but the wild scenes bring glimpses of recollections of it to the traveler, and especially in a country which still appears primitive and from which civilization has not yet entirely effaced the envelope and color of savage life.

But enough of these reflections by the wayside. We are aroused from our romantic meditations—fit preface, however, as they have been to that wild and wonderful scene where tends the chief interest of our journey.

THE NATURAL TUNNEL.

AFTER progressing about three miles from the ford of the Clinch river, and after having repeatedly crossed its crooked tributary, Stock creek, we come to a small mountain or globular hill which is our wondrous destination, for here is the Natural Tunnel. There is nothing which advertises in advance this great wonder, or in any way excites the expectations of the traveler. There is a common road, from which we depart a few hundred yards to make a half circuit of the base of the mountain, that goes clean over the ridge, leading to a settlement some miles farther, called Rye Cove, and which was once the abode of a fierce Indian tribe. This main road goes over the arch of the Tunnel, furnishing a curious conve-

THE NATURAL TUNNEL—THE INTERIOR.

Page 103.

nience to the traveler, of which he would be unaware, seeing nothing through the foliage but glimpses of the mural rocks that guard and sustain the termination of the secret passage-way many hundred feet below him. It is from this convenience that the neighboring people name the gigantic work of nature we are proceeding to explore a natural bridge. But this name is certainly insufficient and paltry for a rock-work that on one flank at least extends some eight hundred feet, and which if regarded with reference to the breadth of the interval it spans, is, in fact, a complication of bridges, arranged, as we shall presently see, in one single massive spectacle.

The western face of the Tunnel, near which we dismount, continues partly concealed from view, or is imperfectly exposed until we nearly approach it; the immense rock which is perforated being here dressed with the thick foliage of the spruce-pine, and the harsh surface adorned with a beautiful tracery of vines and creepers. At last is seen the entrance of what appears to be a huge subterraneous cavern or grotto, into which the stream disappears; a towering rock rising here about two hundred feet above the surface of the stream, and a rude entrance gouged into it, varying in width, as far as the eye can reach, from one hundred to one hundred and fifty feet, and rising in a clear vault from seventy to eighty feet above the floor. The view here terminates in the very blackness of darkness; it is broken on the first curve of the Tunnel. The bed of the stream, from which the water has disappeared on account of the drouth, the reduced currents sinking to lower subterranean channels, is piled with great irregular rocks, on the sharp points of which we stumble and cut our hands: there is no foothold but on rocks, and it is only when we have struggled through the awful, cruel darkness, holding up some feeble lights in it, and issued into the broad sunshine, that we find we have traveled nearly two hundred yards (or say, more exactly, five hundred feet) through one solid rock, in which there is not an inch of soil, not a seam, not a cleft, and which, even beyond the debouchure of the Tunnel, yet runs away a hundred yards in a wall five hundred feet high, as clean and whetted as the work of the mason.

But we must not anticipate this majestical scene, "wonderful beyond all wondrous measure." Happily, in entering the Tunnel from the western side we have adopted the course of exploration which affords a gradual ascent of the emotions, until at last they tower to the standard of a perfect sublimity. The course of the Tunnel may be described as a continuous curve: it resembles, indeed, a prostrate ∽. For a distance of twenty yards midway of this course we are excluded from a view of either entrance, and the darkness is about that of a night with one quarter of the moon. The vault becomes lower here—in some places scarcely more than thirty feet high—and springs immediately from the floor. The situation is awful and oppressive: the voice sounds unnatural, and rumbles strangely and fearfully along the arch of stone. We are encoffined in the solid rock: there is a *strange* pang in the beating heart in its imprisonment, so *impenetrable*, black, hopeless, and we hurry to meet the light of day. In that light we are disentombed: we cast off the confinements of the black space through which we have passed, and we are instantly introduced to a scene so luminous and majestic that in a moment our trembling eyes are captivated and our hearts lifted in unutterable worship of the Creator's works.

It is that sheer wall of rock which we have already mentioned, where the arch and other side of the tunnel break away into the mountain slope; a high wall, slightly impending; an amphitheatre, extending one hundred yards, of awful precipices; a clean battlement, without a joint in it, five hundred feet high. And this splendid height and breadth of stone, that a thousand storms have polished, leaving not a cleft of soil in it—this huge, unjointed masonry raised against the sky, gray and weather-stained, with glittering patches of light on it—is yet part of the same huge rock which towered at the farther end of the tunnel, and through whose seamless cavity we have traveled two hundred yards. It is in this view that the mystery of the scene seizes the mind, and the last element of sublimity is added to it. It is in this view that the Natural Tunnel we had come to see as a mere "curiosity" takes rank among the greatest wonders of the world. What Power, what possible imaginable agency of Nature, could have worked out this stupendous scene?

Of all the wonders and curiosities of Nature within the breadth of man's discovery, there is always an attempt to construct some theory of a cause. There is some scheme of probabilities, or, at least, of possibilities, that may be adjusted to the case—some ingenuity that will supply something satisfactory, more or less, to the ignorance of man and his demand for an explanation. Thus the Natural Bridge in Rockbridge county has been accounted for on the hypothesis, we believe, of Professor Rogers, once of the University of Virginia, of the worn exit of an inland sea that in some immeasurable time washed its way through the Blue Ridge to the ocean. But neither water nor fire can be taxed by human ingenuity as the cause of the Natural Tunnel—a scene which, having approached in wonder, or even in its lower tones of "curiosity," we are yet compelled to leave in unutterable amazement. Look at the breadth, the magnitude of this scene—an unbroken rock eight hundred feet in length, averaging, say, three hundred feet in height to where the soil clothes it, and measuring nine hundred feet across the face of the lower entrance of the Tunnel: multiply these numbers together for the cubic volume of this *mountain of rock*, and then inquire if it is possible that the Natural Tunnel could have been worn—and worn to such dimensions as we have already given of it, and which we have described as *clean rock throughout*—by the action of water operating under any imaginable pressure or in any conceivable time! But the theory of the agency of water, anyhow, is discredited by a single circumstance—the inequalities of the height of the arch, varying as much as from eighty or ninety feet in some places to twenty in others. Again, the phenomenon fails to strike us as one of volcanic action. There are none of the irregularities of an upheaval; there are no signs of a force rending the mountain and tearing it asunder. The *impression* of the scene—and it is here where its sublimity is unexampled—is not as of some mighty force that has raised the crust of the earth, or that has rent the rock or worn through it or delved in it, but as of some mysterious Power, winged with all the winds of heaven and browed like the thunderbolt, that has *battered* its way through the solid rock, tearing away everything in its path, strewing it with the huge, sharp ruins that now choke the stream, and that has rushed through it all like the screaming, invisible body of a storm, which scatters dismay around and leaves behind it the voiceless,

THE NATURAL TUNNEL—LOOKING OUT.

Page 106

uninscribed monuments of a sublime and inscrutable wonder!

The conception is terrible. The imagination is strained as we stand within the august portals of this scene, meditating a question which ever recurs—feeling that shock which verges on insanity, smiting the feeble mind of man whenever he takes into his hands the dark chain of causation. We let fall in the strange doorway where we stand the links of thought that thrill us too powerfully, and we look to other parts of the scene to moderate our emotion.

Turning our eyes away from the battlement of rock to the opposite side of the ravine, a new revelation of the grand and picturesque awaits us. Here a gigantic cliff, but one broken with rock and soil, and threaded to its summit by a sapling growth of the buckeye, the linden and the pine, rises almost perpendicularly from the water's edge to a height almost equal to that of the opposite wall of rock. A natural platform is seen to project over it, and yet a few yards farther there is an insulated cliff, a cyclopean *chimney*, so to speak, scarcely more than a foot square at its top, rising in the form of a turret at least sixty feet above its basement, which is a portion of the imposing cliff we have mentioned. It is at once perceived that here are two points of view that will give us new and perhaps the most imposing aspects of the scene. To attain these points, however, it is necessary to make a circuit of half a mile; and the sinking sun admonishes us to defer this new interest of the scene until to-morrow.

*   *   *   *   *   *

It was well that we did so. After a comfortable lodging in a farm-house two miles away, where a substantial supper, flanked with the invariable milk and honey of the mountains, and a bed of snowy-white linen, attesting that cleanliness so beautiful when found beneath the rude roof, and yet so common in all the homes of the mountaineers, had refreshed us, we remounted for the Tunnel in the early morning, and were soon to find that the rising sun was to give a new and unexpected glory to the scene. This time we ascend the mountain instead of deflecting as before. The road is easy; there are no difficulties of access to the points of view from the top of the Tunnel, and they are undoubtedly the grandest. We pass to the platform before described by a few steps from the main road. It is a slab of rock projecting from an open patch of ground; a dead cedar tree is standing at its edge, throwing its gnarled and twisted arms, as in wild and widowed sorrow, over the awful scene below. We now see the great opposite amphitheatre of rock in added grandeur, for we see it from above—we see it across a chasm nine hundred feet wide and five hundred feet deep, and the exposure being almost exactly eastern, the long spears of the rising sun are being shattered on it. The effect is inexpressibly grand. But there is one more circumstance to be added to the scene: we do not see from this observatory the arch, the entrance of the Tunnel. A few yards farther the fearful chimney-shaped rock invites to a more commanding view, but the ascent is dangerous; the stone on top is loose, and so narrow that two persons can scarcely stand on it. A single misstep, a moment's loss of balance, and we would fall into eternity. But now the sense of peril is lost, or is rather mingled, in the grandeur of the scene. It is a panoramic view. We have now the whole sweep of the mural precipice opposite; the sun's glitter is incessant on the polished stone; the trees which fringe the bottom appear now scarcely more than shrubs; the entrance of the Tunnel has now come into view, and that which yesterday we thought so high and wide, now appears, from our amazing height, as a stooped doorway. We imagine the gloomy entrance into a cave of Erebus and Death, the broken rocks lying within which look like black and mangled entrails. It is a fearful picture—it is that of a supernatural abode.

It only needed some wild legend to crown and adorn the scene. Happily such is furnished, and, more fortunately for the interest of the reader, *the tale is true.* Some tradition attaching to such a spot is to be expected, and a spot, too, surrounded in past times by the Indian tribes. Romances are easily conjured up or invented in such a scene, and in fact there is scarcely a remarkable cliff that does not suggest some new version of the old story of "The Lover's Leap." But the tradition attached to the chimney-rock we have described was ascertained to be true before the writer was willing to transcribe it; and it furnishes a story and a scene more dramatic than that of Pocahontas, or any of those accounts of Indian life which have been carefully preserved in the earlier settlements of Virginia.

The story was told the writer by a lady of the neighborhood, whose intelligence and manners might have adorned any circle of listeners, and whose dark eyes flashed with the spirit of her narrative. Her uncle, Colonel Henry S. Kane, a gentleman well known and honored in this part of Virginia, and of extreme age, remembers the main incidents of the story, which transpired some years after the close of the Revolutionary war, and which were related to him by persons of the neighborhood. The same incidents were preserved some years ago in a Tennessee paper (we think the *Rogersville Times*). So much for the authenticity of the "Story of Masoa."

In 179-, what is now called Rye Cove, a small settlement near the Natural Tunnel, hemmed in by the mountains, was occupied by a fierce Indian tribe, probably the Wyandots. Masoa, the daughter of the chief, was enamored of a young warrior of her tribe, and their trysting-place was on the wild heights that overhung the subterranean passage of the mountain. Here it was her custom to gather flowers, and to meet her lover in the inspiration of the beautiful and solitary scene. But the old chief had other designs for his daughter: he had promised her in marriage to the chief of a neighboring tribe, and, scrupulous as is the Indian in such affairs, he was relentless to the entreaties of his daughter, and angry when he discovered that her affections had been engaged by another. Masoa told her lover in the accustomed place of their meeting of the fate that had been determined for her; when, it is said, he advised, as the only means of averting their disappointment, that on the day appointed for the neighboring chief to claim his bride, Masoa should escape, ascend the sharp high rock, and there, with her lover, proclaim him as her choice to her father and to the party who would probably pursue her; the two threatening to cast themselves from the rock if compassion was not had on their love, and the maiden released by her father from his hateful compact. It was hoped that the prospect of a self immolation so awful, so instant and so dreadful in its aspect might touch the heart of the old chief and save Masoa and her lover. The day came for the celebration of the marriage which the father had designed: the neighboring chief who was to bear away the prize attended with numerous followers. It was an occasion of barbaric splendor, to which all were invited; but Masoa was missing. Search was instituted: her romantic habit of visiting the wild scene on the mountain was known, and it is said that a little brother who had frequently accompanied her there now innocently directed the party of pursuers. These, to the number of several hundred, had searched through the cavernous recesses of the Tunnel. Assembled in the amphitheatre below which we have described, closely mingled in the ardor of pursuit, an appalling sight fell on their uplifted eyes—Masoa and her lover on the high stem of rock, his strong form uplifted above the screen of woods in clear relief against the sky, and embracing it the affrighted but unshrinking maiden, who had ascended with him this awful altar of immolation. She had commenced to speak to the spectators below, and she was yet speaking loudly and vehemently in the last eager hope of reconciliation with her father and of safety for her lover, when an arrow whizzed through the air. It had been strung by the jealous and disappointed chief below. A stream of blood gushed from the breast of the warrior—that breast from which she had separated herself but a little space to rise to the proclamation of her love: she was seen to clasp him in her arms, to look long and tenderly on his face as if inquiring of the death that passed over and sealed it; and then, embracing him more tightly and uttering a wild, long shriek, she leaped down into the air, falling a mangled corpse on the rocks below, and bearing in her not yet loosened arms the dead body of her lover. The scene is not yet ended; another death completes it. Even while Masoa leaped, her brother, exasperated, in the quick agony of his revenge has stridden behind the assassin chief and planted his tomahawk in his brain. All three of the dead bodies are said to have fallen nearly together.

Such is the story of Masoa—characteristic of the Indian nature, its strength and ardor, containing no violent improbability, assured by such living testimony as has given us those many narrations of Indian life which we do not hesitate to believe, and so vivid and dramatic, its natural arrangement falling in such a form of tragedy, that we may congratulate ourselves on saving it to the literature and romance of Virginia.

A more modern and a more homely adventure is related of another part of the scene. It happened within the memory of the neighbors. In the perpendicular wall of rock at the lower entrance to the Tunnel occurs what is apparently a small cave or fissure. A man of the name of Dodson determined to explore it, as it was not unlikely that it might contain nitrous earth, since found to abound in the caves and grottoes of these mountains, from which saltpetre is extracted. Anyhow, Dodson was determined to take a look into this opening, and he was accordingly lowered from the top by a rope running over a log and let out by several men. The rope was eked out to a sufficient length by some plaited strands of the bark of leatherwood; and on this perilous tenure, supported around the waist, he commenced his descent. The precipice shelves considerably here, and to draw himself to the edge of the fissure, Dodson had provided himself with a long pole having a hook at the end. Throwing this on the edge of the fissure, he had nearly pulled himself there when he lost his hold and swung like a pendulum out into the middle of the ravine, suspended by an imperfect rope two hundred feet above the bed of rock below. At this moment, when he was performing his fearful oscillations—so fearful that one of his neighbors, standing at a point on the opposite cliff, described it as if his body had been *slung* at him across the abyss, causing the spectator to draw back instinctively—an eagle, scared from its nest in the fissure and excited to protect it, flew out and attacked the already alarmed adventurer. Having dropped his pole in his consternation, he yet managed to defend himself with a pocket-knife; but while stabbing at the eagle over his head, he severed one of the strands of his bark rope. The accident was unperceived by those who held the rope above, who were only notified that something fearful had happened by the screams of Dodson—"Pull! for God's sake, pull!" He was saved, but the agony of suspense was too much for him; and as the men caught hold of him by his shoulders and dragged him over the top of the precipice, he fainted. The opening he had ventured so much to explore has since been found to be nothing but a shallow pocket in the rock.

"THE CAVE OF THE UNKNOWN."

THE interest of Scott county to the tourist does not end at the Natural Tunnel. But half a mile from this scene, which we leave unwillingly, is a cave in the mountain side, arranged in chambers, one of them seventy by ninety feet, and from the roofs of these hang thousands of stalactites of various sizes and shapes. This cave has been but imperfectly explored, and the two rustics who attended us in it with a pair of tallow dips had never ventured farther than where there was easy ingress, and our party was without facilities to make farther explorations. We passed through several chambers, and must have gone more than a hundred and fifty yards through various windings, at times under lofty roofs, again on our knees in low apertures, our lights sometimes flashing on colonnades of stalagmites formed by the calcareous substance brought down by the drip from the roof or arch. In one of the rooms the country people have been accustomed to have their "frolics" by torchlight. A smaller room adjoins this theatre of the dance, laden with the beautiful tapestry-work of the rock, and looking like a bridal-chamber.

Here, for centuries and ages and countless time, deep down in the bowels of the mountain, Nature has done her unremitting work. Nowhere more than in one of these subterranean workshops, where the silent forces toil in darkness, in absolute secresy, do we obtain that sublimest reflection of the universe—the ceaseless and unmeasurable activity of Nature. Busy in the profound darkness, no measure of time in it, no intermission, work every moment, man sleeping and resting and dying, but the hidden structure ever, ever going on—going on as we are looking at it, going on in stony indifference to the lights that we hold up, yet going on when we have turned the scene into darkness and traveled away, and listen to the rock-drips until lost in the distance of our retreat.

We repeat that our explorations could only be partial, as the extent of the cave is as yet unknown, and so little has the curiosity of the neighbors been taxed with this natural wonder that it is yet without a name, except that which our party agreed to bestow upon it—the "Cave of the Unknown." It was said that wild animals had been chased into it, and it had been found impossible to discover their retreats. There were several apertures noticed by us, which might be increased so as to admit the body of a man, and stones cast through some of these gave a hollow sound, denoting enlarged spaces beyond. But our short and feeble lights, and the ignorance of our guides, caused us to make a hasty and somewhat anxious return to the light of heaven. One of the guides once sent a thrill of horror through us, already chilled in those awful depths of cold air, and impressed by the scenes and pictures, as of another world, that looked at us in the broken darkness and from the saffron walls, calling out to his companion who had wandered into another gallery, and saying, after a painful hesitation, that he believed we were lost. But the cheerful light of day soon shows us its welcome again; and right glad are we to emerge into it, although the atmosphere—and it is that of an October day—is almost stifling as we pass too suddenly into it from the cold and buried air of the cave.

The fact is, the structure of the whole country about here is cavernous. What we heard of caves and grottoes and tunnels and subterranean chambers was enough to give me a crusty sense of insecurity in traversing such a country. Near the house of a Mr. Horton, about three miles back on the road, returning from the Natural Tunnel to Estillville, we were pointed to the partly-choked exit of a tunnel, presenting little that was curious or grand as seen from the roadside, and that might have been passed without notice, but which we were assured opened into an irregular passage-way two hundred feet high in some of its parts, and at one point wide enough, as a countryman described it, to turn a six-horse team in it, and extending a mile and a half through the mountain ridge. We were also told that there was a body of water in it, through which some boys had swam.

BLOOMING ROCKS.

The narrator of the wonder just mentioned, an old countryman, displayed considerable though uncultivated vigor of mind in expatiating on the attractions of the country. If he did not altogether murder the "King's English," he yet persistently knocked an *i* out of "curiosity." There were "cur'osities" innumerable in this region. He would like to sell to the writer (whom he evidently mistook for a Yankee speculator) a thousand acres of them.

"Why, sir," he continued, pointing with animated gestures to a wooded height near by, "there is rocks blooming up there—rocks that bloom all the time."

"What!" we exclaim. "Oh, you mean various colored mosses on the rocks."

"No, sir. There is mosses plenty; but there's yaller blooms—some little as your hand, and some big as a bushel's head; the brightest yaller you ever saw—*in* the rocks. I can show you a mile of them, all blooming round you same as a flower garden."

Here, indeed, was a new feature of mountain scenery, a new wonder; and when we had ridden to see it we found that the old countryman had really supplied a graphic word, and that he had had the unconscious elements of poetry in his rude description. There were rocks which bloomed. We could trace a well-defined ridge of rock, running a mile and a half, on which there were not only patches of rich mosses, black and purple, but spots and irregular spaces of the most brilliant yellow crusted in the rock, their colors apparently as live as those of the richest plant or flower. At certain times of the year the colors of these crusts are found to fade, and then they brighten again as the flowers do, so that the term bloom is even more vividly correct than we had at first supposed. It was a new and strange appeal to the imagination. The long ridge which the eye might follow running away through the foliage, its spots of black and purple and yellow glittering in the sun, lay like the knotted length of a monster serpent, its stripes and patches of different colors glancing through the leaves.

It is a pity to spoil such pictures by hard words of mineralogy; so we propose to leave work so unwelcome to the iconoclast of science, and to proceed thankfully on our journey.

THE HOLSTON SPRINGS.

THREE or four miles south-west of Estillville, and immediately on the North Fork of the Holston river, another curiosity of this region invites the traveler. It is the Holston Springs; and what is most remarkable is, that here, within an area of four or five feet square, one may stand and drink, within reach of his hand, of four different kinds of water. There is a common limestone water, a chalybeate water, a thermal water, and a white sulphur water; and the traveler may drink of each within a common enclosure, without getting out of his tracks. The chalybeate water is weak, but is said to have become so from imperfect tubing. The white sulphur, though not very strong, is a bold spring, and the water cool and pleasant, and efficacious in many diseases. But the most valuable spring in the group is the one known as the "warm spring." Professor Hayden analyzed this water in the summer of 1843. From his report the following extract is published in an advertisement of the Holston Springs property:

"The uniform temperature of the spring, $68\frac{1}{2}°$, being fifteen or sixteen degrees higher than the average temperature of the springs in the vicinity, renders it a natural medicated warm bath, subserving all the purposes of health and luxury, without being sufficiently high to give it the usual disagreeable flavor of warm water. One wine gallon of the water contains 41.14 grains of saline matter, consisting of chloride of sodium and muriate of alumina, 1.51 grains; sulphate of soda, a trace; sulphate of magnesia, 12.75 grains; phosphate and sulphate of alumina, a trace; carbonate of lime, 6.42 grains; sulphate of lime, 20.46 grains. Total, 41.14 grains."

The water is represented to be actively diuretic, and under favorable circumstances determining to the skin by mild diaphoresis; with many it is mildly purgative. Drs. Clapp, Trigg and Preston, respectable physicians of Abington, speak favorably of its use in diseases which have their origin in a disordered state of the digestive organs, in rheumatism, mercurial diseases and scrofula, as well as in diseases of the skin, affections of the urinary organs, and in some of the diseases of females.

When we visited the Holston Springs the property was very much out of repair, and it had been offered for sale in consequence of some litigation. It is to be hoped that the place will be improved. The virtues of its various waters, its bold, rugged mountain scenery, and its pure, bracing air are great natural attractions, which, employed and improved by an enterprising proprietor, might class it among the most popular resorts in the mountainous region of Virginia. There are unsurpassed facilities afforded here for the sportsman. The mountains are full of game, and the beautiful river that flows within fifty yards of the hotel is alive with fish.

CHAPTER VII.

THE MONTGOMERY WHITE SULPHUR SPRINGS, AND THE YELLOW SULPHUR SPRINGS.

Locality of the Montgomery White Sulphur Springs—Beauties and Attractions of the Place—Medical Description of the Water—Reputation of the Springs for Social Gayeties—A Criticism on Southern Society—A GALA DAY AT THE MONTGOMERY WHITE SULPHUR—Description of a "Grand" Tournament—"Gander-pulling"—A Knightly Defence of the Tournament—A Beautiful Illumination in the Mountains—A Night Picture—THE YELLOW SULPHUR SPRINGS—Analysis and Virtues of the Water—Within Sixty Feet of the Alleghany Summit.

ACK from our rugged explorations of Nature to scenes of social gayety, unexcelled in our summer life in Virginia.

The Montgomery White Sulphur Springs are only ten miles from the Alleghany Springs, occupying a central position among the mineral fountains of the South-west, and situated near the Virginia and Tennessee Railroad; but although so accessible, our visit to them was deferred until we had "done" the extremity of the South-west, and it was only after having doubled on the railroad, from Bristol to "the Springs Station," that we were set down in this delightful place to recruit from the wear of our horseback travel in Scott county, and to refresh ourselves with observations of gay and fashionable life in the mountains.

These springs, although, like the Alleghany, of recent

discovery and improvement, are among the best known in Virginia. The grounds are but a mile and a half from the Virginia and Tennessee Railroad, whence the visitor is pleasantly conveyed by a tramway reaching to the threshold of the reception-room. The situation is beautiful, there being two exits by valleys which are formed by small streams that ripple in miniature cataracts over stone bottoms. The wild scene is not without its legendary history; old residents of the neighborhood recollect its early name of "Devil's Dell," and the curious visitor is pointed to a grotesque mass of rock within stone's throw of the reception-room, which has been designated for years as "the Devil's Arm-chair"—a seat which, we must hope, has been long since unoccupied, and which, for ourselves, we were not disposed to invade.

The lawn of the Springs is one of the most beautiful in the mountains—a large elliptical plain planted with ornamental trees, here and there a monarch of the forest, the ground divided by a stream flowing through deep, worn banks, and cutting down clean to the gravel; and bounding immediately this view a broken rim of the Alleghany, while at its very foundation runs a road as hard and level as a race-course. The buildings are unexceptionable; and although less pretentious than those of the Greenbrier White Sulphur, or less substantial than those of the Old Sweet, they have their equals nowhere in the mountains of Virginia, for pleasant architectural effect and for the practical designs of comfort. They are said to have cost one hundred and forty thousand dollars. They suffered during the late war, having been abused for the purpose of a hospital; but it is absolutely astonishing how the energetic efforts of the present proprietors have restored the place to its former condition of attractiveness and comfort, and are already designing additions and improvements. The buildings, as they now appear, are spacious and on a large scale, consisting of elegant cottages sufficient to accommodate at least a thousand people. The central building, which includes the dining-hall, ball-room and parlor, is equal in elegance and spaciousness to any other in the South, and the "cabins" may be put down as a misnomer, as they are in all respects equal to first-class residences, having two stories and galleries, and all suitable appurtenances.

As yet, no analysis of the waters of these springs has been made. They are of two classes—one a strong sulphur water, apparently of like qualities and effects with the famous Greenbrier White Sulphur; and the other a chalybeate water, of a strongly tonic character. Of the first, the medical information which we have is, that it is "a bland and pleasant beverage, well adapted to the cure of a large number of chronic affections that are known to be advantageously treated by sulphur waters generally. It is somewhat less cathartic, and also less stimulant, than many sulphur waters, and hence may be used with more freedom and with greater safety than such waters by delicate and excitable persons. This mild and slightly operative character of the water, while it constitutes it a safe beverage for the delicate invalid, very happily adapts it, as a mild alterative and depurative agent, to a large class of cases in which alterative effects are demanded for the cure of the case."

But it is not so much as an invalid resort that these springs are famous; and the proprietors appear to have the good sense to understand that, after all, the invalid patronage of watering-places is but a small proportion of their profits, and have therefore determined to keep their place in a style of elegance and comfort that will afford to that large portion of the public in motion in summer an attractive resort and a social rendezvous. For the gayeties of their seasons the Montgomery White Sulphur have a peculiar and unrivaled reputation among the watering-places of Virginia. There is nothing of the sapless and uninteresting life of an invalid resort. The social life here, high as it is, is peculiarly *Southern;* drawing its animation from the principal Southern cities, such as New Orleans, and having little of that Northern shoddyism which it has been attempted to import into some of our summer resorts in Virginia. Our Southern belles might, perhaps, improve their taste in decoration, but we are sure that people of fashion in the North might improve their own style by imbibing some of that earnest and natural gayety and enthusiasm, that unconcealed sense of happiness and enjoyment, which characterizes the more impulsive and demonstrative people of the South in places designed for pleasure and recreation.

A GALA DAY AT THE MONTGOMERY WHITE SULPHUR.

A SOCIAL occasion of more than usual magnitude and brilliancy served to divert the writer a day's space from a journey otherwise planned. For some weeks past we had been promised an unparalleled entertainment at the Montgomery White Sulphur Springs, in one of the "grandest" tournaments that had ever yet been witnessed in Virginia, at which Mr. Walker, the governor elect of Virginia, was to preside, to be followed by an illumination and a ball of more than usual magnificence. Governor Walker was delayed, and thus disappointed the curiosity of the multitude; but many other distinguished persons were present, and we doubt whether a similar occasion has ever been excelled in Virginia for real pleasure and brilliancy. The number of visitors at the springs was increased to some six or seven hundred; a special train from Lynchburg brought additions to the crowd, and the gentry in the neighborhood attended in such a number of private conveyances, and there was such a collection of horses, that we were confounded on first entering the extensive ornamental grounds of the springs to hear

"Steed threaten steed with high and boastful neigh."

On the day of the tournament the expanse of the lawn was covered with gay crowds, while nearer the crescent course of the tournament the long line of ladies, thus provided with the best views of the game, might be likened to a wreath of beauty twisted with picturesque confusion on the front of the scene. There are twenty-eight knights entered for the lists, who ride about as if practicing their steeds, while the unlucky pedestrian who escapes them is bewildered by the rattling of carriage wheels, the cracking of whips and the vociferations of the gentlemen to the negroes who accompany them. But in a moment all is silence and expectation, for the herald has sounded the trumpet; the knights are "charged" by a sage, bald-headed orator, and the exciting exercises of the day are commenced.

Some account of the tournament, which for many years has been a peculiar sport in Virginia, and which is evidently becoming one of the popular games of the South, is likely to be new to some of our readers, and not uninteresting. The Southern people are remarkable for their affection for the horse; but they differ from those of the

North in their regard for this animal, to the extent that they esteem him only for his uses in displaying their horsemanship, and not, as the cavaliers of the North generally do, for the qualities and "points" of the animal considered as a creature by itself. To ride a fine horse in this country is a mark of aristocracy, although the writer can scarcely go so far as a certain Virginian, who, speaking in an agricultural society and urging the raising of fine stock, declared that "no man could habitually ride a fine horse without being a gentleman." In the South the trotter is unknown or despised, while the running horse, or one trained to the tournament and sports of the field, is valued for display and exercise. In this sense the Southerners are probably the most equestrian people on the civilized face of the earth; and when the question of a design for their flag in the late war was debated—a question which was vexed and undecided to the last—John M. Daniel was persistent in recommending a horse's head, or the heraldic equivalent of that noble animal.

In Virginia the display of horsemanship has for many years taken the form of tournaments. Farther South a coarser and more vulgar equestrian exercise, which has happily fallen into disrepute, is known by the name of "gander-pulling." One of the feathered tribe is suspended by the head from a cross-beam or gallows, his long neck being cleanly stripped of feathers and well greased; and the feat of the horseman is, riding at full speed, to wring the neck of the fowl, that is yet alive, and to bear off his body as a trophy of his skill. The achievement is a severe trial of horsemanship; the rider is often jerked from his horse; there are ludicrous mishaps, and sometimes severe accidents—the latter, as Mr.

Bergh and his school of humanity might consider, well deserved by the cruelty of the sport.

But for many years there has been no *gander-pulling* in Virginia. The tournament is of another order of diversion. It has no feature of cruelty, and it is designed to practice every resource and grace of horsemanship—in speed of the animal, steadiness of the eye and hand of the rider and a peculiar movement of agility. Ordinarily, the game is to pierce, with a long, metal-shod spear, a ring about an inch and a half in diameter, barely encircling the spear. The ring is suspended on a shallow hook; the knight rides at full speed, being timed by the second to complete the course, which is usually some two or three hundred yards. If he succeeds in bearing off the ring, he is yet to perform the most difficult part of the feat, which is to "cast" the ring, throwing it, by a quick and adroit movement, from his spear within ten, twelve, or fifteen feet of the beam whence he has taken it, as the rules of the game may determine. In the instance of the Montgomery tournament we have commenced to describe there was no casting of the ring, but, as a multiplication of skill, three rings were suspended at intervals of about twenty paces, and the game, which consisted of five courses, was decided by the number of rings and "tips."

The successful knight having been proclaimed, and the choice of Queen of Love and Beauty having been bestowed upon a lady of New Orleans, the most interesting part of the programme remained to be carried out. At night the coronation took place amid the dazzling lights of the ball-room, the knights in their picturesque costumes, and the fair queen fluttering under the attentions that surrounded her throne, displaying perhaps not much of regal self-assertion, but preferably exhibiting the tender and modest grace of a youthful virgin queen. The coronation speech was made by a member of the Lynchburg press (Mr. Edward S. Gregory), a rising young poet of the South ; and, although the writer is not prone to praise, he must say that there was an exquisiteness of expression, a freshness of treatment, a nice felicity of words in the orator's effort, such as he had seldom heard on similar occasions, where the inspirations are necessarily trite and unreal. He referred to some modern efforts to burlesque the tournament, and then eloquently proceeded to vindicate it in its various respects as a game of manly skill, a school of refinement, a social opportunity and an inevitable association of the virtues and graces of real arms. And the reader may believe that the veriest mocker of such sports, witnessing its unusually brilliant and picturesque display on the occasion of this Montgomery tournament—the aspects of reality given to it ; the romantic circumstances of a mountain amphitheatre and the wild scenes loosely bound by the dusky combs of the distant Alleghany ; the evident refinement of sentiment which it inspired in a vast and promiscuous crowd, and, more than all, the real abounding joy of all who participated in it—might relent from his disposition to ridicule and conclude that, after all, there might be real and healthful uses in the tournament.

'But the most brilliant of all the scenes of this festive occasion, and one unequaled in its surroundings by even what the imagination can originate, was the illumination at night of the vast lawns and adjoining grounds of the springs. More than a thousand Chinese lanterns, procured from the most picturesque that could be bought in New York, were hung in the trees. In the midst of these fireworks were exploded, rockets fired. Back of all this display was the dark, ominous mountain, rising in the night, black as a bank of thunder-clouds, anon striped with the ribbon flights of the rocket; above all a star-spangled sky, and in the distance the weird cries and echoes of a night in the mountains. The illumination to such an extent was a happily-conceived idea, and I do not know that it has ever been before so well displayed in the mountains of Virginia. Nowhere could the effect be so well repeated as here, where there is a natural amphitheatre of mountains, and where the variegated plain mingles so abruptly with the wooded height and mural precipice that already, from the elevation of more than three thousand feet above the sea-level, lift themselves to scale the last ascents of the Alleghany.

THE YELLOW SULPHUR SPRING.

FIVE miles south-west of the Montgomery White Sulphur is the Yellow Sulphur Spring. It is most conveniently reached by stages passing over four miles of well-graded turnpike from Christiansburg, on the Virginia and Tennessee Railroad.

We are now in the most elevated part of Montgomery county. The spring rises on the east side of the Alleghany and flows into the head waters of the Roanoke river, two miles away. We are surrounded by variegated and interesting scenery; but what is most remarkable and the most pleasant distinction to the visitor, who already feels his translation into a new atmosphere, is the great altitude of the spring. It is not more than sixty feet above the summit-level of the mountain from which it flows. In consequence of this elevation, the air, as may be well imagined, is elastic, pure and invigorating during the hottest days of summer; and the advantages of a salubrious climate are added in more than ordinary measure to the virtue of the water, to which Nature has given a place so lofty and secluded.

As yet the Yellow Sulphur is but in the infancy of its fame, although the water was locally known and was visited by invalids sixty or seventy years ago. Within recent years the public has obtained some scientific knowledge of the water, and it is already indicated by medical men as one of the most valuable in the Springs Region of Virginia. It derives the name popularly given it from a yellow-brownish sediment, which is often quite perceptible on the sides and at the bottom of the spring enclosure.

The following is an analysis of one gallon of the water:

Carbonic acid	9.360 grains.
Sulphuric acid	53.383 "
Phosphoric acid	0.013 "
Magnesia	7.723 "
Lime	32.150 "
Oxide of iron	0.432 "
Alumina	1.729 "
Potash	0.119 "
Soda	0.359 "
Chlorine	0.092 "
Organic extractive matter	3.733 "

The range of usefulness of the water is to be found in its valuable *tonic* properties. It is a very pleasant beverage, lying lightly and comfortably upon the stomach, even when taken in large quantities. Seven to eight tumblers, taken at intervals, constitute the usual day's allowance of the invalid. The water is beautifully transparent, and, what is a better recommendation to the thirsty, it is delightfully cool, remaining at 55° in the hottest days of summer. The smell of sulphur is not perceptible; the taste is slightly astringent or styptic, and the water, after being used but a short while, is generally preferred by visitors, as a common drink, to the limestone water of the neighborhood.

The accommodations at this spring are as yet limited, their capacity scarcely exceeding a hundred persons. But the buildings are new and very comfortable, and the table furnished by the bountiful proprietors is one of the best in the mountains. All of the visitors of the season of 1869 will testify to the good living of the Yellow Sulphur—the wholesome and substantial beef, mutton and chickens, the splendid bread, and the abundance of good milk, cream and butter. The grounds have a natural beauty to which architectural designs (however we might wish an extension of buildings for the accommodation of a larger number of visitors) are not necessary to add. The shade of magnificent forest trees, whose tops are even with the summit of the Alleghany, makes a shelter glorious and luxurious enough for a summer day; and we leave it unwillingly as the cool nights drive us into our "cabins" and to a refuge under two blankets even in August.

I

CHAPTER VIII.

A TRIP TO NEW RIVER, SALT POND, BALD KNOB AND LITTLE STONY CREEK.

Plan of a Trip into Giles County—Crossing the Mountain—A Ride through a Night-Storm—The Adventure of a Lost Hat—Benighted in the Woods—Singular Experience with a Mountaineer—One of "Nature's Noblemen"—EGGLESTON'S WHITE SULPHUR SPRINGS—SCENERY OF NEW RIVER—"Pompey's Pillar" and "Cæsar's Arch"—"The Narrows"—"Hawk's Nest"—New River compared with the Rhine—LITTLE STONY FALLS—Terrific Leap of the Water—SALT POND—A Lake of Fresh Water suspended among the Clouds—A Submerged Forest—Part of the Lake Unfathomable—An Old Lady's Theory—An Emigrant Company of East Tennesseans—Talks with them—A Picture of Solitude—BALD KNOB—Looking into Five States—Effects as compared with the View from the Peaks of Otter—Cloud-ships—A Fog-ocean—A Hospitable Rest.

HE Salt Pond, one of the "sights" of Virginia, if curiosity is to be reckoned, is thirty-two miles from the Montgomery White Sulphur Springs; and around the terminus of a journey so brief cluster other objects of even surpassing interest. In the neighborhood of this mysterious lake one may get glimpses of the matchless scenery of New river; or he may climb to Bald Knob and get the grandest of mountain views; or he may pursue the swift and contentious course of Little Stony Creek, of which Mr. Fisher, fresh from the art colleges of Europe, has said, "If it was in Germany, we would see a hundred artists sketching on its banks." All these scenes may be compassed by a trip of three or four days. Salt Pond, the centre of them, is

about equidistant from Christiansburg and the Montgomery White Sulphur; the road from the latter place passing into the Christiansburg pike, and constituting the great stage thoroughfare between the springs of the South-west and those of Monroe, Greenbrier and Bath counties. Stages run on this line of travel three times a week, and pass in view of Salt Pond.

A journey which promised so much we were not slow to undertake. With Warren W——, the guide and dear companion of other journeys in Virginia, I was soon equipped for the road, it having been determined not to take the stage-coach, but to travel in our own way, so as to make a more thorough and leisurely exploration of the country. Warren was mounted on a horse—or, as they say in the mountains, by a singular pleonasm, a "horse-beast." I bestrode a mule; "Jacky" being recommended as sure-footed, a regular "dog-trotter," and the pet of the stable.

Our road extended through the richest and most cultivated parts of Montgomery county. It was a vision on either side of broad acres, wide, warm fields, the yellow harvest bound with the garniture of woods, and groves in which stood the square brick houses indicative of the country gentry of Virginia. Leaving Blacksburg, eight miles on our way, a pretty village which boasts a "college" of some sort, we were soon ascending the Brush Mountains. There is nothing like a ride in this elevated atmosphere; the beautiful day is a benefaction—long-forgotten poetry comes to our lips. For miles on the flattened summit of the mountain we gallop along, high in the blue ether and drunken with it, clouds of snowy white over us and the birds of the mountains in their majestic flight.

It had been determined in our leisurely plan of journey to leave the main road within a few miles of Salt Pond, deflecting to Eggleston's White Sulphur Springs, and to spend the night there. We had been told that the hotel accommodations at the Pond were vile beyond description; while Warren, who had spent a former season at Eggleston's, assured me, with good reason, as I afterward found, that it was the most delicious and comfortable of resorts in the Mountain Region of Virginia. We should sup on broiled pheasant, drink the most famous of whisky toddies, and go to sleep on the banks of New river and in view of "Pompey's Pillar" and "Cæsar's Arch," the magnificent rock-work throwing its shadows through our windows. So it was decided to spend the night at Eggleston's, and to devote the following day or days to Salt Pond, Bald Knob, Little Stony Falls, etc. It was a well-planned journey, but, alas! how many such "gang a-gley!"

At Blacksburg, where we tarried and lunched, we had been told that from Newport, nine miles across the mountains, it was but three miles to Eggleston's. We had thus been in no hurry to pursue our journey; the greater part of the way up and down the mountain ridge we had ridden very slowly, and the sun had been set for a quarter of an hour when we reached Newport, a settlement of twenty or thirty board houses on a little pad of soil at the bottom of a funnel-shaped cup formed by the high hills or mountains. As we passed through the toll-gate here, we asked the distance to Eggleston's Springs.

"It's *nine miles!*" was the reply, not a little to our consternation.

The night was gathering, the sky had become overcast

with clouds, but we determined to press on in view of the cheer that awaited us, much to be preferred to that suggested by the tarnished signboard of the Newport hotel that creaked dismally over our heads. We had ridden about three miles, when one of those rain-storms which spring up so suddenly in the mountains absolutely engulfed us in darkness. It was so dark that I could see nothing before me, not even "Jacky's" ears. The roar of the winds through the mountain pines was terribly grand—a solemn diapason that drowned our voices; the air of the night had become so cold that my benumbed fingers could scarcely feel the reins of the bridle; there was no sign of human habitation near; and, to suggest the real perils of our situation, we could hear through fitful intervals of the storm of wind and rain the sound of rushing waters below us, telling us that our road overhung the deep channel of a river. We rode on in single file, "Jacky" bringing up the rear, faithfully keeping the pace of the horse in front, but absolutely refusing to move a peg when the attempt had been made to put him in advance.

Presently a glimmering light was descried in the encircling sea of darkness, in which were absolutely obliterated all our ideas of distance. We could only tell that we approached it by its growing larger, and could only infer that it signified that a house was near.

We shouted at the top of our voices: "Are we in the road to Eggleston's Springs?"

"Yes," came in reply a gruff voice: then followed something indistinct about a "fork" in the road and keeping by the side of a fence.

"But, my friend," I remonstrated, "I can't see any fence—I can't see anything."

"I can't help that," was the boor's reply; and the door must have been slammed to, for the light suddenly disappeared.

There was evidently no prospect of any hospitable resource here. We rode on through the darkness and the rain, Warren, in front, trusting to the eyes and instinct of his faithful steed. In miserable plight we toiled through the storm, blind, wet, dogged, with the cold wind smiting our faces, insensible now to its really sublime effect, as, like an invisible army with chariots, it rumbled far away up the mountain sides. We must have gone a mile or so, when, just as a blast of wind cut fiercely over our heads, I heard a sharp exclamation in front—

"I've lost my hat!"

Expressions of sympathy were of no avail. Warren could not spare his hat, but in such a storm it might have lodged near by, or it might have been blown a quarter of a mile away. I found that Warren had dismounted, for he felt his way to me, and requested me to hold his horse while he attempted to light a match under the folds of his cloak.

"What in the world are you going to do?" I asked.

"I'm going to find my hat," was the reply.

A match was lighted after repeated failures, then a wisp of paper, which showed a fence near by. The rails were torn down, and we soon had, by aid of the wind, a fierce fire burning. It was a wild scene—the fire hissing through the rain, and throwing its twisted arms up into the black sky; Warren, his head bound by a white handkerchief, flourishing a pine torch as he traversed the road for a hundred yards, searching for the lost hat; while far away some alarmed dogs bayed at this unexpected apparition of the night. We had searched in vain for a full half hour, and were on the point of despairing, when I heard a glad cry from Warren. He had found his hat: it had been lodged fifty yards away in a corner of the fence.

Having warmed ourselves at the fire before extinguishing it—and not before, weary and disgusted, I had proposed to spend the night by it—we remounted for the prosecution of our journey. Warren was sure that it was a plain road to the springs; the horses would easily find it; the rain was diminishing, and it was yet early in the night. We plucked up our spirits, and ventured a jogtrot in the darkness. Our steeds had their own way, except occasionally an application of the spur when they showed an unwillingness to proceed.

We had just supposed we had gone far enough to look out for the lights of the springs, when "swash," "swash," came something in my face, then a stroke on the knee, and then some obstruction overhead that nearly dragged me from my saddle. The evidences were unmistakable: I had been smitten by boughs of trees: we were *in the woods!* Nothing could be seen around us; it was pitch-dark, and the rain was yet falling. I twisted a piece of newspaper out of my pocket to make a torch. Warren had but one match left. It fizzled, and then expired before I could reach the paper to it. In dogged desperation I would have rolled from my mule, have put my back against a tree and have waited for the morning. But Warren was more resolute and vigorous. Having dismounted, he twisted a white handkerchief around his hat as a signal in the darkness, and commenced to *feel* for signs of a road. I could only follow helplessly through the darkness after the white speck, holding out my hands for fear of limbs of the trees that might strike me. After groping about some time, Warren was sure that he had got into some sort of a road. It was strewn with the loose and rotting soil of the woods, but he could feel hard earth at times, and prints of wheels in it. It afterward proved, as we learned next day, a mere wagon trace to bring out wood cut in the forest; and that my companion should have discovered this exit was, as he claimed, sheer luck, although in the confidence he had now established in me I was disposed to give him credit for some of that mysterious woodcraft which is supposed to be learned in the mountains.

It was only by signs of feeling that Warren, after a while, could determine that we had come out into a main road. The question now was, which way to turn. In this instance Warren's luck forsook him, for we turned to the right, exactly away from the route we should have pursued to Eggleston's Springs, the lights of which, as we discovered next day, were not half a mile to the left, under a hill on the brow of which we had hesitated. We must have traveled three miles: not a light visible, not a sound heard but the groanings of the dying storm or the splashes of the feet of our slow steeds through puddle and mud, assuring us that we were on a well-traveled road. Suddenly, Warren drew rein and commenced hallooing. He told me to join in, and for several minutes we yelled like madmen, although I had no idea what the demonstration was intended for. A distant barking of dogs at last replied, and I found that Warren had ingeniously sought in this way to find whether any human habitations were near. We rode toward the sound of the barking, exciting it whenever it ceased by renewed yells, so as to get fresh indications of our way. Soon the barking became furious, and we judged that we were near some house. We hallooed with increased zeal; there must have been half a dozen dogs barking in line before us, but there was no reply of any human voice.

"This won't do," exclaimed Warren; "let us make our way through the dogs and find the house." I could hear him urging his horse forward. From a passionate exclamation I understood that the animal recoiled, and that he had dismounted to lead it. Suddenly the white crown made by the handkerchief around his hat disappeared, as if swallowed up in the ground.

A laugh reassured me. Warren had tumbled some six feet down a bank, but was uninjured, and was already on his feet.

Just then a strong but kindly voice quieted the dogs and greeted our ears. "Why, stranger, what's got hold of you?" The owner of the voice, as far as he could be perceived in the dark when he had come up to us, was a large man, bareheaded. He had been aroused from his bed evidently in haste. We explained our situation. The man replied he had "no shelter fitten for strangers," but very civilly gave us directions by which we might make a circuit on main roads two miles and a half to the springs. But he added that, the springs being in the next valley, there was a rough path over the ridge of the mountain that might take us there in half a mile.

I told him I was distressed and in poor health, and unwilling to trust the road. Would he guide us by the near way? and I would pay him anything he asked for the service.

"Well, gentlemen," he replied, "I will take you across the mountain." Taking hold of Warren's bridle, he struck out in the dark, my mule following (for I had found that I could always trust the beast for *that*). I could tell that we were ascending a mountain only from the spasmodic action of Jacky's back and the necessity of clutching his scant mane. We were half an hour making the ascent. Then the mule commenced stepping down, down, as into a gulf of darkness, and as if its lowest depth never would be reached. But I had become desperate; the reins dangled loosely on Jacky's neck, and I no longer thought of precipices or chasms.

Presently the mule's feet sounded on a hard, level road, and the cheerful lights of Eggleston's Springs were seen not a hundred yards away. I rode to the side of our faithful guide. The noble, hardy fellow, to my surprise, had come bareheaded all the way. I felt his shaggy hair drenched with the rain as I reached out my hand in the dark to grope for and to grasp his hard fist in token of my gratitude. I asked, "What shall I pay you, my good sir, for your great kindness?"

"*Not a cent*, stranger," he replied, quietly. "I am jes' glad I got you out of bein' lost."

Again and again we pressed money upon him, or that he would come to the springs and let us entertain him for the night. He would take no reward, and must return to his house. The beautiful and touching grace of the act of kindness done by this simple mountaineer was that he made nothing of it, and seemed to be surprised that we thought it remarkable. Yet this man had left his comfortable bed, gone out in the darkness to strangers, who might have been murderers or marauders for aught he knew, and at their simple request had gone with them, uncovered, through the rain, toiling in mud up and down a rough mountain; and now, storm-drenched, at midnight, having to make his way back home, this poor fellow—a man who worked hard for his scanty bread— who perhaps bitterly knew the value of money—refused the least reward for what he had done, and was satisfied to take with him on the dark, rough path on which he was to grope back through the unceasing storm, the consciousness of having done a kindness to strangers!

Truly this world is made up of different people; but never have I been so touched by the lesson of something good and noble in human nature, never have I thought better of my fellow-men, never more sincerely thanked God for what there is in this beautiful world, than when shaking by the hand this rough inhabitant of the mountains, this true nobleman of Nature found in the forest.

The name of this man is George H. Williams; and I record it here as an expression of gratitude and of admiration, which I am sure the reader will respect.

. . . The attention and kindness of our bustling host of the springs soon consoled the fatigues of our journey. It is sufficient to say that the prospects of good cheer which Warren had held out were more than fulfilled; and when, long after midnight, I retired to bed, coiled in clean and delicious sheets, it was with a sense of well-earned rest, a *luxury* of fatigue even sweeter than the sleep that blunted it.

EGGLESTON'S WHITE SULPHUR SPRINGS—SCENERY OF NEW RIVER.

WHEN next morning I put aside the curtain from my window, it seemed that I had been transported into Fairyland. The experiences of the journey yet bewildered the brain; the black night, the voices of the storm, the dark, muttering mountains—and I woke out of these to see a beautiful river carrying rich freights of the morning sunshine by my window, and washing what, partially seen, seemed to be the broken, scarred wall of a ruined castle.

I was looking at some of the most beautiful cliffs of New river. Eggleston's Springs is situated on a green knoll. New river bends here nearly to doubling, but a calm, majestic bend, with no anger of the stream at loss of distance, not a ripple to show that it is disturbed in its course, no sign of vexation in the graceful movement.

The scene is at once lovely and grand. My first surprise was, that a resort so attractive had been found out by so few seeking health and pleasure in the mountains of Virginia, for the water of the spring is said to be of unsurpassed virtues, and completes the attractions of the place. The water has not been analyzed, but it is strongly sulphurous, perhaps more so than the famous Greenbrier water—so strong that we were told that in *ante-bellum* times, when the happy custom was of carrying silver coins in the pockets, they would be found tarnished from the insensible perspiration after a few days' use of the water, so thoroughly did it saturate the system. There were only about seventy visitors here in the summer of 1869, although the excellent accommodations might have admitted more. It is a pity that the place is so far removed from the railroad; but there has recently been discovered a mode of access to it which we think far preferable to the stage-coach, and of so inviting and romantic a nature that Mr. Eggleston might well advertise it as a new sensation for the tourist in Virginia. It is to leave the Virginia and Tennessee Railroad at New river bridge, and to float down the stream twenty-five miles in one of the batteaux which navigate it, the current of the stream taking the boat slowly down through a scenery most grand and picturesque, upon which the eyes of the floating passenger may constantly feast. It is a journey that may be done in six or seven hours of daylight; and the batteau may be rigged with a shelter from the sun, and may be easily equipped with whatever comforts may be required. Some ladies from New Orleans had adopted this mode of reaching the springs; they had had music on the water; there were wonders to tell of a scenery such as they had never seen before, a diorama of the banks of New river; and they were enthusiastic in praises of the delightful and romantic conveyance, which they had preferred to that ordinarily adopted by the traveler.

Yet they had only got glimpses of the scenery of New river. It is a wonder for a hundred miles. Just at the springs there is a picture of rock-work the effects of which are absolutely startling. The various forms of it are designated by such classical names as "Pompey's Pillar," "Cæsar's Arch," "Vulcan's Anvil," etc. Just where the river bends it is one hundred and twenty yards wide, and towering clean out of the blue water are majestic cliffs of clean gray rock two hundred and ninety-five feet high. The stream is one hundred and fifty feet deep at their base. The grotesque shapes of the cliffs startle us with resemblances; it is a Titanic world by moonlight; and we may imagine the slow, sinuous water creeping under the shadow of a giant's castle.

Following the stream a few miles from Eggleston's, we come to the "Narrows," where it passes through Peters' Mountains. This ragged defile was a well-known strategic point in the late war, and the headquarters of the Northwestern army of Virginia was kept near it until Cox's raid in 1863. The scene is about three miles north-west of Parisburg, the county seat of Giles. The town is at the extremity of a mountain, which rises over the scene, and which is poetically named "Angel's Rest." From the banks of New river it appears to be a peaked summit scantily garnished with shrub-like trees, but there is said to be a beautiful piece of flat and open land on top.

Yet many miles farther away there rises another characteristic landmark in the gallery of scenery which New river affords. It is Hawk's Nest, ten miles from where New river joins with the Gauley and makes Kanawha river proper—a scene beyond the boundaries of our tour. Although not afforded a visit here, the writer may complete what he has designed as a rapid sketch of the remarkable scenery traversed by New river with a description of Hawk's Nest, or Marshall's Pillar, credited to a European traveler. His impressions standing on this observatory are thus recorded in beautiful and thoughtful language: "Beneath and before you is spread a lovely valley. The peaceful river glides down it, reflecting, like a mirror, all the lights of heaven—washes the base of the rocks on which you are standing, and then winds away into another valley at your right. The trees of the wood, in all their variety, stand out on the verdant bottoms, with their heads in the sun, and casting their shadows at their feet, but so diminished as to look more like the picture of the things than the things themselves. The green hills rise on either hand and all around, and give completeness and beauty to the scene; and beyond these appears the gray outline of the more distant mountains, bestowing grandeur to what was supremely beautiful. It is exquisite. It conveys to you the idea of perfect solitude. The hand of man, the foot of man, seem never to have touched that valley. To you, though placed in the midst of it, it seems altogether inaccessible. You long to stroll along the margin of those sweet waters and repose under

LITTLE STONY FALLS.

Page 143.

the shadows of those beautiful trees; but it looks impossible. It is solitude, but of a most soothing, not of an appalling character—where Sorrow might learn to forget her griefs, and Folly begin to be wise and happy."

Beautiful, generous river, that bestows such scenes on the lover of Nature and gives such noble places for the meditations of man, the purification and strengthening of the soul of the wanderer! It should be the pride of Virginia, as the Rhine is of Germany. "The Rhine! the Rhine! a blessing on the Rhine!" sings its worshiper. And a blessing, too, on our beautiful Virginia river—not, like it, flowing by ruins of ancient castles grim and hoar, and "reeling onward through vineyards in a triumphal march, like Bacchus crowned and drunken," but passing in solemn pace the eternal rocks which Nature has sunk deeper than man ever made foundations for his work, the shadows of enduring castles on its silver breast, and its pure waters washing like a sacrifice the feet of the great mountains.

LITTLE STONY FALLS.

LITTLE STONY CREEK is a tributary worthy of New river. We had to ride seven miles from Eggleston's Springs to find it, hid, as it is, in a deep and narrow valley. Hitching our steeds at a saw-mill worked by the beautiful stream, we provided ourselves with redoubtable pilgrims' staffs to assist on the rugged path to the Falls, half a mile below.

The path was by or near the side of the stream, the sound of which, tearing through a channel piled with rock and broken into a succession of small falls, guided us through the thick laurel, even when the swift and clamorous water was not in sight. The stream averages a width of fifteen or eighteen feet, but the descent is great, and the water rushes through a deep channel with the volume and contention of a mountain torrent. At times it darts by us with arrowy swiftness; a cape of rock wounds its side, and it writhes for a moment on it; again it passes into cascades, with here and there a divided current wandering playfully away to a worn basin, and throwing drops of silver water up into the air.

The path was rough and difficult enough to please any romantic notions. At one place, where we had to cross the stream, we found the rude bridge had been swept away, and our only resource was to "coon" a small tree, thick with branches, that was found lower down, fallen across the chasm. The process is to straddle the tree and work the body along by the hands, with the necessity of "spraddling" in a very ungraceful manner whenever a limb putting out from the body of the tree is encountered. I was some time working my passage, and I found that Warren, who was in my rear, had been amusing himself making a pencil sketch of the performance.

But there was no time for idling, for the sound of the great Falls was already in our ears. Spanning a turn of the stream, we come to a decayed wooden walk just on the brow of the Falls, and affording an excellent view. The water descends sixty feet clear, and then breaks in wild confusion upon a succession of short falls, and then rocks itself in a wide, worn basin fifty feet deep. The impetuosity of the stream has before been spoken of, but here it is grand; it does not fall, but it *leaps* far out into the air, and we might easily stand between it and the wall of black rock that measures the descent. With a fierce, almost deafening sound the stream springs over the chasm. It is fearfully lifelike, and makes one involuntarily shudder as the torrent, with frothy lip and wild scream, leaps by us to the torture of the rocks below.

At the foot of the Falls the scene and sounds are less terrific. We hear the incessant trampling of the waters on the succession of the short falls below. There are graceful shadows on the rocky face of the cliff; miniature rainbows hang around the falling waters; and for a hundred yards, such is the force of the main fall, the mist floats in the sunbeams and dances in our faces. The framing of the picture is curious. The entire structure of rock is seamed like masonry, and the abutments are almost as well defined as if the hand of man had reared them there. But the yet further surroundings of the scene overpower the suggestion of Art having intruded here. A mountain crested with towering plumes guards the scene, and Nature reigns in unbroken grandeur around.

SALT POND.

THREE miles farther we had to go to see Salt Pond, and we proceeded across the country at a rapid pace, so as to get a view of it before the expiration of the day.

The first view of this wonder of Nature, as obtained from a turn of the road half a mile distant, was a disappointment. It looked like any large mill-pond, and there was nothing in the contracted surroundings—this strange water being sunk in a cup, as it were, deep in the mountain side—to tell us that we were looking upon a lake suspended four thousand five hundred feet above the level of the sea. A nearer view disclosed some beauties in the scenery. The bright, translucent water is held sparkling in a bowl of forest green, a shaded walk winds along its banks, and from a surface smooth as a mirror arise the dead tops of giant trees that the water has submerged without overwhelming.

The lake is three-quarters of a mile long, and will average a third of a mile in width. It approaches the form of an ellipse, with one side flattened or bent into a shallow crescent. Contrary to the suggestion of its rude and inappropriate name, it is a lake of pure *fresh* water, not the least saline trace in it. It obtained its name from the circumstance of a tradition that there was once a famous "salt lick" here, frequented by immense herds of elk, buffalo, deer and other wild animals.

The interest that attaches to the lake is the mystery of its source. There is no visible stream to feed it. At its eastern termination it is enclosed by a huge pile of rocks, and there is no exit but one recently made by an act of vandalism of some wretch, who has cut out a "race" to drain its waters for a saw-mill. As yet, the diminution of the water has not been considerable from the act of this savage, although we could perceive that it had fallen some two or three feet from the old water-line on its banks. However, when we consider the *mysterious depths* of this wonderful lake, we can have no fear of its disappearance unless from yet hidden causes that Nature commands. It is said to have been forming and to have been gradually enlarging for more than sixty years, its first appearance having been noticed in 1804. It has been steadily increasing since then, having risen twenty-five feet within the memory of persons living near it. It has never been affected by drouths; and although the water has not the least trace of stagnation, and is fresh enough to be taken to our lips, it has never been inhabited by fish, and it is said that all of the finny tribe placed in it have not died, but strangely *disappeared*.

The surpassing wonder is that in some parts it is *unfathomable*. A boat carried us over this enchanted water. At some places we could look down, down into its translucent depths, and see the great trees which it had submerged, crooked and dwarfed by the refracted light—a weird, leafless forest yet rooted in its original soil. The effect was indescribable; it was that of the glimpses of a strange, solemn world of shapes that looked heavy as stone or bronze, and was yet suspended in the water. Rowing into the middle of the lake, we were told that thereabouts the water had been sounded by a line three hundred feet long and that no bottom had been touched. I wrenched a thin silver band from my pencil and cast it into the water. It made a cord of beautiful white light, let down, down—no end, no circlet to tell that it had stopped, until the eye, straining after a diminished strand, then a vanishing point, could see no more, and quivered on phantasms of its own creation in the depths of the water that mocked it.

What can account for this mystery of a bottomless lake suspended among the clouds? A popular but inadequate explanation is, that the trampling of the herds in the bottom or sink, where they came to lick the salt, kneaded and packed the earth until it held the water that gradually collected from springs which the area contained. Indeed, we were informed that a common practice of making ponds in this region is to select a "springy" bottom, and use it as a place for salting cattle until the soil is beaten so as to hold the water that rises in it. But this explanation does not account for the immeasurable depth of water we have referred to. That suggests a subterranean river, the opening of lower depths, or whatever the imagination may supply of "caverns measureless to man, down to a sunless sea."

I had been amused by an anecdote I had heard at Montgomery White Sulphur Springs. Some ladies there had planned a trip to Salt Pond, escorted by gentlemen. The anxious mamma of one of the former insisted upon exacting a promise from the gentleman who was to escort the treasure of her hopes that on no account should she be permitted to venture into a boat and go upon the water. The gentleman remonstrated that there could be no possible danger in this part of the amusements that had been designed. "I don't know about that, Mr. A——," rejoined the old lady: "it is a curious sort of thing, that pond, and if I was on it I should feel all the time as if *the bottom might fall out!*"

Altogether, Salt Pond is a great curiosity to the common traveler, and may be much more to the man of science. If an enterprising Yankee had hold of the place, a large and pleasant hotel would be built here; there would be the finest boating imaginable on the water; the delightful mountain air and the scenes it encases would invite hundreds of visitors; and all these attractions would be afforded immediately on the great thoroughfare of the Springs Region of Virginia, the stage-coaches which traverse it passing in sight of the Pond and just under the brow of Bald Knob. As it is, the accommodations here for the traveler are not worth the name. Poverty and filth surround the place. What is called a "hotel" we found to be a single dreary house built like a barn, the cattle housing under the front portico, and a muddy scow, pushed from the slime of the bank in which it was rotting, was the only conveyance we could get on the water. The large, bleak house, cut up into rooms, hotel-fashion, appeared to be deserted. It was only when we entered it that we were surprised to find a swarm of unsavory humanity hid away in it—men, women and children pigging together in the dirty rooms, and scarcely aroused to notice the appearance of strangers or to answer our questions except in sullen monosyllables. An emigrant company of East Tennesseeans had come to make a settlement here, and for the present inhabited the hotel. It was a dreary collection of the old and young of a people whom poverty had driven to new adventures in the wilderness. A pitiful, shrunken woman, a specimen of the "respectable" poor, entered into conversation with us. Warren asked her how she liked her new home. "It is a hard life," she replied; "but" (with an air of superiority) "what I mind most is that there is no *society* here." We were not disposed to deride the aspiration of the poor woman. A country where we may ride for miles without seeing a house, even a log cabin, where in the stillness of evening we may look from the road-side or the mountain over unbroken forests stretched to the stained sky and hear no sign of life—not the bark of a dog, not the tinkle of a bell—may give momentary emotions to the passing traveler, and he may exclaim in the silence around him, "How grand is this solitude!" but to live in it, to bind up our life and work in such a scene, is a thought that appalls, and in a moment the solitude has become changed and oppressive when we realize it no longer as a passing picture, but as an allotted home.

BALD KNOB.

The sun was sinking when it was proposed to complete the emotions of the day by a view from Bald Knob, the top of the mountain on the high shoulder of which Salt Pond is placed. It was only half a mile farther to the mountain's summit, and we could go up on horseback. I had but little anticipations of the scene that awaited me, and, fatigued as I was, was almost tempted to decline any farther explorations. I had imagined that no other view in Virginia could compete with what I had seen from the Peaks of Otter; but I was yet to see an even surpassing image of sublimity, differing in aspect and perhaps in kind from the former experience of mountain scenery, and realizing how various is Nature, even when we select to explore but a single feature of its wealth or grandeur. If I had not gone to Bald Knob, I would have missed what by far most rewarded our journey, and I would not have my present reflections, that the finest mountain view in Virginia is comparatively unknown, and is yet to be advertised to the tourist.

The top of the mountain we should judge some thousand feet above Salt Pond, and our impression was of an elevation quite equal to that of the Peaks of Otter, although we had no means of measuring it. The summit is very differently formed from that of the Peaks: it is a globular surface, having on the north a broken crown of rock, with a field of some acres of dark soil on the blunt top, thickly covered with undergrowth. What appear to be bushes a foot and a half high are really dwarfed oak trees, bearing acorns. A slight rain had fallen just before we commenced the ascent of the mountain, and the leaves of the dwarfed forest we have described still held drops of water, illumined by the glancing rays of the setting sun, and giving the effect of a jeweled veil twisted on the scant and deformed head of the savage mountain.

We had ascended up out of the cup formation of Salt Pond, its narrow circumscription of scenery, to the sudden view of a new world, where we could see a hundred miles away. We could look into five States— Virginia, West Virginia, Kentucky, Tennessee and North Carolina; we could see the systems of mountains in all these States—parallel ranges of mountains, mountains running transversely, sierras, single mountains, mountains near by thatched with rock and shrub, mountains in the distance whose even line of summit looked sharp as a knife edge, and mountains which peeped ever yet beyond on the farthest banks of the infinite sky. The scene was hung with strands of raveled clouds; a variable purplish tint rested on the mountains; the sun was throwing across them the last lengthened javelins of the day. It was a scene of surpassing width and grandeur. The wildness of it exceeded that of the Peaks of Otter. There were no patches in it of cultivated fields; there were no round and milky-bosomed hills in the foreground. The savage grandeur of mountain scenery was spread around us and lifted up into the sky. Our eyes seized, twenty miles away, a glittering object. The light of the sinking sun must have flamed on a cupola in a distant village, for in a fold of the purple robe of the mountain there shone something like a single star, bright as a diamond—fit clasp to the regal attire of the scene. New river, too deeply sunk in its valley to catch the last rays of the sun, appeared but as a silver thread. Everywhere a new feature of sublimity appealed to us. We could speak only in exclamations. The mind was squandered by the extent of the scene.

On the Peaks of Otter the writer has referred to an effect experienced there—that of immensity of space, looking from the cribbed earth below up into the blue, unfathomable sky overhead. The sensation on Bald Knob was quite different, and so from a singular circumstance. The sky was half covered with clouds; they were just over our heads, and the effect was as if we had been thrust right up under the dome of the heavens—the result of measuring the clouds and the blue spaces together, as in the same plane of distances. The eye, in a little while, searches through this delusion, but the first impression is that of being just under the sky, and it is one of grand, unspeakable terror. As we watched the scene a great white cloud swept near us, looking like a flying ship. We were near enough to have thrown a stone into it. I could almost imagine that I could hear the sound of its passage through the air. So much to see, so much to think of, in a scene that changed every moment, and was now passing, with shadowy grandeur of the dying day, into the blackness of night!

> "Many are the thoughts that come to me
> In my lonely musing;
> And they drift so strange and swift,
> There's no time for choosing
> Which to follow; for to leave
> Any, seems a losing."

. . . Such a scene called for another visit; and even at a cost of a night of wretchedness in the Salt Pond hotel, we were determined to see the next sun rise from the observatory of Bald Knob. We had some biscuits and cold meats in our bag, and a thick traveling shawl spread on the floor, with our satchels for pillows, was found sufficient for the little time of night we gave to sleep. We asked only shelter of the Tennessee emigrants, and that was given us in an apartment used for a wood-room, in which we fortunately had abundant materials for a good fire, grateful enough in this mountain atmosphere.

The morning was raw, and so dark that our watches only had informed us when it broke. When we had walked up the mountain (choosing this mode of ascent for its superior exercise), the sun must have been up; but, although we could not see it, Nature had prepared for us a superior scene, and no happier circumstances could have been imagined than those which rewarded us. The air was filled with a dense fog, and, as at last we ascended above it on the summit of Bald Knob, we found that what appeared to be a great ocean had engulfed the scene, and that we stood upon a small island raised above its immensity. The fog hung below us, around us, a shipless ocean—not an object discernible upon it but the summit of the Cumberland Mountains in the distance, not yet quite submerged, and looking like a thin rim of coast seen far away at sea. Presently the fog rose above this too, and drowned it, and we stood upon a single island under the hollow sky, in a vast, solemn ocean—no sail upon it, no white caps of waves, no sound of water—a gray, limitless, breathless sea. It was hours before this sea broke up, and when it did, it was as the apparitions of another creation issuing out of chaos. The mountains arose, and took shape gradually; the valleys were spread out and garnished; the eternal rocks were planted and the river traced; and when at last the sunlight streamed in full joy and conquest over the scene, there was naught of the fog but some shreds twisted by lances of the sun, as they retreated slowly with sullen steps of defeat up the mountain side.

We had seen Bald Knob in its various glories. The following night we were happy in telling our recollections of the scene. We spent the night by invitation at the beautiful residence of Mr. W——, who did not need the recommendation of being "the richest man in Giles county" to establish the elegant hospitality and refinement of his home. There was a company of ladies visiting here from neighboring counties, such reunions being common in the hospitable practices of Transmontane Virginia. The next morning we were returning to the Montgomery White Sulphur, going back to its places of fashionable gayety, yet places holding for us no fairer, sweeter faces than those we had left in the mountain home behind us—a transient, but unforgotten vision.

CHAPTER IX.

TAZEWELL COUNTY, THE SWITZERLAND OF VIRGINIA.

How to go to Tazewell County—Descriptions of the Route—Saltville—The Alps of Virginia—"THE PEAK"—An Indian Battle-Field—Dial Rock—Climbing the Cliffs—VALLEY OF THE CLINCH RIVER—View of it on a Summer's Evening—Burke's Garden—Abb's Valley—The Flora of South-west Virginia—The Tazewell Historical Society—Was Tazewell County ancient Xuala?—Social and Literary Culture in the Mountains—Romance on Horseback—A RIDE THROUGH THE MOUNTAINS—HOMES OF THE MOUNTAINEERS—Comparison of the Mountaineer and the Lowland Rustic—Dialect of the Mountains—Traditions of the Early Commerce of South-west Virginia—"Uncle Billy"—Isolation of the Mountaineer's Home—An Observation of Mr. Horace Greeley—Simplicity of a Primitive Society—A COMEDY IN THE MOUNTAINS—"Sal's" Courtship—The "beatingest" Dog—A Lock of Hair—Reflections on the Mountain Maid—A Vision of Beauty.

E were meditating a journey to the upper tier of Virginia watering-places—approached as this part of the Springs Region is from Staunton, or by stage routes crossing from various points on the Virginia and Tennessee Railroad in the direction of the Greenbrier White Sulphur Springs—when we were advised that we had not completed even the most obvious interests of South-west Virginia until we had made an incursion into Tazewell county, described as the Switzerland of the Old Dominion. The whole country is a tossed bed of mountains. Clinch Mountain, which derives its name from Clinch river, which heads here, extends through the entire length of the county; the Cumberland Moun-

tains also traverse it, the "Great Flat-Top" in the northeast corner of the county being a spur of this range, and the whole of Tazewell may be described as broken up into a succession of mountain and valley. The mean height of the arable soil of the county is about two thousand two hundred feet above the level of the ocean. Without either a railroad or a navigable stream, the condition of Tazewell is one of singular isolation; it suffers greatly from the distance of markets; and, glancing at it on the map, we would imagine that it would be impracticable to the traveler.

But an easy route is to be found to the scenes of Tazewell—one that may be recommended to the tourist, not only for its convenience, but for the agreeable circumstances of the wayside. This route is by way of Glade Springs Station. There we leave the Virginia and Tennessee Railroad; a branch railroad runs eight miles to Saltville, itself an object of interest. Passing through a rugged defile of Walker's Mountain, we enter the beautiful valley in which the great salines of Virginia are situated. The settlement is at the foot of the mountain, and overlooks one of the most charming valleys in the world, in the centre of which is the curious basin of salt water, eighty per cent. in strength, from which a large portion of the country is supplied with salt.*

* In a recent account of these salines, published in the interest of an emigration company in Virginia, there is a sketch of their history; and it may gratify the curiosity of some of our readers to trace the steps of this now important manufacture of salt. At the advent of the whites decisive evidences of the prior presence of the Indians were furnished by the *débris* of an Indian village or encampment immediately contiguous to that part of the valley where the soil is most sensibly impregnated with salt. These consist of pieces of broken pottery, arrow-heads, and other rude commodities of stone which

We then commenced a delightful ride on horseback to Jeffersonville, the seat of justice for Tazewell county, eighteen miles distant. We say delightful, for the road then abounded, and are yet by no means infrequently turned up by the plough, not only about Saltville, but at the foot of both gaps of Walker's Mountain, opening into the valley from the south. But the presence at the lick of numerous little pits or basins, fashioned by the tongues of animals in the soil, besides other reasons unnecessary to state here, would indicate rather nomadic than permanent settlements there of the aborigines, allowing occasionally in the interim uninterrupted access of wild beasts. Manifestly the spot was to the Indians an invaluable preserve of game. There are many proofs of the countless numbers of animals which used to resort to it thickly underlying the soil in large spaces. The Indians, too, must have found their supplies of salt here, although we cannot say whether it was used concrete or in brine. The pits would often, no doubt, be found to contain little pools of brine, trickled into them from the surrounding earth, and in warm seasons, or where long overlooked, crusted at the edges or at the bottom with grained salt. To the more instructed whites these natural processes pioneered the way to their own first rude salt-works—excavations of a few feet, into which the brine, saturating the adjacent soil, gradually flowed, whence, transferred to some iron household vessel, it was boiled down to salt. At length some more adventurous innovator enlarged and deepened these excavations, carried finally to a depth of eight or ten feet, and, obtaining larger kettles, commenced the business of making and selling salt. The sweep now, instead of the dipper, was needed for these larger operations, and, raising the brine, swung it around to monster twenty-gallon kettles at convenient distances. This description of operations belongs to a period of time between 1780 and 1800.

Toward the close of the last century, a stalwart, fine-looking man, a Scotchman, with his pack on a little white pony, appeared on the scene. He sought and found employment with the parties then engaged in making salt. A piece of land lying adjacent was, soon after his arrival, offered for sale. His employer, the proprietor of the salt-works, refused to buy it, because it had been already stripped of timber, which alone gave it value in his eyes. Here was the golden opportunity. For the slight requital, as a well-authenticated tradition goes through the grandest and most various scenery, and at the beginning is signalized by the sublime picture of a grand mountain gateway, through which one of the tributaries of the Holston river breaks its channel. We are in the Alps of Virginia; and never were the shifting

assures us, of an indifferent horse and rifle, the Scotchman became the purchaser of a future principality. He set up a little store, but immediately commenced, also, exploring for salt, opening a large well, which, at the depth of about two hundred feet, rewarded his sagacity and enterprise by the disclosure of the finest brine ever yet discovered, and in unlimited quantity. This almost penniless wayfarer was William King, whose salt and mercantile establishments were soon known to fame, far and wide, through Virginia, Tennessee and North Carolina. The property of his former employer, General Preston, extended to the immediate neighborhood of King's well. He, too, a short distance off, now dug for and found, finally, a similar brine. Sometimes separately, sometimes unitedly, these two wells have been operated to the present time.

The value of these salines to South-western Virginia and East Tennessee is at all times very great; but how greatly they concern the most vital interests of both these States in particular, as well as those of the Carolinas and Georgia, and how deserving they are of the favor and fostering care of them all, can only justly be estimated by adverting to the part they have played in times of war. In that of 1812, interrupting as it did the supply of foreign salt, wagons were sent to them from almost all parts of Virginia—certainly from as far east as Richmond and Petersburg; and during the late civil contest, both sources of competitive supply being cut off—that from Liverpool and that from the Kanawha Valley—the salt from these works was almost the sole resource of the whole Confederacy lying between the Mississippi and the Potomac. At one period of the civil war the product of them was near ten thousand bushels a day, or between three and four millions a year; and it deserves mention that this great draft upon the wells was met by them without apparent strain or material deterioration in the quality of the brine. Still, the present annual supply, restricted by the costliness of fuel, may be stated at but from four hundred thousand to five hundred thousand bushels.

panoramas of mountain scenery more conspicuous and vivid. The ascent of the Clinch Mountain, associated with Indian memories, interests the traveler at every step, and at its highest altitude discloses visions of rare beauty. A sudden burst of the majesty of the landscape demanded the pause and tribute of silent admiration. The wayside is diversified with clusters of laurel in bloom, and deep, dark defiles with overhanging cliffs bristle with mountain pine.

Jeffersonville is a village of a few hundred inhabitants, situated on an elevated plain in Clinch Valley, about one mile from the river. It is a grateful retreat in mid-summer, and from its streets we may see the pinnacles of one of Nature's mountain-temples. A gentle tranquillity reigns around the ancient village, and the sweet incense of fields and meadows is wafted from sequestered altars.

THE PEAK.

Here we are in the midst of a scenery that invites us on every hand, its grandest and its loveliest displays being within a circuit of a few miles. Immediately south of the village is "the Peak" (or, as it is more commonly called, Wolf Creek Knob), and the view is notable from its summit, looking west and south-west. As the warm season closes, the summit of this mountain is frequently covered with snow, while verdant grass is seen lower down its sides. But when we visited it the mountain was beautifully decorated even to its top with laurel and ivy blossoms. The view is grand and full of associations. We see rising up the abrupt and rocky heads of innumerable mountains; the large hills are intermingled in the picture; and a singular opposition of mountain ranges, rising up steadily against each other like the ranks of two great armies, has its story of a fearful Indian battle—a scene of savage war on the very antitype of a convulsion of Nature. They are parallel ranges of Clinch Mountain and Rich Mountain, and here occurred, just one hundred years ago (1769), one of the most desperate and terrible battles between the Cherokees and Shawnees, those two powerful tribes that so long contested the possession of South-west Virginia. The battle was witnessed by a single white settler, of the name of Carr, who furnished ammunition to the Cherokees. It lasted two days, during which the fiendish yells of the savages might be heard echoing over the rugged cliffs and deep valleys, while the nearer ear caught the sharp crack of rifles and the ringing of tomahawks striking against each other. The Cherokees, who had their breastwork on the Rich Mountain range, were the victors or remained holding their advantage; but after the battle both tribes left Virginia for their homes in the South and West, and the disputed territory was left open to the encroachments of the white man, alike their common enemy and their common master. But before the savages left the bloody ground a large pit was opened in the intervening valley, and a common grave received those who had fallen in this last battle fought between red men in this part of Virginia.

Another object of interest near to Jeffersonville is Dial Rock. It is three miles east of the village, and tradition has it that on one of the rocks of the three heads of East River Mountain is a natural sun-dial. We could see no traces of this wonder, but from a naked cliff, rising more than two hundred feet above the summit of the mountain, which again is fifteen hundred feet above the valley of the Clinch, we beheld a scene of wild grandeur that awed and affrighted the eye that dared to overlook it. There are a number of these cliffs, among which we climb, alternately ascending and descending, at times peering into dark caverns, and again holding on to rocks lying on thin scales so loosely that apparently the slightest blow would sever the props that uphold them, and precipitate us into one of the black mouths of the mountain side yawning for its prey. Traversing this beautiful though terrible array of cliffs (on the top of one of which a basin of clear, ice-cold water quenches our thirst), it is not until we have climbed the sixth that we have reached the highest point of view, the pinnacle of Dial Rock. It is again a view of mountain and of valley. The eye is directed down to the valley beneath, with a disposition to shrink back, so precipitous is the chasm; while, looking another way, mountains rise above mountains in endless succession, until far in the smoky distance the vision ceases to distinguish the faint outline of the Cumberland and the Tennessee ranges.

VALLEY OF THE CLINCH RIVER.

But the view of largest combination and of most varied charms in Tazewell county is, the writer is persuaded, one that he obtained in an evening ride, and which may be described as the head of Clinch Valley, looking west, four miles east from Jeffersonville. It is a view in which mountain and valley are combined, in which the highest effects of natural scenery are obtained, in which it is difficult to tell where the line of beauty passes into that of the sublime, and to distribute to each part of the picture its appropriate emotion. The mountains of Tazewell are all around us, and in the distance may be seen the mountains in Russell county; while again and again runs across this scene the breadth of sublimity, or the passing grace of a beautiful valley with its interlocked hills and flashing streams. These hills, so round-bosomed, this circle which the grove describes with the severity of a mathematical line, these trees grown up in rows so even or in clusters that a landscape gardener might have designed, are not of Art, but of that infinite variety of Nature which sometimes mingles the regularity of what is apparently human work with the most excessive wildness of its creations.

It was a lovely summer evening when I ascended the mountain that overlooked this scene. I had climbed to a voiceless pinnacle two or three thousand feet above the valley for the purpose of making a sketch. It was done with a feeble hand. It was a scene only to be painted in the variegated and brilliant hues of Nature's own dyes, and where the hand was to be guided by a more than human inspiration. The sun is sinking behind the distant mountains, clothing them in purple, gold and amethyst. Away in the distance to the north the beautiful Clinch river

"Winds like a blue vein on sleeping Beauty's breast."

I turn my eyes to the east, to a scene in which I must falter in the description. Huge mountains loom up, piercing the sky. They stand firm, grim sentinels of God, guarding the sleeping emerald valleys below. On a former visit to Tazewell I had seen them in winter. They were then shrouded in death-like garments of snow; the "frozen music" of the torrent on their breasts. Now their rock-braced sides are bathed in a warm violet glow, and their rugged brows are bound with a golden band of light; while here and there along the pearly heavens glide the satin clouds, their purple slowly mingling in the pale, tranquil twilight sky. And now

> "The golden gates of day are closed,
> And darkness drapes the world."

The open lands of Tazewell county are fit complements to its mountain scenes—stretches of beautiful and fertile valleys contrasting with the stern aspects of the mountains which interlock and guard them. Burke's Garden, a refreshing and poetic name, is the Eden of this region. It is about twelve miles east from Jeffersonville—an enclosure, being almost entirely surrounded by lofty mountains, save a narrow pass, through which runs Wolf creek, a small rippling rivulet. It is about ten miles long and five wide, and is a beautiful, perfect level. Abb's Valley (so-called from Absalom Loorey, the first white man who occupied it), about fifteen miles northeast of Jeffersonville, is another delightful tract in the county. It is a narrow but beautiful and fertile valley, in which it was formerly observed, as a singular phenomenon, that there was no running water; but later investigations have discovered a subterranean stream of considerable size running in its hidden course the entire length of the valley, about twelve miles. The soil of these fertile tracts is the celebrated blue-grass soil, strongly impregnated with lime, and very productive.

There is one interest in the aspects of Tazewell, and of other parts of South-west Virginia, that the writer should not omit because of his inability to use a scientific technology. He refers to the rich and abundant *flora* of this region. A physician of Tazewell, accomplished beyond the usual limits of his profession, thus refers to the subject: "The botany of Western Virginia is not surpassed by that of any other section in the temperate zones. 'This region,' as Torrey says, 'may be called a garden of medicinal plants.' Ornamental plants, as well, are here scattered with a profuse hand. To every disease of this region Nature seems to have furnished a remedy. If in any country botany can be studied with advantage, it is here, for flowers of the same class, genus and species are blooming for several months—those in the valleys first, and those found upon the ascent of the mountains later. Many have been the pleasant days which I have spent in botanical rambles on the mountains, where from frost till frost flowers are ever found."

The county of Tazewell is, as we have already suggested, a field for the historical explorer, having many traces of traditionary history of the Indian tribes who contested this territory, and frequently dyed its soil with bloody massacres of the early settlers. Located on the line of the great Indian road from the Ohio to the Western settlements, it was naturally invaded at frequent times, and it is said that no county in Virginia has such a list of Indian massacres. Within recent years a historical society has been instituted in the county to collect the memorials of its early history. As an illustration of its industry, we were informed that evidences had been collected to show that the territory of Tazewell and the adjoining counties had been crossed by De Soto (1540) in his exploration from the Santee to the sources of the Tennessee river; that the region was then occupied by the Xualans, who were afterward driven out by the Cherokees; that, in fact, Tazewell county was the ancient Xuala of the New World, the inhabitants of which had a certain sort of civilization, and of whom the modern inquirer of the Tazewell Historical Society asks, "Might not the natives have been originally from Egypt, having been driven thence after embracing the religion of the Hebrews?"

Here is a nut for the archæologists. But seriously, and to come down to our own times, the institution of such a society in Tazewell (which, indeed, has been very profitably employed outside of the times of De Soto) is a singular evidence of the cultivation and literary patronage of its people. There is a social and literary cultivation in this mountainous country which often takes the stranger by surprise. The hospitality of some of these homes is elegantly dispensed. Some of the finest private libraries in Virginia are found here. The daughters of the wealthier proprietors are sent to distant cities to be educated, and it is not unfrequent to find them giving that excellent grace to the social circle which we may expect from the real refinements of culture without the affectations of fashion. But what is remarkable of Tazewell, and of other parts of Virginia rudely called "The Mountains," is, that with such a degree of intelligence and refinement as that noticed we should find the most violent and grotesque mixture of the abjectest ignorance. The contrasts in this respect are of the sharpest and most painful sort. What may now be the scale of popular intelligence in Tazewell I do not know; but before the common-school system was instituted in Virginia it was estimated that of 3317 persons in the county over twenty-one years of age, 1490 were unable to read or write!

The country is yet wild enough to afford many romantic rides through it, not only in the interest of its natural scenery, but in that other interest of the observation of a singular people, many of them yet living in circumstances of the original settler of the forest. I had determined, as part of the journey I had planned, to mingle with this people, to "rough" it in their homes, and to give myself the fresh sensation of a ride on horseback at random through the mountains. I had provided, indeed, a delicious sensation, with contrasts in it of bodily discomfort only sharp enough to increase the zest. There can be no enjoyment like that of a horseback ride through these grand and beautiful mountains, inhaling the pure, fresh air, casting the eyes upon constantly-shifting scenes, and catching the inspirations of Nature rejoicing around us. It is summer, but the pointed, glittering lances of the sun no longer bar the pathway; blunted and distempered in the cooler air, they are broken in the foliage and lay a golden spoil in the forest. We descend the mountain by a faintly-discerned path; a deer starts from the copse at its base, gazes in beautiful alarm for a moment, then gathers its slender limbs and bounds away. Again, we are climbing toward distant summits bathed in golden light, while the virgin dress of Nature flutters on our path, disclosing some new beauty and inviting pursuit, even through the dark, solemn forest, matted with vines and almost excluding the light of the day. Now we are come to a mountain stream. The horse's feet splash musically in it, and we see the bright, speckled trout flirting the crystal waters with their glittering fins. The forest is alive with songsters; and the sun, which has parted the locks from the mountain's brow far above, does not neglect, in dissipating far and wide the fog and the dew, to stoop and kiss from the cheek of the humblest wild flower its mark of grief.

But enough of these pictures. We had come to see the people of the mountains, to study the ways of a sequestered life and the manners of a strange society. The subject is large enough to group upon it a number of observations, and we should treat it as a distinct field in our tour.

A RIDE THROUGH THE MOUNTAINS.—HOMES OF THE MOUNTAINEERS.

The people who inhabit the wild country which breaks into a succession of mountain and valley in the southwestern corner of the State are designated generally as "Mountaineers." They are a peculiar class, with very strong marks of character and manners upon them. They differ widely from the lowland rustic in the freedom of their manners, their superiority to the bashfulness and slouching manner of the bumpkin of Eastern Virginia, and the energy and even sharpness of their discourse. When you ride to the cabin of a mountaineer, there is no scampering of an astonished family, and no unpleasant incident of small uncombed rustics peeping through the intervals of brush-heaps or through the cracks of fences at the sudden apparition of "the stranger;" no whining, distrustful greeting of "Mister;" no feeling on your part that "the man in store clothes" is on exhibition in a curious circle of unmannerly wonder. The master of the house advances to meet you with a free manner: he has not much to say, but generally his words are meet and sufficient: you discover that while he has the stoicism, he exhibits the *nil admirari*, the silence, the self-collection, of the red man of the forest; and it is only when he discovers you to be as unaffected and natural as himself that he warms into discourse, yet speaking with a strange energy, in loud, distinct, decisive tones, and with a brevity and sententiousness that sometimes really rise to the dignity of a literary study.

"Look here," said I, "old man" (a term of dignity always appreciated by the mountaineers), "why do you smoke so much?" for I had observed him filling pipe after pipe, without a moment's intermission in the space of an hour. "Well, sir, I live *here*"—tapping his pipe: "I has my pleasure in whatsoever I is at for de time I am at it." Could there be any more brief or pregnant exposition of the philosophy of *carpe diem?*

In an intercourse of some days I found that the dialect of the Virginia mountaineer was not without peculiarities. If he wishes to explain that he is well and in spirits, he is "hunky;" but if he wishes to give you a very emphatic assurance of his feeling very agreeable, he is "hunky-dory." Whatever is not sweet and fruitful is "flashy." The peaches were "flashy" on account of the drouth. But the word of greatest pregnancy—that used to convey the most extraordinary degree of worthlessness—that in which the eloquence of contempt is boiled down, strained and compressed—is "extrornificacious." It was explained to me as the derivative of a verb meaning to build up and to pull down. A worthless busybody, a man busy but with little results, is "extrornificacious;" and woe to the unhappy wight upon whom the weight of this word is laid— to whom this fearful adjective once attaches in the critical distribution of the mountaineer's opinions and judgments of men!

From the roads running through Tazewell county, the writer, being conveniently on horseback, turned off several times to explore the irregular tracts of mountains on the wayside, and to claim the hospitality of their singular inhabitants. That hospitality was never once denied. Indeed, its abundance was at times embarrassing. "Stay all night," and then the addition, "I'll treat you as well as any man," was the unfailing invitation on our journey. Once, when I had said, "Good-evening, gentlemen," after having mounted my horse, my companion replied, as we rode away, "*Gentlemen* indeed!—for I offered one of them a dollar for having pursued and caught my horse up the side of the mountain, and he actually refused it, as if he had been hurt by the offer."

The county of Tazewell is, as we have observed, far away from markets: the people sell only those things which "walk away"—meaning cattle, horses, swine, etc. In midsummer the farmers begin to gather their cattle for the drovers, who start usually about the first of September on their way to the Eastern markets. Before the war, this county exported, annually, about seven thousand head of cattle, and it was not unusual to see the roads lined with them for miles, many of them passing to market through the county from Kentucky and Tennessee. The traditions of the commerce of Tazewell are among the most interesting of South-west Virginia, and the modern traveler gathers from stories of the old settlers many curiosities of the early history of this part of the State. One of the early settlers, yet remembered by name (James Witten), had one day, at a house-raising, jocosely inquired of his comrades what they would think if, in twenty-five years, wagons actually came into the county and passed along the very valley in which they were at work. "We think," they replied, "you are a fool." Yet in less than twenty-five years there were roads in Tazewell county, and wagons traveled to it from cities hundreds of miles away. The local historian, Dr. Bickley (of

Knights-of-the-Golden-Circle fame), says: "Goods were then wagoned into Tazewell from Philadelphia, one wagon-load generally supplying the whole county. About the year 1800, a sack of coffee, for the first time, was brought into the county. It was kept by Mr. Graham, the merchant, a year and a half, and sent back as altogether *unsalable*." The mountaineers had not yet learned the use of the prime staple of the breakfast-table—which is yet an uncommon consolation of their poor descendants—a consolation which, adulterated at the cheap grocery and stirred up with the native sugar of the maple, is by no means an unmixed one.

But what is most surprising to the modern tourist is the size and value of farms (mostly devoted to grazing purposes) owned by rude men living in smoked log cabins, whose appearance would betoken them as dire, half-nude children of poverty. There is many a feudal proprietor here in the guise of hickory shirts and disproportioned pantaloons. "Uncle Billy"—the avuncular title is only one of dignity—owns twelve hundred acres, a beautiful domain on a broad tableland, probably three thousand feet above the sea-level. There is a natural park here of chestnut and white pine, some of the trees fifteen to twenty feet in girth, fit to be the ornament of a nobleman's estate: there are bursting granaries; the broad fields are picturesque with cattle; there are storehouses of hides, tallow, butter and wool; yet "Uncle Billy" goes in his shirt-sleeves, lives in a log house, and having taken several drams villainously sweetened with maple sugar on the day we alighted at his cabin, whines dismally, "Ole Billy is poor, but Ole Billy, you know, doctor, is bound to have his spree; and Ole Billy had his jaws slapped at the saw-mill last night by one of the boys; and Ole Billy cussed him to h—ll and back again; and Ole Billy has a white man's principle," etc., etc. But Uncle Billy is happy and contented in his own way: he raises the finest cattle to be found in the Eastern markets, and he puts the money in more lands, which he farms out on shares to "the boys"—a characteristic of these mountaineers being an ambition of tenantry and an extreme tenacity of landed property.

It is painful to notice the seclusion in which these mountaineers—even the better class of them—are satisfied to live. It is a seclusion which nurtures some virtues, but which begets a habit of life, a slipshod industry, difficult to be understood in the populous and cultivated old Northern States. A mountaineer will live in what he esteems comfort, and in what he exhibits as contentment, in a cabin to which there is no access but a hogpath, and cut off by unbridged mountain streams, which, swelled by freshets, may imprison him for weeks. The blacksmith, the harness-maker, the wagon-maker, are unknown in his neighborhood. He will do his work of all sorts—cobble harness, work a farm with one poor worn-out plough—and will have about as many tools for five hundred acres of land as a live Yankee will require for fifty. The loneliness of his life never troubles him. Mr. Horace Greeley, traveling in another part of Southwest Virginia (Pulaski county), says: "Coming down from the mountains to Wolf creek, our party struck the clearing of a pioneer who had probably lived here fifteen to twenty years, had cleared twenty to thirty acres, and had most of it in grain, yet who had no outlet but a bridle-path—no sign of cart, sled or wagon-track—to the road, half a mile distant and perhaps three hundred feet below him, through a forest of superb oak, where a good week's work would have made a very passable cartway." This is a picture which we may see in almost any mountain hollow of South-west Virginia—a bridle-path going up dry beds of streams and along precipices to a mean log house squat in a recess, the master of which, though comparatively a man of means, has been satisfied for years to plod the same way to his dwelling as when he first picked his steps through the forest and made a clearing for his home.

Altogether, the mountaineers of Virginia are remarkable for a simplicity of primitive life—a simplicity of some hardy and manly aspects, quite unlike that mere want of cultivation or that degeneracy which, among the opportunities of more populous communities, designates the lower and ignorant classes. There is nothing of the squalor or wretchedness of poverty in the mountains. It is the native simplicity of the lives of this people that interests us, not the vicious or slouching poverty that comes from loss of caste or neglect of opportunities in other societies. There is nothing in common between the poorest mountaineer and the "mudsills" of the lowland community. The poverty of the mountain is picturesque; it is hardy, healthful; it is a school of rude but independent manners, not one of degradation or of mendicancy, as elsewhere. One excellent trait in the life of this people will be testified to by the observant traveler. It is the exceeding cleanness of even their humblest homes. The exterior of the log dwelling is uninviting enough, but it would be unjust to omit the surprised experience of the traveler at the neatness and comfort he finds across the rough-hewed threshold. The few articles of furniture are well arranged. The bed, which is always found in the main room where strangers are received, is almost uniformly spread with a coverlet of snowy white, forming a contrast to the dingy log walls and rough floor of boards or puncheons. The dress of the inmates, though often scanty, is clean homespun. Their appearance is healthful : the men gaunt, muscular, remarkable for the want of color in the face, but having nothing of the sallowness of a sickly or ill-conditioned people.

There are some humorous aspects in the primitive life of this people. But they are simple, refreshing comedies, at which we may laugh without contempt or bitterness. Our recollections of a night in one of the log cabins we have described are preserved among the incidents of a journey in which we had much to be thankful for, and in which I would not indulge humor at the expense of gratitude.

A COMEDY IN THE MOUNTAINS.

WE had ridden far and the day was closing, when, taking one of those unmistakable crooked paths in a mountain hollow which always lead to a house, we alighted at a double-story structure of logs, and asked shelter for the night. An old woman, in a very strait dress of linsey-woolsey, received us rather doubtfully, and said she would call "the old man." While awaiting the presence of the individual thus designated we were seated in the main room; and the old woman, evidently to relieve that embarrassment which people sometimes suffer from poverty of conversation, commenced firing off the wildest and most incomprehensible questions about the "'tater crop." I noticed that, whatever was the woman's nervous want of something to talk about, we were never once asked where we were from, or where we were going, or what was our business, or any other questions commonly prompted by a vulgar and impertinent curiosity.

Presently a gawky, healthy, great girl bounced into the room, and bounced out as quickly at the sight of strangers.

"Don't be skeered, Sal," called the mother after her.

Sal, reassured, entered the room, but insisted on sitting near the door. Her first singular exhibition of modesty was to tuck her skirts very closely around the lower portion of her body, and then to gaze on vacancy. The girl had some wild flowers in her hands, and H. (the wag of our company) soon commenced: "I see you are a lady of taste; you love flowers, the poetry of earth, as the stars are of heaven!"

"Ah, stranger, and more'n that—they smell so purty," replied Sal.

The old man came in—a splendid specimen of his class—a stalwart son of the forest, of Herculean stature, bent as he stooped through the door; a simple, ignorant mountaineer, but his grizzled looks framing a majestic and impressive countenance that might afford a study to a painter. He greeted us kindly, said he would look after our "horse-beasts," and returned to ask us to supper in an adjoining log structure, which looked about as big as a hen-house, but proved to be the kitchen, as well as a bed-room for the children. The supper was of pones of corn-bread, venison and sassafras tea, to the latter of which I declined the addition of "long sweetening," *i.e.*, maple sugar. After supper we were thrown again on the resources of conversation.

Generally speaking, the mountaineer is hospitable in

his way, but his lonely habits unfit him for many of the offices of this virtue, and the host is sometimes put to awkward emergencies. On the present occasion our host was anxious to acquit himself of the embarrassment of finding topics to entertain his visitors. The man was greatly at a loss to find something to talk about, and thus put himself at ease in a strange company. At last he hit upon the expedient of acquainting us with the extraordinary accomplishments of one of his dogs, who happened to be out at the time. There was never such a dog as "Wolf:" he would do anything at the command of his master; he was almost "like folks;" in short, he was the "beatingest" dog in the world. Wolf supplied the conversation for hours; and whenever it flagged the mountaineer wished Wolf were only present to exhibit some new accomplishment for us—the scale of his accomplishments rising at each renewal of the subject, which the poor man thought it necessary to make to entertain his visitors. But, as ill-luck would have it, just in the middle of his discourse, what should we see but Wolf returned, slinking through the door—a mangy cur, flop-eared, wet and covered with mud. His first exhibition of sagacity was to shake himself in the doorway, scattering his filth right and left, and spoiling H.'s broadcloth. "Go out, sir!" commanded his master, stamping his foot, and anxious no doubt to get him out of sight. But Wolf was obdurate: he had an eye for his accustomed place under the bed. As he made for it, his master took in the situation at a glance with the lightning inspiration of the genius of a great commander, and in a yet severer tone of authority and with a triumphant look toward us, exclaimed, "Go under the bed, sir!—right under the bed, sir!" And Wolf *did* go right under the bed. But, as the reader may well imagine, he was not called from there for any other exhibition of his master's power over him, and not another word was heard of "the beatingest dog you ever seed"—the old man suddenly jumping up and exclaiming that he must go out to look after the cattle. I could not help reflecting that the incident was not without instruction, and that it might apply with hearty effect to some pretenders in the world, who have just as much real influence in directing events as Wolf's master exhibited in the obedience of his dog.

The old man having disappeared after his experiment in conversation, and the old woman having bustled back into the main room, we were left in the kitchen alone with Sal and with some big-eyed, wakeful children, who insisted upon sitting up with the strangers.

H. was gallantly inclined, and renewed his rhapsody or rigmarole, evidently with increased effects. From the undertones of his voice and the quizzical glances cast toward us, we could understand that he was making steady approaches to the heart of Sal, while a giggling sound from that young lady and the stuffing of her apron into her mouth told that something was working inwardly. Occasionally there was a deprecating wriggle of the body, and a sigh struggled out. We could overhear but a portion of the dialogue.

H.:
"I love you,
And I feel a seal is set
Upon the fountain of my heart,
To keep its waters pure and bright for thee."

SAL:
"Go on, stranger, it sounds so nice!"

Before we retired to our shake-downs in the loft, I

found that H. had entreated a lock of hair of the gentle
Sal—"yea, had begged a hair of her for memory." The
next morning, as we mounted our horses to ride away, I
noticed a package of brown paper slyly put in H.'s hand
as Sal bent over it in parting. When we had got out of
sight I accused H., and the package was produced—its contents a great rusty rope of carroty hair, that might have
plaited a halter for our gay Lothario. Poor Sal! The
last we saw of her as we went over the hill she was waving
a white bib and hallooing—no doubt, as she had informed
H. at parting, "ready to bust a-cryin'."

But what, asks the gentle reader, of those female beauties of the mountain pictured in poetry and read of in
romance—creatures with gazelle eyes, "hair flowing
like Alpine torrents," cheeks wooed by the breezes, etc.?
Is there any antitype in reality of the mountain maid, or
is she but the ideal, the wood nymph of poets and
romance-writers? In fact, it is to be confessed that the
female of "the child of Nature" is not commonly prepossessing; and, shocking as it may be to our poetical
preconceptions, the girl of the mountain is usually found
to be sallow, ungrammatical and altogether unlovely, a
gawky specimen of ill-dressed humanity, having ropy hair,
standing in clouted brogans and furnished with great red,
clawing hands. The disillusionizing process is sharp and
painful enough. But stop: we must not be too hasty in
our induction. Rare as may be the mountain maid of
the rural school of poetry, there *is* such a being. And
when Nature, in her infinite variety of gifts, *does* plant a
flower of female beauty in the mountains, does out of this
remote and uncultivated humanity mould a face and form of
loveliness, the creation is as infinitely exquisite as it is bold.

When this creation is found, the type of beauty can only be described by the word "exquisite," and we find ourselves wondering more at the perfect finish of the picture than at any separate feature. The most *perfectly* beautiful girl the writer has ever seen was from one of the mountain homes of Tazewell. The description is merely that of an artist: he knows nothing of her but a name casually mentioned in a crowd. She was standing in the gathering of an agricultural fair at Lynchburg. She was dressed in the simplest merino, and a wisp of the commonest shawl had fallen from her shoulder and was twisted around the firm hip, whose form Fashion had never disguised. The pose was that of the unconscious grace of a classic statue. A wealth of hair, of yellowish-dark color streaked with red—that *tawny*, amorous hair so seldom seen—floated down her shoulders, and was matched by the warm light of young desire that glowed on the cheeks and made pensive half confessions as it swam like the mouldering fire of a sacrifice in the golden-blue depths of her eyes. The face was oval, classic, but warm from the glow of a perpetual and insatiate love, and the rich lips appeared constantly pouted for kisses, that could never be satisfied. It might have been supposed that there was some mark of uncultivation, of rusticity, to mar the picture and to break the spell of the admirer. But no: Nature had done her work with a completeness that left nothing to be desired. The feet were small and exquisitely formed. The unjeweled hands were as dainty as those of a princess. Looking back at the face, the expression of a pure, unconscious voluptuousness that swam over it, yet contained in the severest classical types of virtue and modesty, was perfect. I have attempted no description of the eyes. Mr. Longfellow has done it in *Hyperion:*

"Eyes like the flower of the night-shade, pale and blue, but sending forth golden rays." Such human orbs are seldom seen. They haunt us for ever: the form is withdrawn, the face is absent—"only her eyes remained."

CHAPTER X.

LEXINGTON, AND THE VALLEY OF VIRGINIA.

From South-west Virginia to Lexington—COYNER'S SPRINGS—Reputation of the Water—LEXINGTON AND ITS SURROUNDINGS—"The Athens of Virginia"—Its Educational Institutions—General Lee's Professorship—THE GRAVE OF STONEWALL JACKSON—A curious letter from a former Governor of Virginia—THE ROCKBRIDGE BATHS—A Buoyant Water—THE ROCKBRIDGE ALUM SPRINGS—Mountain Views—A Remarkable Advantage of the Watering-Places of Virginia—Testimony of Dr. Cartwright—THE VALLEY OF VIRGINIA—Its Physical Geography—Peculiarity of Minor Formations—The Luray Valley—View from Thornton's Gap—A Recollection of the War—Mineral Springs on the Flanks of the Alleghany—The Valley of Virginia, as a Fancy and as a Reality.

TO the traveler looking from that part of Virginia we have been traversing (the South-west) toward the Springs Region lying north of him, on the inner slopes of the Valley of Virginia, there are two available routes. He may go by rail on each of the lines making the angle which we have heretofore described as containing the range of the tourist in Virginia—that is, he may go to Charlottesville, and thence take a new departure by the Chesapeake and Ohio Railroad, passing through Staunton, etc. Or he may cross the angle by stage-coaches from a series of points on the Virginia and Tennessee Railroad, extending from Bonsack's Dépôt to Newbern. The latter mode of conveyance is recommended for those who have leisure and taste for the wild scenery traversed by the coach, and for the opportunities it offers to deflect to intervening places and to find recreation by the wayside. If preference is determined for the coach, a most agreeable route may be marked out from Bonsack's Depôt, taking the delightful Coyner's Springs, only one mile away from the railroad; thence to Lexington; thence to the baths and springs of Rockbridge county; and emerging into the cluster of watering-places in Bath, Greenbrier and Monroe counties by striking the Chesapeake and Ohio Railroad at Goshen Depôt, or other points west of Staunton. The route is recommended for its many intervening opportunities; the coaches are "slow" and inelegant, but they are comfortable; and if we lack other companionship, Nature affords us communion and thought in the various scenes which spring to our view at every turn of the devious mountain route.

COYNER'S SPRINGS.

THE traveler will make his first rest at Coyner's Springs, on the western base of the Blue Ridge. The convenience of access to these springs is all that can be desired, and they are a favorite resort of the people of Lynchburg, being but fifty miles from that city. The buildings are spacious and comparatively new, the management of the hotel is exceptionally good, and as a social resort the place is known as one of the gayest in Virginia.

The waters are sulphurous, and are, of their class, mild and pleasant. They are recommended in cases of difficult, imperfect or painful digestion, enfeebled condition of the nervous system, chronic diseases of the bladder or kidneys, salt rheum, tetters, indolent liver, with deficient or vitiated secretions, and in some of the affections peculiar to females.

The place is a new candidate for the favor of summer visitors in Virginia; and to judge from the energy and tact of its manager, and the reputation it has already acquired for its elegant social entertainments, as well as for the value of the water, it is destined to become better known. The hotel accommodations, we repeat, are excellent. The situation is on the borders of one of the most delightful and fertile regions of Virginia, being immediately on the line of the counties of Botetourt and Roanoke.

LEXINGTON AND ITS SURROUNDINGS.

THE town of Lexington is, by the pike, forty-two miles from Coyner's Springs. It affords another convenient place of refreshment on a tour to the springs and through the mountains of Virginia, being distant twelve miles from the Natural Bridge, ten from the Rockbridge Baths (which the correspondent of the London *Times*, visiting during the late war, pronounced unequaled in virtue and brilliancy by anything of the sort in Europe), and seventeen miles from the Alum Springs, which are on the direct road to the Warm and Hot Springs of Bath county. The town is also one of the most interesting in Virginia. The extent and success of its educational institutions have won for it, from the red-brick and harsh-looking town of Charlottesville, the title of "The Athens of Virginia."

There were two hundred and seventy cadets of the session of 1869 at the Virginia Military Institute. It was vacation term when we visited the place, at which time the cadets usually go into camp and undertake all the discipline of regular soldiers, performing each evening in dress parade. But owing to the want of tents, which the State, in its financial difficulties, had not furnished, the encampment had been intermitted on the year of our visit; and, as nearly two-thirds of the cadets were on furlough, there were no parades or other exercises, and there was but little to repay the visitor beyond the examination of the buildings, which have, in the main, been reconstructed since General Hunter's raid. The success of this military academy has greatly increased of late years, since, from being an exclusive State institution, it has extended its benefits of instruction to pupils from all the States of the Union. It originated from a slight germ. Formerly a guard of soldiers was maintained, at the expense of the State, for the purpose of affording protection to the arms deposited in the Lexington arsenal for the use of the militia of Western Virginia. About the year 1836 some zealous friends of education, among whom was Governor McDowell, thinking that the arsenal might be converted into an educational institution without any increase of expense to the State, and afford at the same time equal security to the public arms, applied to the Legislature to make the necessary change. After various delays the application resulted in the establishment of the Virginia Military Institute in the year 1839. Since then its success has been such as to fulfill the wishes of its warmest friends.

Here also is situated Washington College, which in 1869 numbered nearly five hundred students, exceeding the State University, and which has progressed from a beginning as humble as the military school in its neighborhood. It is one of the oldest literary institutions south of the Potomac, having been established as an academy in the year 1776, under the name of Liberty

Hall, by the Hanover Presbytery, then embracing the whole of the Presbyterian Church in Virginia. Liberty Hall received its charter from the State in the year 1782, and in 1796 it received its first regular endowment from the hands of the "Father of his country." The Legislature of Virginia, "as a testimony of their gratitude for his services" and "as a mark of their respect," presented to General Washington a certain number of shares in the old James River Improvement, a work then in progress. This, Washington, unwilling to accept for his own private emolument, presented to Liberty Hall Academy. To perpetuate the memory of this act the name of the institution was, by the unanimous vote of the trustees, changed to Washington Academy; and in the year 1812, by an act of the Legislature, still further changed to Washington College. Subsequently, there were other bequests to the college, among them one from the Cincinnati Society of Virginia. Within late years the course of instruction has been enlarged by a professorship founded by Mr. McCormick, the inventor of the reaping machine; and still another professorship, recommended by General Lee, the president of the college, has been added, through a donation made by Mr. Peabody, the last of the public gifts of this distinguished philanthropist.

The college is now flourishing mostly on the strength of the name of General Lee as president. It is a brilliant head to an advertisement; but we cannot help comparing the obscure names of the professors which follow with the gilded top line of "Robert E. Lee, President." One absurdity of the institution is to be laughed at—that is, a "professorship of journalism"—the man who is to make our future Greeleys and Raymonds and Danas, the individual called to this high station of instruction being the editor of the village weekly paper, which recently showed its appreciation of the mission of journalism by devoting its columns to a long discussion by two opposing village wiseacres of the question, "Does Prayer bring Rain?"* Lexington has not made up its mind on the subject.

The country around here is interesting in its natural features and in its population. It is especially so as the abode of that Scotch-Irish stock and "true-blue" Presbyterianism which yet in Rockbridge and Augusta counties, and in what is called the upper portion of the Valley of Virginia (although geographically the lower), making its head near Staunton, exhibits traits and influences as distinct and cherishes traditions as peculiar and dear as the Puritanism of New England. From the Scotch-Irish stock of this portion of Virginia have sprung some of the most remarkable men of the nation. We may name Stonewall Jackson, Sam Houston of Texas—who was born in a small house six miles north of Lexington—and Rev. Archibald Alexander, D.D., president of the Theological Seminary at Princeton, New Jersey, who was a native of this county, and married a daughter of the "Blind Preacher."

* Everybody in Virginia was talking of the drouth in the summer of 1869. The writer recollects, once on his tour, to have made this discovery from the conversation of a minister at the hotel table—that he had marked out on the map the lines of the prevailing drouth, which much of the South was then deploring, and found them all the way through Virginia, Tennessee and the Carolinas adjacent to the railroads; and that was convincing proof, to which he should call the attention of the next conference, of the special displeasure of Almighty God at the carrying of mails on Sunday! This discovery should have been communicated to the Lexington *Gazette* before it closed its columns to the discussion of the pluvial theory. The pious gentleman who figured it out gave us his address in North Carolina.

THE GRAVE OF STONEWALL JACKSON.

An interest which may be much greater in future times than now, attaches to Lexington as the resting-place of all that was mortal of the great warrior-spirit of the South, that issued from the quiet shades of the Military Institute here to its meteor-like career in the late war. The grave of Stonewall Jackson is in the Presbyterian burying-ground, which lies at the extremity of the town. There was only a board imitation of marble, with rude lettering, to mark the place where the hero slept.

Indeed, the neglect of the grave of Stonewall Jackson and inattention to his memory on the part of the State of Virginia, the Commonwealth his life shielded and adorned, are almost incomprehensible, and, it must be painfully confessed, throw a reflection of suspicion upon the vaunted generosity of her people. We cannot doubt that there are many hearts in Virginia that hold proudly and tenderly the memory of the departed warrior. But we cannot forget that, one year after the war, the household goods of the dead hero were allowed to be sold in the town of Lexington under the hammer of the auctioneer, and that his family have been unnoticed in their poverty, except by the benefaction of a citizen of another State; despite, too, the lessons of generosity which might have been derived from the reviled North, which has abounded in attentions and gifts to the families of those public men who have died poor in her service.

Yet, more strangely, it has remained for the North, though at the instance of a Virginian, to testify to the illustrious nature and ennobling qualities of Stonewall Jackson, and to vindicate his name and fame from the cloud left upon it by a defeated cause. The movement to this end is reported to have commenced with the following letter from an ex-Governor of Virginia:

"LEXINGTON, VA., 1869.
"COL. JACOB HYLAND, PHILADELPHIA:

"MY DEAR SIR: The admirers of the virtues and exalted character of the great Christian soldier, Lieutenant-General Stonewall Jackson, propose to erect at the Virginia Military Institute, where he served fourteen years as a professor, a memorial chapel, to testify the respect and honor with which his name is cherished, and to transmit to after generations the veneration due to so renowned a hero. It is estimated that twenty thousand dollars will erect a monument.

"I am truly your friend,
"JOHN LETCHER."

It does seem hard that Mr. Letcher should have felt compelled to go beyond the State of Virginia, and to first besiege a Northern city (Philadelphia), for the sum of twenty thousand dollars for the memory of Stonewall Jackson!

At the date of our writing it is reported that a subscription among the citizens of Philadelphia, in response to Mr. Letcher's appeal, has amounted to five thousand dollars, and that citizens of New York have offered to guarantee twenty thousand dollars for the object proposed in the above letter. Such responses are, in some sense, a subject of congratulation; they do infinite honor to the magnanimity of some of our Northern brethren, and show that section in an elevated light that cannot fail to instruct the mind and touch the heart of the South; and they are powerful and eloquent testimonies to the memory of the great man whose fame has so soon surmounted the prejudices of the war. Whatever of painful comparison is in them is for the State of Virginia. It is a stinging reflection that this movement should have commenced with the strange and unbecoming letter of Mr. Letcher, and that the North should have led off in a work which reverent hands in Virginia should have been the first to undertake. To be sure it is said that Mr. Letcher, encouraged by the eager and generous contributions of the North, now proposes to enlarge the scope and object of the plan first designed in his letter, and to give the testimonial to Stonewall Jackson a *national* significance, by inviting the South to join in contributions to it. But the afterthought will hardly redeem the commencement of the enterprise. To say the least, an ungraceful thing has been done in directing the first appeals for a monument to the hero of Chancellorsville to citizens of the North; and if Virginia ever really proposes to repair her public neglect of the memory of the greatest of her dead, she should at least lay the foundation of it in gifts and contributions of her own.

THE ROCKBRIDGE BATHS.

WE leave Lexington *en route* for the watering-places in the Valley of Virginia. The Rockbridge Baths are midway between the town of Lexington and Goshen Depôt on the Chesapeake and Ohio Railroad, being, say, twelve miles from either place. They are within a few feet of the banks of North river, and the road toward Goshen Depôt pursues these banks through mountain chasms of the most picturesque effect. There are two springs, which supply two bathing establishments, the water being impregnated with iron and abounding richly in carbonic acid gas. The bath is so buoyant with this gas that one floats easily lying in its brilliant and refreshing water, which is five feet deep and affords a surface of forty by twenty feet for the swimmer.

The bath is medicinally classed as *tonic*. It is adapted to nervous diseases, general debility and to that large class of cases in which stimulative and tonic effects are required. The testimony of physicians is that the Rockbridge Baths will be found highly efficacious, especially after the use of alterative mineral waters.

Within two miles of the baths is a strong sulphur spring in an islet in North river; the cup or basin of rock which holds the mineral spring rising just in the middle of the stream of fresh water, and from depths below its channel. It is a bit of curiosity, and it is visited for medicinal effects in addition to those of the baths.

THE ROCKBRIDGE ALUM SPRINGS.

THE Rockbridge Alum Springs are situated in the northern part of Rockbridge county, seventeen miles from Lexington, and are reached thence by the main turnpike which traverses the county, leading to the Warm Springs in Bath county. Access in another direction is from the Chesapeake and Ohio Railroad, which runs five miles from the springs, but discharges its passengers bound for this watering-place at Goshen Depôt, eight miles distant, whence comfortable stage-coaches transport them to their destination. The springs are thus within easy reach of the whole Atlantic seaboard and of the North, being brought within twenty-four hours of New York, allowing the Northern passenger to breakfast in Washington City and to sup the evening of the same day in this romantic seclusion of the mountains.

A shallow vale or basin, bounded by hard but picturesque ridges, contains the springs, a row of five fountains issuing from beneath heavy and irregular slate-stone arches. The sloping strata are exposed on the hewn side of the cliff, and on top there is a pleasing crest of green forest. The lawns, which are within a circular drive, are begirt by brick cottages, but there are other houses of greater extent, and buildings on the whole sufficient for the accommodation of six or eight hundred visitors. Mountains skirt the plain in which this retreat lies hidden, and in some parts overhang it. There are pleasing views of the North Mountain and the western wall of the Great Valley and of some lesser ridges, while the near forest, thronged with fine trees and enriched with a luxuriant flora, invites the visitor into seclusions as complete as those of a wilderness remote from man and untouched by his inventions. The remark attributed to a distinguished gentleman from the North, spending his first season in the Springs Region of Virginia, and aware for the first time of its attractions, may be very justly applied to the scenes we are describing: "It is one of the singular advantages of these Virginia watering-places that, by walking for three minutes, you can plunge yourself at once into glens and tangled wilds."

The water of these Alum Springs is found useful in a number of diseases. Dr. Cartwright, of New Orleans, whose fame as a physician will occur to readers in all parts of the Union, thus speaks of the value of the water, stamping it with the authority of an opinion derived from a special study of the various spas of both continents: "In truth, I know of no water in Europe or America so rich in medical substances as that of the Rockbridge Springs. My attention was first attracted to it some fifteen years ago, by observing that the sojourners at the Rockbridge Springs were generally composed of invalids from Virginia, while those at the other springs were mostly from distant parts of the Union, more in search of pleasure than health. Most of these other springs in the Virginia mountains have a deservedly high reputation for the efficacy of their water in a variety of chronic ailments; but I am satisfied that the Rockbridge Springs have not yet attained that wide celebrity they deserve, from the circumstance of their being regarded as merely *alum* springs, instead of being seen in their true light as the richest of all that class of mineral springs known as the *acidulous ferruginous*—a class of mineral waters to which the most famous springs of the world belong."

The chemical description of the water suggests that "Alum" is a popular misnomer, since its virtue is probably not owing to the alum it holds in solution, nor are its effects the well-known ones of this powerful astringent. The protoxide of iron, sodium, potash, lime, magnesia and ammonia, together with sulphuric, carbonic, crenic, chloric and silicic acids, exist in the water in common with alum. The qualities which result are tonic, alterative, diuretic and aperient, and a remedy is furnished for many of the ills of humanity—one of rare and unquestionable virtues. The therapeutic applicability of the water appears to be well defined. It is prescribed generally for the following diseases: confirmed dyspepsia in nearly all its varieties, except such as are attended with symptoms of acute gastric irritation ; chronic diarrhœa ; leucorrhœa ; scrofulous ulcers and other scrofulous affections of the skin and of the lymphatic glands. A Southern physician speaks of this water as having removed a great reproach from the healing art, in that it has furnished an undoubted cure for *scrofula* (king's evil), a disease that has so long fatigued and baffled the multiplied resources of medical science.

THE VALLEY OF VIRGINIA.

WE shall conclude this chapter, not inappropriately, by a general sketch of the Valley of Virginia, into which we have now entered, and through some of the galleries of which we have undertaken to guide the traveler. We propose to give only the outlines of this famous topographical feature of the State; our object being to introduce a principle of order into scenes upon which we are advancing, and in the midst of which the traveler would see nothing but confusion without a reference to the landmarks which make the third great geographical division of Virginia.

The Alleghany Mountains preserve this name only in Virginia and Pennsylvania. Beyond these States, north and south, they assume the proper geological name of the Appalachian chain, the second or subordinate system of North American mountains. In Virginia and Pennsylvania the range averages one hundred and fifty miles in width; the characteristics, especially in the former State, being the parallelism of the ridges and the uniform level of their summits. Another characteristic, which extends generally through the Appalachian chain, is that these mountains have no central axis, but consist of a series of convex and concave flexures, forming alternate hills and longitudinal valleys, running nearly parallel throughout their length, and cut transversely by the rivers that flow to the Atlantic on one hand and to the Mississippi on the other. It is remarkable that the water-shed nearly follows the windings of the coast from the point of Florida to the north-western extremity of the State of Maine.

The Valley of Virginia properly extends from the wall of the Alleghany to the edge of the terrace known as the Atlantic slope, which rises above the maritime or Atlantic plain—this latter at its extremity south of Virginia joining the plain of the Mississippi. The features of it are ridges of hills and long valleys running parallel to the mountains. It is rich in soil and cultivation, and has an immense water-power in the streams and rivers which, flowing from the mountains across it, are precipitated over its rocky edge to the plains below. It has been calculated that Rockbridge county alone has in water-power and sites a capacity for manufacturing greater than that of the whole State of Massachusetts!

In its limited acceptation, the Valley of Virginia has its head in the tract of country between Lexington and Staunton, becoming well-defined toward the latter place, thence gradually widening toward the Potomac, and debouching into the wide hills of Pennsylvania. In the late war it was a prominent theatre of strategy, as it afforded the most obvious avenue to an attack on Washington, and constantly threatened a flank movement on that city.

The most remarkable flexure or minor formation of the valley occurs near the middle of it. About half-way between Staunton and the Potomac two ranges of mountains run parallel for twenty-five miles, uniting in Massanutten (Mesinetto) Mountain, which divides the branches of the Shenandoah, and ends southward abruptly in Rockingham county. This is *Luray* Valley—a beautiful vale branching off from and thence running parallel to that main gallery through which the troops of Stonewall Jackson marched in 1862, and where that warrior won his first and imperishable laurels. It was terribly devastated at a later day by Sheridan.

This minor formation is the north-eastern limit of the Valley of Virginia. Through its gaps are the communications with the lower lands of North Virginia on the Rapidan and Rappahannock, where Lee campaigned. One of the most famous of these gaps, familiar in the geography of the late war, is Thornton's Gap on the line of Page and Rappahannock counties. It is a wide avenue curving up to the mountain tops, and bounding a view on which the eye is unable to compose itself for the excess of riches spread before it.

It was our fortune once to see this scene as it was lighted up by the glories of the Morning.

> " Day!
>   Faster, and more fast,
>   O'er Night's brim, Day boils at last;
>   Boils, pure gold, o'er the cloud-cup's brim,
>   Where spurting and supprest it lay—
>   For not a froth-flake touched the rim
>   Of yonder gap in the solid gray
>   Of the eastern cloud, an hour away;
>   But forth one wavelet, then another, curled,
>   Till the whole sunrise, not to be supprest,
>   Rose, reddened, and its seething breast
>   Flickered in bounds, grew gold, then overflowed the world!"

We could imagine the presence of the great army of Confederates which had once passed through this scene, catching the light of the morning on their bayonets. For here, even to these secluded retreats, rolled the red-hot lava of the war. The tides of battle which tossed

VIEW FROM THORNTON'S GAP—THE LURAY VALLEY.

in agony around these hills are replaced now by floods of sunshine, which come and go with the peaceful day; and where armies dashed to strife there are now but "light and shade upon a waving field chasing each other." But what memories are for ever bound up in the rock-ribbed sides of the Valley of Virginia! We would not, without occasion, take the seals from these memories—least willingly in such a day, when the glories of the sky are on the earth, and all should be forgotten of the dead but the gentle peace in which they have been laid to sleep beneath the coverlid of green turf and blooming flower.

The beauties of this valley (the Luray) have often been told. For miles around us is the mass of Nature's lives and wonders pulsing under the sun; "the voice of man is on the mountains;" human life touches the scene only to make it more vivid and beautiful. Nothing can exceed the loveliness of the Shenandoah, which flows here. Straying by its banks, we watch its waters rippling in adroit, laughing escape under the mottled arms of the sycamore tree. There is the swell of turf and slanting branches on the hillside; the spaces of the deep blue sky, at which we look from the narrow vales jutting on the stream are edged round with dark tree-tops; and beyond is the forest full of whispered mysteries, within which are the dramas of a thousand creations—the birth, life and death of unseen flowers. The picture must be badly stripped in winter. What differences, indeed, wrought by the seasons on all this "pomp of groves and garniture of fields," and what reflections troop upon the symbols! Now tresses of newly-budded flowers hung up in the forest, now "honeycombs of green," and on the warm fields the freckled wings of the butterfly. Anon the yellow leaves, and the owl's cry of coming winter.

The Springs Region of the Valley of Virginia is near the dividing line of the Alleghany, the springs of Rockbridge and Bath counties being in minor formations—the North Mountain and Warm Springs Mountain being really spurs of the Alleghany—and those of Greenbrier and Monroe counties clinging to the backbone of the great range. The Valley of Virginia is not, as in geographical speculation or in fancy we might take it, a uniform depression running evenly between two ranges of mountains; it is broken and cut up, remarkable, as we have said, for its subordinate formations, a succession of valley and of mountain range. It is only a comparative view of the Alleghany and of the sunken parallel of the Blue Ridge that gives order to the impression and bestows the idea of a valley. The traveler must hold to these great landmarks, or, so far from realizing that he is in the Valley of Virginia, he will imagine himself in a wild, intricate country, where every feature of Nature has been huddled and Disorder reigns supreme.

The effect of the physical geography of the Valley, as we have briefly described it, is a scenery the most various in the world. We have the sublimity of the mountains, where we may stand "ringed with the azure world;" the peace of humble vales; the picturesqueness of the inhabited landscape; the beauty of waving crops on a bountiful soil; streams which seem to flow out of the sky; haunts of romance; the most curious formations of geology; the wonder and magnificence of the subterranean world. On the whole, however, the scenery is inferior in point of grandeur to that of South-west Virginia. It is more varied, but, on a general estimate, it is more quiet. We have not here such scenes as those of the Peaks of Otter and of Bald Knob or of the cliffs of New river—the peaked observatories, the mural precipices and the pictures of great convulsions where rocks have been piled on rocks and timber swept from the earth.

17 *

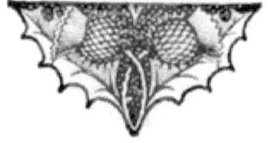

CHAPTER XI.

ROMANCE OF THE VALLEY OF VIRGINIA.

Geographical Fables of the early Virginia Colonists—Mr. Jefferson's Belief in the Mastodon—A Curious Indian Myth—The Barrier of the Blue Ridge—Influx of Pennsylvania Germans into the Valley of Virginia—The Adventures of John Salling—The Lewis Family—Remarkable Result of a Buffalo Hunt—Burden's Grant—Andrew Lewis' Explorations on Greenbrier River—The Shawnees—Death of Cornstalk—Relations of the Germans and of the Scotch-Irish in the Valley—Characteristics of the Scotch-Irish—Their Churches and Schools—Three Generations in the Valley—The Progress of America in Miniature.

IT is difficult for those of the present day to realize the extravagance of the mysteries and the wildness of the fancies with which the colonists of Virginia, even for several generations, invested that part of the world that laid beyond the mists of their mountains. From the time when Captain John Smith sent up a boat expedition to the present site of Richmond, on the James, to discover an outlet to Cathay, the vision of some mystery of land or sea seems to have receded only just as the line of settlement or of exploration passed westward; the romantic wonder of a South Sea, of a land of giants or of a range of unknown beasts being always imagined but little beyond the last discovery. The geography beyond the Blue Ridge was almost a blank; the hydrographic system of the Mississippi was unknown; and who could have imagined that beyond the azure boundaries on the sky, to which the colonists looked with constant questionings and imaginings, there laid the breadth of three thousand miles of continent? The geographical fable of the West had as many interpretations as the imagination could give it. There were bloody romances of the terrible Massawomees; there were stories got from Indian tradition, which even intelligent persons in Williamsburg believed, of Titanic races, of men ten feet high, of strange forms of life; and among other wonders of the mysterious land there was not neglected a new version of the great devouring Beast of the nursery tale.

Even Mr. Jefferson believed in the existence of the *Mastodon*,* and that it had ranged near the Ohio, a creature for which, in his "Notes on Virginia," written in

* It is known in our day that in the great salt deposit which lies in the valley of the North Fork of the Holston river, a vast quantity of fossil remains is dispersed in the soil, probably indicating that it was once the resort of the larger quadrupeds which at some period have inhabited this portion of the earth. Remains, judged to be of the Mastodon (as we may choose to call it), elephant, elk and others, but mainly the larger animals, are almost profusely found in the immediate vicinity. The railroad cut, through a swell in the Valley rising westward, revealed a large bed of them, while in the ditches cut in all directions for the drainage of the lake-like flat below, they were frequently encountered and thrown out by the spade. Of these remains, a pair of very perfect tusks, of the double curve which is said to have marked them as pertaining to the Mastodon, upward of eleven feet in length, were disinterred some years ago; but they fell to pieces by some neglect or from the effect of exposure to the atmosphere, although the parts were carefully collected, and have since been contributed to the Museum of the Smithsonian Institution at Washington. These salines were, no doubt, from time immemorial the resort of numerous animals, whose instincts and necessities led them there; and hunters and pursuers of the wild beasts were guided on the track of their precursors to an object of so prime a value to them. The "lick" of the animals became the

1787, he adopts the calculation of Buffon, as "five or six times the cubic volume of the elephant," and adds: "But to whatever animal we ascribe these remains, it is certain such a one has existed in America, and that it has been the largest of all terrestrial beings." And to reinforce his speculation that such a creature had recently inhabited the Ohio district, the sage of Monticello is found relating an Indian account of this natural wonder, which was expounded at Williamsburg as late as when Patrick Henry was governor of Virginia. It is one of the wildest of the aboriginal traditions, with a mixture of sublimity and grotesqueness that makes it remarkable even to the reader of the period. Some Indians had crossed the mountains to visit Williamsburg, and, after having been entertained by the governor, were asked what they knew or had heard of the animal whose bones were found at the salt-licks on the Ohio. It was an opportunity for *empressement*, such as the Indian orator does not usually neglect. One of the warriors immediately struck an attitude becoming the elevation and seriousness of his subject, and, with great pomp and emphasis delivered himself to the following effect, as reported by Mr. Jefferson: "That in ancient times a herd of these tremendous animals came to the Big-bone licks, and began a universal destruction of the bear, deer, elks, buffaloes and other animals which had been created for the use of the Indians; that the Great Man above, looking down and seeing this, was so enraged that he seized his lightning, descended on the earth, seated himself on a neighboring mountain, *on*

salt springs, doubtless, of the men, hardly less wild, who followed after them—when and how long before the era of the dimly-known Massawomees none can speculate—and is now the brimming "saline" of our day, one of the greatest natural gifts of Virginia.

a rock, on which his seat and the print of his feet are still to be seen, and hurled his bolts among them till the whole were slaughtered, except *the big bull*, who, presenting his forehead to the shafts, shook them off as they fell; but missing one at length, it wounded him in the side, whereupon, springing round, he bounded over the Ohio, over the Wabash, the Illinois, and finally over the great lakes, where he is living at this day!"

Such fables—some of which were believed by intelligent men who have died within the times of those now living—none of which, indeed, are exaggerated illustrations of the geographical myths of early Virginia, a peculiarity of that colony not sufficiently noticed in the common histories—may give us some idea of the romance which attended the footsteps of those who first scaled the mountain barriers of the Old Dominion. For a full century the eyes of the settlers in the distant plains below had been turned with passionate longings and mysterious imaginings to the top of the Blue Ridge, enveloped in a peculiar blue mist, wearing an unusual depth of that beautiful color which gave it its name. The first efforts to surmount it were naturally made in the direction of the settlements on the upper branches of the Rappahannock and in the Northern Neck (the country between the Rappahannock and the Potomac), the ridge declining toward the Potomac, and being less rugged and forbidding in its aspect than it is farther toward the south-west. Here the first exploring parties from East Virginia entered the vale of the Shenando (Shenandoah), planting themselves on the rich, low grounds, but gradually venturing upon the pleasant uplands beyond the river. So slow, however, was the extension of these settlements, and so little was the country subdued, that we are told by Judge Marshall that as late as the year 1756, eighteen years after Frederick and Augusta had been formed into counties, the Blue Ridge was regarded as the northwestern frontier of Virginia, and that the colony found great difficulty in completing a single regiment to protect the inhabitants from the horrors of the scalping-knife, and the still greater horrors of being led into captivity by those who added terror to death by the manner of inflicting it. Carlisle, in Pennsylvania, Frederick, in Maryland, and Winchester, in Virginia, were then frontier posts, the latter continuing to be such until the French were driven out of Canada.

The first settlement of the Valley from Lower Virginia was preceded, however, to some extent, by an earlier tide of immigration coming from Pennsylvania. The eastern part of the Valley was conveniently situated for emigrants from Pennsylvania; and the *Germans* in this colony no sooner heard of the rich vales of the Shenandoah and its branches than, manifesting the characteristic passion of their race for fat lands, they began to join their countrymen from Europe in pouring themselves over the country below Winchester, following the branches of the Shenandoah, and going up the Valley of Virginia as far as the Massanutten Mountain, where these branches divide, being called the South and North Forks. And here, in our distribution of the Valley of Virginia, we must explain that it is habitually described according to its form and the flow of its waters, and in opposition to the points of the compass; the *upper* portion or head of the Valley commencing from the south, and what is called the *Lower* Valley being to the north, where it declines and spreads about Winchester.

This latter division of the Valley, for the space of sixty

miles, had been occupied by the Germans, until, as they pressed toward the head branches of the Shenandoah, their immigrant columns were met by another race, which soon filled up an equal space beyond them, and was destined in most respects to dominate in the new land of promise. The Germans brought with them their energetic language, the simplicity of their manners and a vigorous industry that was to improve in a country where the climate was most delightful and the soil the richest imaginable. Traces of this healthful element of population, tenacious of its customs, are yet to be found among their descendants in Shenandoah and Page counties and other parts of the Valley; but a sensible transition has been going on about the borders of their old settlements, and the trace of the Germans in the Valley of Virginia is much slighter than that of the wonderful and strong stock of emigrants who were to meet them on the branches of the Shenandoah, and who to this day maintain their strongly-marked characteristics not only in Transmontane Virginia, but wherever they continued to spread southward and westward, until, as said by one of their historians, "there is scarce a county in the great Valley of the Mississippi where some of their descendants may not be found."

We allude to the Scotch-Irish element. The importation of this element beyond the Blue Ridge is one of the most romantic stories of American settlements, and is yet preserved with a singular fondness for details and personal anecdotes by the descendants of the old settlers of the Valley of Virginia. We all may know generally of "Burden's Grant," of the explorations and surveys of the Lewises, etc.; but it is a new interest to find the local and traditionary history of the Valley yet preserved in such vividness of coloring and particularity of details among the unwritten memories of its people.

The first explorers of the Valley of Virginia from the eastern portions of the colony appear to have been two traders, who were accustomed to pass from the Northern Neck to the settlements about Winchester. Moved by a passion for adventure, or perhaps by the prospects of trade with the aborigines, they determined to explore the unknown parts of the country toward the south-west. They seem to have passed entirely through the Valley, for they were captured by some hostile Indians on the waters of the Roanoke. One of them, John Salling, after six years of strange and eventful wanderings, the prisoner of various tribes by the event of war, having been shifted from the hands of the Cherokees to those of some Indians from Illinois, and after having accompanied various tribes in distant expeditions to countries then wholly unknown in Virginia, at one time treated with cruelty, and at another with distinction as the adopted son of a chief's mother, ended his strange pilgrimage in Canada, where he was kindly redeemed by the French governor, and returned to Virginia.

He brought back to Williamsburg a stock of wonderful stories that were eagerly devoured by a curiosity whetted with the passion for discovery. He told of a great river in the West, of new countries where he had fallen in with exploring parties of Spaniards, and he is thought to have even looked on the Gulf of Mexico. But the country he described most passionately, and to his glowing description of which his auditors listened most attentively, was the Valley of Virginia, a broad and broken space between parallel ridges of mountains; a country of beautiful prospects and sylvan scenes—lofty mountains, transparent streams, falls of water, rich valleys and majestic woods; its plains covered by a rich herbage grazed by herds of buffaloes, its hills crowned with forests, and the whole interspersed with an infinite variety of flowering shrubs, constituting the landscape around them. To these accounts of this strange and beautiful land, for the most part untouched by the hand of man, and offering unbought homes and easy subsistence to the adventurer, the most constant and interested listener was a stranger from Great Britain. The name of the stranger was John Lewis—the founder of an historic and one of the most romantic names in Virginia, and one honored in every part of the State even to this generation. He not only heard Salling's story with admiration, but he determined to accompany him to this newly-discovered land, and to found a settlement there if it fulfilled the expectations that had been excited in his mind.

Lewis—or, as he was afterward known, Colonel John Lewis—accompanied by his sons, Samuel and Andrew, the latter the brave and beloved General Lewis succeeding to the greatest honors of the family, made a settlement on Middle river, on a creek which bears his name. The large design and high spirit, however, with which he had entered the new country were soon manifested; for while Salling and his companions were dissipating their time in the chase, he set about surveying lands, not satisfied to be a mere pioneer of hunters—indeed, showing a true greatness of soul in laying the foundations of an empire in the wilderness.

In 1736, Lewis visited Williamsburg, desiring to obtain authority to locate lands in separate parcels in the country around him. An accident served him to obtain an influence and a patronage that the most assiduous endeavors might not otherwise have gained. He met with Benjamin Burden, who had lately come over to Virginia as agent for Lord Fairfax, proprietor of the Northern Neck. Burden, pleased with his new acquaintance, who opened to him his views, agreed to accompany him to his home to see the country and to hunt the buffalo—an animal then unknown in Lower Virginia. In one of their hunts a young buffalo-calf was taken by Andrew Lewis, who turned it over to Burden, and in doing so proved himself a provident hunter. Burden, knowing that the shaggy young monster would be an object of great curiosity at Williamsburg, carried it there; and he is said to have won the heart of Governor Gooch by presenting to him this rare pet. Anyhow, the governor was so pleased with the donor and what he told of the country roamed by the monsters of which the pet was a small specimen, that he promptly favored his views for himself and Lewis by entering an order in his official book authorizing Benjamin Burden to locate *five hundred thousand* acres of land, or any less quantity, on the waters of the Shenandoah and James rivers, on the condition that he should not interfere with any previous grants, and that within ten years he should settle at least one hundred families on the located lands.

Here was a princely gift on paper, but there were difficulties in the way of employing and realizing it. The first difficulty was to obtain settlers. The old colonists of Virginia were indisposed to leave their tobacco lands. They lived by the cultivation of tobacco; it was the sole staple of their trade; it was the money of the colony. A life in the new Arcadia, with occupations among green pastures and herds of cattle, had no enticements for them. Tobacco was associated with all their ideas of a prosperous agriculture, and was their measure of the luxuries of life. The common practice was to *roll* the hogsheads of tobacco to market. How could this be done through the rugged defiles of the Blue Ridge? It was readily seen by Burden that he must look elsewhere than to the old settlements of Virginia for a stock of emigrants with which to people his broad possessions. A few months after the governor's concession he returned to England for emigrants, and the next year, 1737, he brought over upward of one hundred families to settle on the granted lands. The Presbyterians in the northern parts of Ireland, in Scotland, and in the adjacent parts of England were at this time greatly stirred by the spirit of emigration. Most of Burden's colonists were Irish Presbyterians, who, being of Scottish extraction, obtained the name of Scotch-Irish. Among the names of the more numerous families settled on Burden's grant occur such as the Prestons, the Paxtons, the Lyles, the Grigsbys, the Stuarts, the McDowells, the Alexanders, the Crawfords, the Cumminses, the Browns, the Wallaces, the Wilsons, the Carutherses, the Campbells, the McCampbells, the McClungs, the McCues, the McKees, the McCowns, etc. Many of these names are yet extant in the Valley of Virginia, attesting relationship with the race which imbibed the indomitable spirit of John Knox, and proud of the distinction which the robust virtues of their ancestors have made for them in the new homes of America.

Of the hardihood and enterprise of this emigrant stock an illustration is furnished in an anecdote which we copy from one of the chroniclers of Virginia:

"Among others (says Withers) who came to Virginia at this time was an Irish girl named Polly Mullhollin.

On her arrival she was hired to James Bell to pay her passage, and with whom she remained during the period her servitude was to continue. At its expiration she attired herself in the habit of a man, and, with hunting-shirt and moccasins, went into Burden's grant for the purpose of making improvements and acquiring a title to land. Here she erected thirty cabins, by virtue of which she held one hundred acres adjoining each. When Benjamin Burden the younger came on to make deeds to those who held cabin-rights, he was astonished to see so many of the name of Mulhollin. Investigation led to a discovery of the mystery, to the great mirth of the other claimants. She resumed her Christian name and feminine dress, and many of her respectable descendants still reside within the limits of Burden's grant."

The supplement to Burden's grant was a new enterprise, the circumstances of which were even more dramatic than those which prefaced the first adventure of the Lewis family into the mountainous region of Virginia. The grant obtained by Burden did not include some lands on the upper branches of the Shenandoah. An opening to further settlements in that direction, however, was obtained by an order of the governor and council of Virginia, giving to a company of grantees 100,000 acres of land lying on the waters of the Greenbrier river; and in 1751 we find General Andrew Lewis, as agent for the company, entering upon the exploration of this country, lying close to the great range of the Alleghany. To his surprise, he found that he had been preceded in the discovery of this new area for settlement, and that there were white men already living in it. The story goes that in the year 1749 a person who lived in the county of Frederick was subject to spells of lunacy, during which he wandered into the wilderness, returning to his home when he recovered a sane condition of mind. This unhappy creature, wandering westwardly, came to the waters of the Greenbrier river. The features of the country here were unknown to the English inhabitants of the then colonies of America. It is true it was claimed by the French, but their settlements were limited to the Ohio and its waters, west of the Alleghany Mountains. The lunatic being surprised, even in his condition of mind, to find waters running a different course from any he had before known, and retaining a recollection of the scene where he had been brought to his senses, told of the phenomenon on his return home, and described a country abounding in game. His wild tale found believers, and soon excited the enterprise of others. Two men from New England, Jacob Marlin and Stephen Sewell, were the first white settlers on Greenbrier river. Having disagreed, they separated and lived apart.

In 1751, General Lewis found these two men in the Greenbrier country—one lodging in a cabin, the other making his abode in a large hollow tree. He inquired what could induce them to live separate in a wilderness so distant from the habitations of any other human beings. They replied that difference of opinion had occasioned their separation, and that they had since enjoyed more tranquillity and a better understanding; for Sewell said that each morning when they arose, and Marlin came out of the great house and he out of his hollow tree, they saluted each other, saying "Good-morning, Mr. Marlin," and "Good-morning, Mr. Sewell," so that a good understanding then existed between them. The neighborly feeling did not last long, for Sewell soon removed about forty miles farther west, where he was found and killed by the Indians. "Sewell's Mountain" is a monument to the name and memory of the rude adventurer.

The General Lewis spoken of above was the hero of the battle of Point Pleasant, 1774, which finally broke the power of the Indians between the mountains and the Ohio; the tribes which had inhabited the Valley of Virginia and the powerful Shawnees having retired down the Kanawha toward its mouth as the white settlements advanced upon them. Here General Lewis pressed them in what was known as "Dunmore's War" (1774), with an expeditionary force of eleven hundred men. In the battle of Point Pleasant were represented the Shawnee, Delaware, Mingo, Wyandotte and Cayuga tribes, the whole force commanded by Cornstalk, sachem of the Shawnees and king of "the Northern Confederacy." The Virginians paid dearly for their victory, about one-fifth of their number being killed and wounded. Colonel Charles Lewis, a nephew of the general, fell in the engagement.*

* The following ballad, obtained from a mountain cabin in this region, appears to have been published in the papers of the time, and is inserted here as a very rare and decided curiosity. The name of the border minstrel does not appear:

>Let us mind the tenth day of October,
> Seventy-four, which caused woe;
>The Indian savages they did cover
> The pleasant banks of the Ohio.
>
>The battle beginning in the morning,
> Throughout the day it lasted sore,
>Till the evening shades were returning down
> Upon the banks of the Ohio.
>
>Judgment precedes to execution,
> Let fame throughout all dangers go,

The removal of the Shawnees from the lovely valley of the Greenbrier is a story throughout of thrilling and beautiful romances. It was not until frequent battles and desperate forays, by which they testified their attachment to their ancient hunting-grounds and the graves of their fathers, that they were finally, after the battle of Point Pleasant, forced to abandon their country and seek shelter with the main body of their tribe, then living on the waters of the great Scioto.

The romantic story of their expulsion is fitly crowned with the death of their great warrior, Cornstalk, two years later, by one of the foulest and most pitiful assassinations that ever drew sympathy for the wrongs of the red man and reflected the fierce and cruel spirit of his conquerors. He was murdered by the garrison at Point Pleasant.

> Our heroes fought with resolution
> Upon the banks of the Ohio.
>
> Seven score lay dead and wounded
> Of champions that did face their foe,
> By which the heathen were confounded,
> Upon the banks of the Ohio.
>
> Colonel Lewis and some noble captains,
> Did down to death like Uriah go,
> Alas! their heads wound up in napkins,
> Upon the banks of the Ohio.
>
> Kings lamented their mighty fallen
> Upon the mountains of Gilboa,
> And now we mourn for brave Hugh Allen,
> Far from the banks of the Ohio.
>
> Oh bless the mighty King of heaven
> For all his wondrous works below,
> Who hath to us the victory given
> Upon the banks of the Ohio.

He had gone there on an errand of peace, and was detained as a hostage, war being expected with his tribe. Of what ensued we have some vivid details in a memoir of Colonel John Stuart, who was in the garrison and sought to prevent the dreadful crime referred to. He writes:

"During the time of our stay, two young men, of the names of Hamilton and Gilmore, went over the Kanawha one day to hunt for deer. On their return to camp some Indians had concealed themselves on the bank among the woods to view our encampment, and as Gilmore came along past them they fired on him and killed him on the bank.

"Captain Arbuckle and myself were standing on the opposite bank when the gun fired; and while we were wondering who it could be shooting contrary to orders, or what they were doing over the river, we saw Hamilton run down the bank, who called out that Gilmore was killed. Gilmore was one of the company of Captain John Hall, of that part of the country now Rockbridge county. The captain was a relation of Gilmore's, whose family and friends were chiefly cut off by the Indians in the year 1763, when Greenbrier was cut off. Hall's men instantly jumped into a canoe and went to the relief of Hamilton, who was standing in momentary expectation of being put to death. They brought the corpse of Gilmore down the bank, covered with blood and scalped, and put him into the canoe. As they were passing the river, I observed to Captain Arbuckle that the people would be for killing the hostages as soon as the canoe would land. He supposed that they would not offer to commit so great a violence upon the innocent, who were in nowise accessory to the murder of Gilmore. But the canoe had scarcely touched the shore until the cry was raised, 'Let us kill the Indians in the fort;' and every man, with his gun in his hand, came up the bank pale with rage. Captain Hall was at their head and leader. Captain Arbuckle and I met them and endeavored to dissuade them from so unjustifiable an action; but they cocked their guns, threatened us with instant death if we did not desist, rushed by us into the fort and put the Indians to death.

"On the preceding day the Cornstalk's son, Elinipsico, had come from the nation to see his father and to know if he was well or alive. When he came to the river opposite the fort he hallooed. His father was at that instant in the act of delineating a map of the country and the waters between the Shawnee towns and the Mississippi, at our request, with chalk upon the floor. He immediately recognized the voice of his son, got up, went out and answered him. The young fellow crossed over, and they embraced each other in the most tender and affectionate manner. The interpreter's wife, who had been a prisoner among the Indians and had recently left them, on hearing the uproar the next day, and hearing the men threatening that they would kill the Indians, for whom she retained much affection, ran to their cabin and informed them that the people were just coming to kill them, and that because the Indians who killed Gilmore had come with Elinipsico the day before. He utterly denied it, declared that he knew nothing of them, and trembled exceedingly. His father encouraged him not to be afraid, for that the *Great Man above* had sent him there to be killed and die with him. As the men advanced to the door, the Cornstalk rose and met them; they fired upon him, and seven or eight bullets went through him. So fell the great Cornstalk warrior, whose name was bestowed upon him by the consent of the nation as their great strength and support. His son was shot dead as he sat upon a stool.

"The Cornstalk, from personal appearance and many brave acts, was undoubtedly a hero. Had he been spared to live, I believe he would have been friendly to the American cause; for nothing could induce him to make the visit to the garrison at the critical time he did but to communicate to them the temper and disposition of the Indians and their design of taking part with the British. On the day he was killed we held a council at which he was present. His countenance was dejected, and he made a speech, all of which seemed to indicate an honest and manly disposition. He acknowledged that he expected that he and his party would have to run with the stream, for that all the Indians on the lakes and northwardly were joining the British. He said that when he returned to the Shawnee towns after the battle at the Point, he called a council of the nation to consult what was to be done, and upbraided them for their folly in not suffering him to make peace on the evening before the battle. 'What,' said he, 'will you do now? The Big Knife is coming on us, and we shall all be killed. Now you must fight or we are undone.' But no one made an answer. He said, 'Then let us kill all our women and children and go and fight till we die.' But none would answer. At length he rose and struck his tomahawk in the post in the centre of the town-house. 'I'll go,' said he, 'and make peace,' and then the warriors all grunted out, 'Ough, ough, ough,' and runners were instantly despatched to the governor's army to solicit a peace and the interposition of the governor on their behalf.

"When he made his speech in council with us he seemed to be impressed with an awful premonition of his approaching fate; for he repeatedly said, 'When I was a young man and went to war, I thought that might be the last time, and I would return no more. Now I am here among you; you may kill me if you please; I can die but once, and it is all one to me, now or another time.' This declaration concluded every sentence of his speech. He was killed about one hour after our council."

But to return from these incidents to the settlements within the boundary of the Alleghany. The battle of Point Pleasant secured these settlements, and it may be considered to have been fought for them. The country between the Alleghany and the Ohio was yet a wilderness, while the Valley had commenced to smile with homes, and was able to send to the battle-fields of the Revolution of 1776 a body of volunteers who made the name of Augusta county (as was then called the immense territory which at the present time comprises four entire States and nearly forty counties of the two Virginias) famous in its annals.*

The following has the authority of tradition, and has appeared before in print:

* "When the British force under Tarleton drove the Legislature from Charlottesville to Staunton, the stillness of the Sabbath eve was broken in the latter town by the beat of the drum, and volunteers were called for to prevent the passage of the British through the mountains at Rockfish Gap. The elder sons of William Lewis, who then resided at the old fort, were absent with the Northern army. Three sons, however, were at home, whose ages were seventeen, fifteen and thirteen years. William Lewis was confined to his room by sickness, but his wife, with the firmness of a Roman matron, called them to her, and bade them fly to the defence of their native land. 'Go, my children,' said she. 'I spare not my youngest, my fair-

Looking over the distribution of the early populations in the Valley of Virginia, we find, first, the German element filling the lower portion of the Valley as far as the Massanutten Mountain; secondly, beyond the line of their settlements, the Scotch-Irish or Presbyterian element extending to the vale of James river, and pushed yet farther to hug the Alleghany, until for seventy or eighty miles along the Valley there was a population scarcely less homogeneous and more peculiar than the mass of Germans below them. The German element, as we have already intimated, was not so strongly marked, nor has it been so retentive of its characteristics, as the Scotch-Irish. It has lost much of its identity in Virginia by dispersion and by diffusion with stronger races, although there are yet to be found in some of the Valley counties German families who are unwilling to give up the language of Fatherland, corruptly as they speak it, or the plain homespun of old times, and who bewail the transition that is going on about their borders, and the Anglicizing disposition of their children, as the degeneracy of their race.

The strong and fruitful element in the population of the Valley has been the Scotch-Irish. The characteristics of these people were strongly marked—not less than those of the Pilgrim Fathers—and they yet survive to a marked degree in their hardy descendants. Their detestation of civil tyranny descended to them from the Cov-haired boy, the comfort of my declining years. I devote you all to my country. Keep back the foot of the invader from the soil of Augusta, or see my face no more.' When this incident was related to Washington shortly after its occurrence, he enthusiastically exclaimed, 'Leave me but a banner to plant upon the mountains of Augusta, and I will rally around me the men who will lift our bleeding country from the dust and set her free.'"

enanters of Scotland; and on the dispute between the Colonists and the mother country, they were Whigs of the firmest and most invincible spirit. They were a sober and thoughtful people; and it is remarkable that they never showed any disposition to join the bands of white hunters who formed a sort of connecting link between the savage aborigines and the civilized tillers of the soil. A striking peculiarity of manners which they had in common with the Puritans was that certain self-continence, which, mistaken by a superficial observer for phlegm or dullness, is sometimes found covering an enormous strength of character, held in reserve and capable of putting forth the most strenuous and persevering exertions when demanded by occasion.

Another characteristic of these people was their rigid Calvinistic morality. Founded on a religious principle, this morality was sober, firm and consistent, though in some of its aspects stern, and too disdainful of persuasions to virtue. They had none of the gay amusements common among the Eastern Virginians. There was, indeed, as has been observed, but little communication with these, and not until roads and navigation offered new facilities for trade, and the Eastern planter was somewhat weaned from his devotion to the culture of tobacco, did the Valley cease to repel settlers from the lowlands of Virginia.

The Scotch-Irish were a God-fearing pople. No sooner had the immigrants provided necessary food and shelter for their families than they began to provide for the regular and decent worship of God. They built churches of the solid limestone of the Valley, and they called pastors as far as their limited means would admit. The difficulties sometimes experienced in raising these religious structures, where there were no roads, wagons or saw-mills, may be illustrated by a relation which tradition yet preserves, that the Providence congregation packed all the sand used in their church from a place six miles distant, sack by sack, on the backs of horses; and, what is almost incredible, the fair wives and daughters of the congregation are said to have undertaken this part of the work, while the men labored at the stone and timber.

The social intercourse of the early homes of the Valley was chiefly religious. The meetings of the presbytery, held in turn by the principal churches, drew together a large concourse, and were celebrated as the chief religious festivals of the country. Except these solemn festivals, and the weekly meetings at church, the families of the country had but little social intercourse. The careful and religious education of their children was one of the most important features of their domestic polity, and was the first concern of the infant society. Common schools arose among them as soon as their settlements were founded, and increased as the state of population warranted them.

Of the early institution of learning that preceded Washington College the following account is yet preserved in a manuscript local history of one of the oldest inhabitants:

"The school-house was a log cabin. Hither about thirty youths of the mountains repaired 'to taste the Pierian spring' thirty-five years after the first settlement of Burden's grant. Of reading, writing and ciphering the boys of the country had before acquired such knowledge as primary schools could afford; but with a few rare exceptions, Latin, Greek, algebra, geometry, and such-like scholastic mysteries, were things of which they had heard—which they knew, perhaps, to be covered up in the learned heads of their pastors—but of the nature and uses of which they had no conception whatever. The institution was a log hut of one apartment. The students carried their dinners with them from their boarding-houses in the neighborhood. They conned their lessons either in the school-room, where the recitations were heard, or under the shades of the forest, where breezes whispered and birds sang without disturbing their studies. A horn—perhaps a real cow's horn—summoned the school from play and the scattered classes to recitation. Instead of broadcloth coats, the students generally wore a far more graceful garment—the hunting-shirt—home-spun, home-woven and home-made by the industrious wives and daughters of the land. Their amusements were not the less remote from the modern tastes of students—cards, backgammon, flutes, fiddles, and even marbles, were scarcely known among these home-bred mountain boys. Firing pistols and ranging the fields with shot guns to kill little birds for sport they would have considered a waste of time and ammunition. As to frequenting tippling-shops of any denomination, this was impossible, because no such catchpenny lures for students existed in the country, or would have been tolerated. Had any huckster of liquors, knick-knacks and explosive crackers hung out his sign in those days, the old Puritan morality of the land was yet vigorous enough to abate the nuisance. The sports of the students were mostly gymnastic, both manly and healthful, such as leaping, running, wrestling, pitching quoits and playing ball. In this rustic seminary a considerable number of young men began their education who afterward bore a distinguished part in the civil and ecclesiastical affairs of the country."

No wonder that such nurture and education produced one of the most vigorous and manful populations in America. Amid the many changes that have passed over the face of their country, and affected, too, the social organization, the people of the Valley of Virginia are, as we have already said, still distinguished for many of the virtues ascribed to their ancestors. And how great and multitudinous have been those changes! It has often struck us that in no part of America is there to be observed so striking an epitome of its progress, in all phases, as in the enclosure of the Valley of Virginia, so distinctly marked are the epochs on this well-defined and measurable theatre.

Let us take three generations for our survey. Toward the close of the last century we find here the "backwoodsmen"—a type but little visible in Pennsylvania and New England—leading a nondescript life between civilization and barbarism, yet one of singular virtues drawn from each. This life was rude, even in its highest development toward civilization, but in its harshest aspects there was a sort of purity and romance. The men of the Valley of these times wore the hunting-shirt and moccasin; the common household furniture was the noggin, the trencher and the wooden bowl; their life was scanty but not nomadic, and where we might have expected the shiftlessness of the hunter-state, we are surprised to find men with steady industry planting homes in the wilderness. Their principal agricultural instrument was a harrow with wooden teeth, and their common vehicle the sled. In the rude and ponderous industry of this primitive people we see something grand, even while we smile at the grotesqueness of some parts of the picture.

Another generation comes upon the stage. In 1833,

Mr. Samuel Kercheval writes: "The linsey and coarse linen of the first settlers of the country have been exchanged for the substantial and fine fabrics of Europe and Asia—the hunting-shirt for the fashionable coat of broadcloth, and the moccasin for boots and shoes of tanned leather. The dresses of our ladies are equal in beauty, fineness and fashion to those of the cities and countries of Europe." With yet greater complacency he writes of the miracle of turnpike roads over the mountains: "The horse-paths along which our fathers made their laborious journeys over the mountains for salt and iron have been succeeded by wagon roads, and these again by substantial turnpikes, which, as if by magic enchantment, have brought the distant region, not many years ago denominated the '*backwoods*,' into a close and lucrative connection with our great Atlantic cities. The journey over the mountains, formerly considered so long, so expensive, and even perilous, is now made in a very few days, and with accommodations *not displeasing to the epicure himself!*"

The last scene comes in panoramic succession; and what do we see in our day and generation? Miles of country, far and wide, smiling with a cultivation the most luxuriant in America; busy towns; the most splendid institutions of learning in the South; a people practicing every refinement of dress and manners; villas that Cicero or Sir Walter Scott might have envied; the telegraph set up where formerly had been the Indian's trail; and for sled and stage-coach, the arrowy car, that is soon to bear by the doors of beautiful and animated homes the trade of a continent!

CHAPTER XII.

THE GREENBRIER WHITE SULPHUR SPRINGS.

The Railroad through the Mountains—Site of the White Sulphur Springs—Pleasing Scenery—The Springs in 1772—Hotel Improvements—The Grounds—Analysis of the White Sulphur Water—Remarks on the Use of Mineral Waters—Popular Errors on the Subject—Debauchery in Mineral Waters—A Guide to the Use of the White Sulphur Water—The Theory of *Fresh vs. Stale*—The Bathing Establishment—Life at the Springs—"Jenkins" in Virginia—A Ball-room Conversation—A Southern Editor on Society and Comfort at the Springs—Why Virginians "can't keep Hotels"—An Anecdote of Boniface—The White Sulphur Hotel, a Superior one.

HE ride by rail from Staunton to the White Sulphur Springs is not the easiest and most joyous in the world. Near the latter the Chesapeake and Ohio Railroad surmounts its greatest physical difficulties, and is elaborate with engineering skill; and whatever may be the safety, there is yet a feeling of insecurity on being whirled through the deepest of cuts and over the loftiest of trestles. The tunnels in a short distance aggregate two and one-eighth miles. One of them, "the Big Bend," is sixty-four hundred feet long. Some of the longest ones were yet incomplete, and in the haste to complete the road to the White Sulphur for the summer's travel of 1869, a temporary track had been laid around them and around incomplete trestles.

The location of the springs is on the immediate confines of the Valley of Virginia, being but six miles west of the Alleghany chain, which divides the waters that flow into the Chesapeake Bay and those which wander westward, carrying their tribute to the Mississippi. It is enclosed in one of those small valleys, branches of minor formations, which we have noticed as characterizing the geographical system of the great Valley. The immediate confines are Kate's Mountain and the Greenbrier Mountains, and the intervening country is beautifully embosomed with hills. The valley opens about a half a mile in breadth, and winds with graceful undulations beyond the eye's reach.

As a hunting-ground of the Shawnees, and as the limit of settlements founded by the famous Lewis family when competing with the Pennsylvania Germans for the possession of the Valley of Virginia, we have already glanced at the surrounding country, which is yet strewn with many ungathered traditions. The county of Greenbrier is now within the boundary of West Virginia. In the year 1778 it was separated from Botetourt county. The reputed origin of the name is a little curious. The county is named from the river, and it is said to have been named by old Colonel John Lewis, father to the late general, and one of the grantees under the order of council, who, in company with his son Andrew, exploring the country in 1751, entangled himself in a bunch of greenbriers on the river, and declared that he would ever after call the stream Greenbrier river.

The locality of the White Sulphur Springs was known to the Indians as one of the most important licks of the deer and elk. As early as 1772 a woman was brought here on a litter forty miles, whose disease had baffled all medical skill. A tree was felled, and a trough dug and filled with the mineral water, which was heated by putting hot stones into it. In this the patient was bathed, while, at the same time, she drank freely of the fountain. In a few weeks she went from her bark cabin perfectly restored. The fame of this cure attracted many sick persons to the springs, and they soon commenced throwing up rude log cabins. But the dreariness of the mountains, the badness of the roads, and the poverty of the accommodations, repelled all but the most anxious from these health-giving waters till 1818, when they fell into the hands of a Mr. Caldwell. From that time the place has continued rapidly to improve.

At the time of this writing the Springs' property is leased, but it is owned by a joint-stock company of great resources and enterprise. This company has already erected the largest building in the Southern country, its dimensions being four hundred feet long, by a corresponding width, and covering an acre of ground. This immense structure is of brick, and is appropriated for receiving-rooms, dining-room, ball-room, parlors, lodging-rooms, etc. There are also numerous cottages for families. With these improvements, together with a new and capacious bathing establishment, and the removal of many of the old buildings to new localities, by which the lawns are enlarged and adorned, the property in capacity and in the elegance of its arrangements will compare with some of the most pretentious of Northern watering-places. The interior appointments of the hotel are imposing and elegant. The dining-room is upward of three hundred feet long, with a correspondent width, and conveniently seats at one time more than a thousand persons.

The fountain issues from the foot of a gentle slope, terminating in the low intervale upon a small and beautiful stream (Howard's creek) which is tributary to the Greenbrier river. It flows with unusual boldness from rock-lined apertures, and is enclosed by marble casings five feet square and about three feet deep. The ground ascends from the spring eastward, rising to a considerable eminence on the left, and spreading east and south into wide lawns. These have been improved by the construction of broad serpentine walks, among which the most popular is "the Stroll," and the most romantic, "the Lover's Walk;" the latter with many a winding, and measured by such stages as sweet "Hesitation" and downright "Acceptance," while a dark and angular recess, where unhappy hearts are slain, takes the name of "Rejection."

The White Sulphur water was analyzed in 1842, by Professor Hayes, of Boston, with the following results:

50,000 grains (about seven pints) of this water contain, in solution, 3.633 water-grain measures of gaseous matter, or about 1.14 of its volume, consisting of—

Nitrogen gas	1.013
Oxygen gas	.108
Carbonic acid	2.444
Hydro-sulphuric acid	.068
	3.633

One gallon, or 237 cubic inches of the water, contains 16 739-1000 cubic inches of gas, having the proportion of—

Nitrogen gas	4.680
Oxygen gas	.498
Carbonic acid	11.290
Hydro-sulphuric acid	.271
	16.739

P

50,000 grains of this water contain 115 735-1000 grains of saline matter, consisting of—

Sulphate of lime	67.168
Sulphate of magnesia	30.364
Chloride of magnesium	.859
Carbonate of lime	6.060
Organic matter (dried at 212° F.)	3.740
Carbonic acid	4.584
Silicates (silica 1.34, potash .18, soda .66, magnesia and a trace of oxyd iron)	2.960
	115.735

The temperature of the water is 62° Fahrenheit, and remains uniformly the same during winter and summer. The principal spring yields about thirty gallons per minute; and it is notable that this quantity is not perceptibly increased or diminished during the longest spells of wet or dry weather.

With reference to the use of the White Sulphur waters in the sense of a discriminating or pathological practice, there may be conveniently prefaced here some reflections on the use of mineral waters generally; which, so far from being a technical treatise, will, following the *popular* design of our work, be found a familiar and intelligible experience among those accustomed to resort to these natural provisions of health.

The most common difficulty in the use of mineral waters is an impatience for sensible and obvious effects— the eagerness of the invalid to witness the progress of his cure. This disposition, so natural that it can scarcely be severely censured, is yet an unfortunate one, and sometimes very injurious. The patient is impracticable; he cannot be reconciled to the use of small and inoperative quantities of the water; or he debauches himself with excessive draughts of it. These are common errors, and yet they are founded on an ignorance which a little reflection and a little observation of analogies within the general experience, even without the aid of a medical adviser, might readily remove.

The best effects of mineral waters generally are not those of sudden disturbances. The intelligent physician will admonish the invalid, eager for immediate and visible results, that it is far better that the water should lie quietly upon his system, not manifesting much excitement upon any of the organs, but rather silently putting *the inner man* to rights, and giving it its natural and healthy motion. The technical word that describes this effect is "*alterative*." As the celebrated Patissier—one of the few learned physicians who is content to use a popular language rather than the technology of his profession—has explained: "In the general, mineral waters revive the languishing circulation, give a new direction to the vital energies, re-establish the perspiratory action of the skin, bring back to their physiological type the vitiated or suppressed secretions, provoke salutary evacuations either by urine or stool, or by transpiration; they bring about, in the animal economy, an intimate transmutation—*a profound change*." The common springs' parlance of "saturated with the water," as a desirable condition, is an unconscious popular endorsement of the pathology of the learned professor. And again, the common experience of impatient invalids of being "no better while at the springs, but beginning to mend soon after leaving," is another familiar tribute to this true theory of the action of mineral waters.

The medical world appears to have pretty well concluded on the modern discovery, properly dated since the days of miraculous cures, that the real curative action of mineral waters is the *alterative* action. This is held to be especially true of sulphur waters; and yet, more especially, Doctor Moorman says of the Greenbrier White Sulphur Springs: "Indeed no article of the materia medica has more decided alterative effects." He claims that the water has these effects by being absorbed, or, in other words, entering into the great circuit of the circulation, and thus exercising the specific or peculiar action of its constituents in promoting the various secretory and excretory processes, and thereby restoring the diseased system to a physiological condition.

Between the action of *mercury* and of the more powerful of the sulphur waters on the organic system the most striking similarity exists. Dr. Armstrong long since remarked the resemblance between mercury and the sulphur waters of Europe, and confidently expressed the opinion that the latter are equally powerful as the former in their action upon the secretory organs; and with this very important difference, that while the long-continued use of mercury, in chronic disease, generally breaks up the strength, that of the sulphur waters generally renovates the whole system.

The principal ground of discrimination in the use of the White Sulphur waters proceeds from the general considerations already advanced; it is perfectly intelligible, and the invalid may constantly refer to it, in the absence of those details of instruction for which there is no place here, and for which he should have recourse to his medical adviser. The leading guide is simply to determine the preference for sensible medicinal effects or for the alterative action; and on this depends the practical question which every visitor is called upon to decide—whether to use the water fresh as it flows from the spring, or deprived of its gas, or with its quantities modified.

This question, it seems, has always had its partisans at the White Sulphur, and it is the first one that is proposed to the visitor. Doctor Moorman, however, thus intelligently decides between the two opinions, giving to each of the methods of using the water—*fresh* or *stale*—its proper allotment:

"For some patients, the White Sulphur as it flows from the spring is too *stimulating*, and hence, before the *non-stimulating* method of using it was introduced, many such patients left the spring either without giving the water a trial, or actually rendered worse by its stimulating influence.

"In cases of nervous persons, and especially in those whose brain is prone to undue excitement, we have often found it necessary, either by *freezing* or *heating* the water, to throw off its gas completely before it could be tolerated by the system; and some of the happiest results we have ever witnessed from the use of the water have been achieved by it after being thus *prepared*.

"Our object in prescribing White Sulphur has been to pursue a discriminating or *pathological* practice. We regard it as an active and potent *medicine*, and believe that, like all such medicines, it should be used with a wise reference to the nature of the case and the state of the system. *We must not be understood as advancing the opinion that this water is always to be preferred after the escape of its gas.* We entertain no such opinion; on the contrary, for a large class of visitors we think it preferable that they should avail themselves of the use of the water either at, or recently removed from, the fountain, and as it naturally abounds in its gases."

And the conclusion is plain and emphatic—that the water, to be used safely and most beneficially in very many cases, must be taken with strict reference to its *fresh* or *stale quality*; or, in other words, to its *stimulating* or *non-stimulating* qualities.

Without attempting a set of rules for the invalid, preceding and other reflections on the use of the White Sulphur may be reduced, for distinctness and for readiness of reference, to such obvious propositions as the following. All the "points" are deducible from the main theory:

1. The water is always more *stimulant*, and generally *less purgative*, when taken fresh at the spring and abounding in its gas.

2. The *alterative* or changing effects of the water are by far its most valuable effects, and are those which, more than all others, give to it its distinctive and effective character.

3. If the water produces *active purgative* or *diuretic* effects, its *alterative action* is correspondingly delayed.

4. An active and long-continued *diuretic effect* is generally useless and frequently hurtful, and hence when in much excess should be arrested. This may be effected with the utmost certainty by a modification in the quantity or periods of using the water, and by gentle medical means that divert from the kidneys and determine to the liver and skin.

Of diseases in which the White Sulphur may be usefully prescribed, we may adopt again a summary paragraph from Dr. Moorman's work:

"Various diseases of the stomach, liver, spleen, kidneys and bladder, as well as some derangements of the brain and nervous system generally, are treated successfully by this agent. To the various affections of the skin, unattended with active inflammation, to chronic affections of the bowels, and to gout and rheumatism, it is well adapted. In hæmorrhoids, in some of the chronic affections of the womb, in chlorosis and other kindred female disorders, in mercurial *sequelæ*, and especially in the secondary forms of *lues* and ill-conditioned ulcers in depraved constitutions, it constitutes the most valuable remedy to which the invalid can resort."

An aid to the internal use of the water is supplied in the excellent bathing establishment which the present lessees of the White Sulphur have added to their other extensive improvements of the grounds. The water used for bathing flows from the sulphur spring of which the visitors drink. Looking at the analysis of the water, and finding it to contain about one hundred and fifty grains of active medicinal salts to the gallon, we cannot fail to see that, so far as the medication of waters can favorably affect the bath for which they are used, the White Sulphur baths must be remarkable. It is said that no other waters in America that are used for bathing, except the Washita Springs in Arkansas, are so highly impregnated with mineral salts.

These baths, in connection with the drinking of the sulphur waters, although not required in every case, are of great importance in a large number of cases, aiding to produce the best effects of the waters.

Impressed with the great value—in fact the absolute necessity to some invalids—of the baths in connection with the drinking of the water, the proprietors of the springs have recently enlarged and remodeled their bathing establishment, so as to make it satisfactory in every respect. The bathing-house is large, affording ample accommodations. The rooms are spacious, airy and comfortable, and in addition to the usual tub-baths there are erected *douche* baths, for the application of streams of hot or warm water to parts of the body; and there are also set apart rooms for the administration of *sweating* baths.*

The company at the White Sulphur has always been distinguished for its numbers and culture, although we cannot go as far as the description of Doctor Moorman—in which there is an unpleasant evidence of the *afflatus* of the advertisement—and designate the place as "at once the Athens and the Paris of America." Heretofore, these springs have had a larger patronage than any other watering-place south of the Potomac. Their reputation for gayeties and fashionable display stands in stead, or in preference, of even more solid attractions to draw a

---

* The new and improved method of heating the water for bathing deserves to be noted. This is effected by *steam* in the vessel in which it is used, and is a great improvement over the old method of heating mineral waters for bathing. Under the old plan of heating in a boiler and thence conveying the water to the bathing-tub, much of its valuable saline matter was precipitated and lost. By this improved method of applying steam to the water in the tub, the heat is never so great in raising the water to the bathing point as to cause any important precipitation of its salts; hence they are left in their natural suspension in the water to exert their specific effect upon the bather. Not only so, but by this improved method hot steam may be let into the tub from time to time as the water cools, so as to keep it essentially of the same temperature during the entire period of bathing—a consideration often of no small importance. This method of heating mineral waters in the tub in which they are used, in connection with the *douche* and *sweating* baths, brings *hot* and *warm bathing* at this place in favorable competition with bathing at naturally hot and warm fountains, and promises to be productive of the same good effects that are experienced from bathing in such fountains.

crowd, of which the invalid element is by no means the larger.

While the White Sulphur has been such a social rendezvous, there has recently been some displeasure at the development of a vulgarity and a nuisance there which was supposed to belong only to certain promiscuous watering-places in the North, which we unwillingly notice here, and to which we would not refer except to point out a source of detraction which we would be glad to see removed. We refer to the representation of "the press" tolerated here in the persons of low reporters sloughed off from the city journals during the summer season, and of editors of country *Phœnixes* and *Trumpeteers*, the encouragement of weak editions of "Jenkins," and a feeble apishness after the watering-place literature of the North. We had hoped that "Jenkins" was altogether a Northern institution, or at least that his tribe that threatens our Virginia watering-places would not be quite so underling and paltry as those who figured in the *fiasco* of the "Press Ball" of 1869. The proprieties of our Southern manners do not permit such liberties of the press as have been practiced recently at some of our springs, while common sense rejects their frivolities. To criticise the dresses of ladies; to print estimates, in dollars and cents, of jewelry worn at different balls; to publish the names of ladies in full, without even the small decency of asterisks, and with no more misgivings than those of ballet-dancers on a play-bill; to tell how Brigadier General Bombastes Furioso, released from the cares of conducting his great gift establishment of "real diamonds and plated ware," and of giving certificates of prizes to negro barbers, made happy at fifty cents a head, spends his valuable time, and what anecdotes he tells of his fugacious military career; to describe how the wife of the man who gave buttermilk to John M. Daniel, of the Richmond *Examiner*, as a peace-offering, conducts herself as the clothes-horse or other unfeminine thing to display a silk dress that cost several thousands of dollars, —are certainly not the most valuable or interesting things that could be written, or even the most tolerable things that should be written of a society of Southern ladies and gentlemen.

But "Jenkins" defends his privileges. He puts in the plea that the ladies, however they disclaim it, are delighted to have their names and dresses published broadside in the newspapers, and that their protest of "*No*" is merely the feminine of "*Yes.*" One of the ingenious tribe thus reports a conversation in the ball-room to illustrate and sustain his position:

REPORTER. "Miss ——, have the kindness to describe your costume to me."

MISS —— (shocked and blushing at the idea of being put into the paper). "Oh, indeed, don't put my name in. It's a horrid way. Now, really, you mustn't."

REPORTER. "Oh, certainly, Miss ——, of course not, as you wish otherwise."

MISS —— (startled and turning pale at the idea of *not being put in the paper*). "Well—but—at any rate—*if you should*, say that I wore," etc. And there followed a catalogue a half page long.

On which we have only this commentary to make: that we fear that the dear creature "interviewed" by Jenkins was not the very best exponent of the culture and gentleness and unaffected modesty of the daughters of the South.

There is something undoubtedly of "shoddy" at the

White Sulphur (as at all famous places), and something, we must add, of undue adaptation of the system of accommodation and entertainment there to the mere bacchanalism of society. A correspondent who cannot be suspected of Jenkinsism—it is the editor of the New Orleans *Times* who writes—thus indicates the hotel life here, with a glance at the accommodations of the place:

"I missed, in the ball-room, many of the old characteristics of our Southern women. There is quite too much overdressing and emblazoning, and the air of conscious beauty, splendor and attractiveness. The prettiest feature of a pretty woman is the unconsciousness of her charms. This is a great natural endowment or a high achievement of art. I do not perceive much of it here. I can read too distinctly in the face of the leading belles the idea which is predominant in their minds—that they are exciting great admiration and producing certain effects. The overdressing is awful, and may well alarm the political and social economists of the South for the future of our section. What a terror to aspiring bachelors to contemplate the potent agencies of bankruptcy which flutter and glitter around them! But I am venturing upon a dangerous sea of moral disquisition, and return to the more agreeable one of expressing my great admiration for certain of the beauties here who are regarded as rightful aspirants for the apple of Paris. Kentucky, Illinois and Virginia may be considered as the three goddesses who enter the list. Each of these States is represented by a magnificent specimen of female beauty and elegance, and a most perplexing task it would be to determine between their respective claims. . . . . Whilst I do not underrate the value and pleasure of the drawing-room and ball-room pleasures and amusements, it is an obvious criticism of this establishment that this line of business is overdone, and that there is a woeful lack of other pleasures and conveniences for quiet enjoyment for which people flock to such resorts. There is no drawing or reading-room for gentlemen, not even a sitting-room, which is not shared with the servants and hangers-on. This is an enormous hotel, and friend Hildreth, who is here, says it has the largest dining-room in the world, and a ball-room of corresponding dimensions. And yet no sitting or reading-room for the many quiet old gentlemen who would like to hold pleasant converse without the necessity of dressing in full ball costume, or mixing with the rather miscellaneous crowd in the bar-room or the office. In fine, this hotel is, both in design and management, far from what it ought to be as the principal spa of the South."

Yet it is to be admitted that the present lessees, Messrs. Peyton & Co., whose fame is eminent in the hotel directory of the country, have already done wonders in improving a resort so popular; and we doubt not, considering their present rate of progression, they will before long make the entertainment of the White Sulphur complete at all points. The modern hotel is a small monarch, but in Virginia the lines of succession are too short and uncertain to accomplish the highest degrees of improvement and prestige.

Indeed, however defective may be the hotel establishment of the White Sulphur, it is so far superior to the common run of what we get at the Virginia springs that criticism in this connection is unjust; and we have made such only in comparison with the accommodations to be found at Northern watering-places. The Virginian, with all his virtues and accomplishments, does not, generally speaking, understand keeping a hotel; and when we descend from the cities to his rural entertainments, his deficiencies in this respect are yet more painfully perceived. The comparative aversion to the watering-places of this State is, we are persuaded, greatly due to distrust of the accommodations. We too often meet at these country hotels, in the character of host, a man above his business, who has a provoking air of indifference as to whether his guests are pleased or not; who treats them rather as pensioners on his civility, bound to be grateful for what they get; and whose manners, on the whole, are those of a man dispensing a doubtful, languid hospitality to half-welcome visitors, rather than of one getting a *quid pro quo*—the individual who is really served in the transaction—he who is indebted to his guests, rather than they to him.

The White Sulphur is cosmopolitan in comparison with some other summer hostelries in Virginia. An experience in the worst of these is a curiosity in its way, although we doubt whether any one would be willing to renew the discomforts of the investigation for the information gained. The fiction of the Virginia country hotel is that you are *guests*, and that the "General," "Colonel" or "Judge," or however may be called the gentleman who takes your money, is at the head of a private dinner-party. You must observe his ceremony and be thankful. Imagine ceremony—and though the ceremony of provincialism and ignorance, yet of the stiffest sort—in a country hotel! Here is an example for the doubting reader: On one occasion in his travels, the writer took breakfast in a company of some thirty or forty persons. The breakfast was served on a long pine table draped with a dirty cloth, persons taking their seats along the board at whatever intervals they pleased. The writer had finished his meal on strong bacon and doubtful eggs, and was about retiring, when the proprietor and a colored waiter rushed to him, on either side, whispering mysteriously and with *empressement*. "Don't get up yet," said Boniface. "You mussen't move," responded Cuffy. Surprised, alarmed at the expostulation delivered in such anxious manner—imagining, even, some tragedy taking place in the next room from which he was to be debarred access—the writer asked, in broken tones, "What's the matter?" "Sir," whispered the landlord, in tones of wounded surprise, "*the ladies! the ladies!* don't you see they ain't done eating yet?" It was only when the last female had licked her chops that Boniface gave a signal, by beating a little iron rod on a triangle, and his company of guests were then dismissed to their respective avocations.

Generally speaking, we believe that wherever assurances can be made of good hotel accommodations, the Virginia springs will obtain visitors in proportion to their other attractions. Let the liberality of the springs' proprietor begin at home, with himself, in founding hotel establishments which are neither wayside inns, cocked up in boards, nor yet too scant "mammoth" structures, large without comfort and garish without elegance, and he will have less to complain of the liberality of the public, and of the slight put upon the summer resorts of Virginia for those where Nature has done less, but man more.

CHAPTER XIII.

THE SPRINGS OF MONROE AND BATH COUNTIES.

The Springs Region described from the White Sulphur as a Centre—Surrounding Scenery—View from Dry Creek—THE OLD SWEET SPRINGS—A Ride through the Rain—An Aristocratic Resort—Medical Description of the Old Sweet Water—THE SALT SULPHUR SPRINGS—Observations of Dr. Mütter—THE RED SULPHUR SPRINGS—Reported cures of Consumption—THE BLUE SULPHUR SPRINGS—Analysis of the Water—Routes from the Greenbrier White Sulphur Springs into Bath County—THE CASCADE OF THE FALLING SPRINGS—Views through a new Atmosphere—THE BLOWING CAVE—Thomas Jefferson's Description Incorrect—THE WARM SPRINGS MOUNTAIN—Looking from " Flag Rock "—THE HOT SPRINGS—Virtues of the Thermal Baths—THE WARM SPRINGS—An Indian Tradition—THE HEALING SPRINGS—Beauties of Scenery—Pleasures of Trout-fishing—Dr. Burke on these Springs—THE BATH ALUM SPRINGS—Effects of the Water—Painful Aspects of Invalidism at the Springs.

A RADIUS of about forty miles, sweeping from the Greenbrier White Sulphur as a centre, will describe a circle containing the most important part of the Springs Region of Virginia. Within this circle we have to the north the famous cluster of springs in Bath county—the Hot, the Warm, the Healing and the Alum Springs; the distance to the former measured by the common route of travel being thirty-five miles; to the east, the Sweet Springs, seventeen miles from the common centre; to the south, the Salt Sulphur Springs, twenty-four miles, and the Red Sulphur, forty-one miles; and to the west, the Blue Sulphur Springs, twenty-two miles.

In leaving this centre of the Springs Region in any

direction we can scarcely escape refreshing views of mountain scenery. They lie on every hand. A general description might suit them all, and we were not disposed to select any of them for our sketch-book, with but one exception. This—the sketch which faces this chapter—is taken from the vast environments of the scenery of the Greenbrier through which our road lies. It is on Dry creek, a few miles from the White Sulphur, and may be taken as an eminent representative of the extent and combination of mountain views in this part of Virginia. The mountains are not so high as, and they are more sloping than, those where the Alleghany ridge is more severely defined; for we are on the decline of this great feature of the State and its rude pictures of grandeur. On this decline the views are softer, and comprehend a variety peculiar to the situation. There is more breadth of landscape; there is more for the eye to distinguish and to combine; and the distant mountains, instead of being thrust up as boundaries to our vision, "swell from the vale," and are lost in pleasing indistinctness near the rim of the horizon. In fact, each of the characteristic pictures of mountain scenery in Virginia has its merits: that which rises in clear and abrupt outlines against the sky, and ends boldly on distinct effects, and that, such as we have attempted to show on the neighboring page, which in infinite variety of landscape reaches to the limits of vision, and with its mingling of effects yet prefers the picturesque to the sublime.

THE OLD SWEET SPRINGS.

But we must turn aside from sight-seeing of this sort to explore in another interest the neighboring country.

VIEW ON DRY CREEK.

Page 240.

The common routine of the visitors of the Greenbrier White Sulphur Springs is to supplement a season there with one at the Old Sweet. There are said to be good medicinal reasons for the transfer; and the invalid after undergoing the alterative effects of sulphur water is frequently advised by his physician to complete his treatment by using the more tonic and nervine waters that are placed within his reach, they being adapted to strengthen the animal fibre and to give vigor and security to his convalescence. On the other hand, the change of scene and of company are obvious inducements to those who seek pleasure rather than health at the watering-places; and thus it is usual to find all the springs of Virginia which lie conveniently close to each other profiting from an interchange of visitors, and instead of indulging in rivalry, manifesting the best relations of good and kindly neighborhood.

The road to the Old Sweet is an interesting one. There is a station called "Crows," midway between it and the Greenbrier White Sulphur, and where it is not uncommon for parties from the two watering-places to appoint a rendezvous for pic-nics and other amusements, returning in the evening to their respective abodes. A few miles farther on is the Red Sweet Springs, a pretty object by the roadside, but rather neglected since the superior attractions, or at least the larger accommodations, of the Old Sweet await the traveler at the farther distance of only one mile.

The term "old" is not inviting. As one of the travelers, jolted on the top of the lumbering stage-coach and grumbling under a dilapidated umbrella, remarked by the way, "The word brought visions of a rickety country-tavern-looking place, badly-patched and worse-kept invalid resort, where an old fellow with a patch over his eye nodded 'good-morning' to a rheumatic spinster, and a scrofulous infant disported with a mangy kitten." It afforded, indeed, an agreeable surprise to find at our journey's end an array of buildings the most tasteful and neat that we had yet found in the mountains of Virginia— a crescent shape of brick cottages stretching away for two or three hundred yards, with pleasant avenues in the rear (Broadway and Elbow Row), and the pleasing effect surmounted by a hotel, which, though much inferior in dimensions to the caravansary at the White Sulphur, proved to be the best appointed and most comfortable in which we had rested since we had left the Virginia House at Staunton. The buildings are all of brick; and the distinguished boast of the proprietor is that he has introduced what has heretofore been a novelty in the hotel accommodations of Virginia watering-places—the use of *gas*, which is manufactured on the premises and is supplied in every room. In fact, the Old Sweet has certain claims to being an aristocratic spring; the company we saw there, not more than two hundred and fifty persons, about one-third of the capacity of the accommodations, were decidedly distinguished; and our impressions of the "style" of the place were early confirmed when on our arrival we were met in the dining-hall by an elegant colored gentleman in a full-dress suit, not omitting the white vest, who persuaded us that we would be doing him a favor to eat, or, as he might have expressed it, to condescend to the gratification of our appetites in his presence.

The locality of these springs is a charming valley in the eastern extremity of Monroe county, the lofty Sweet Spring Mountain rising on the south, while not a mile away towers the Alleghany. The ground swells gradually on either side, and a fine sodding of grass affords agreeable walks beneath the shades of a primitive forest which the axe of the woodman has not yet despoiled.

These were the earliest known of the mineral springs of Virginia, their reputation dating back to 1764. The water is chemically described as the best acidulous water found in the United States. A marked characteristic is the predominance of carbonic acid (fixed air), which gives the water a peculiar briskness. It is prescribed in the varieties of dyspepsia accompanied by gastrodynia or spasms, with pains occurring at irregular intervals, and heart-burn; in secondary debility of the digestive canal from the exhausting heats of summer; and in chronic diarrhœa and dysentery without fever, or not sustained by hepatic inflammation. As a *tonic* the water is successfully used in chronic diseases connected with debility, as in certain forms of dyspepsia, amenorrhœa, chorea and hysteria, etc., and in passive hæmorrhage. In dropsy, from its union of tonic and diuretic qualities, it is eminently useful. In sterility, especially when connected with membranous menstruation, it is regarded almost as a specific.

Another feature of the sanitary arrangement here, and a very important one, is the bath. A stiff building, of a military appearance, faces the main hotel, about two hundred yards distant, having a quadrangular shape, with two high towers. On the right, looking from the hotel, is the ladies' bath, and on the left the gentlemen's, each sixty by thirty feet, and four, five or six feet deep, as the bathers may choose. The bath, which is fed from the spring, is reported to have made some remarkable cures in sub-acute rheumatism and in neuralgic attacks; and the external application of the water may be aided by the use of the spout directed to the diseased part. Immersions are also prescribed in calculous and nephritic complaints; and in such cases it has been remarked by a distinguished physician that no mineral water promises greater benefits. To persons in average health the bath is stimulating, and, after the first slight shock, leaves the most agreeable impressions.

THE SALT SULPHUR SPRINGS.

THESE springs are near Union, the county seat of Monroe, and are completely encircled by mountains—having Peters' Mountain to the south and east, the Alleghany to the north and Swope's Mountain to the west. There are three springs here—one known as "The Iodine;" but the virtues of the Salt Sulphur proper are best known, and constitute the chief attraction to the invalid. Dr. Mütter, some time the resident physician at this resort, thus describes the water, giving a touch of poetry to the medical detail:

"Its odor is very like that of a 'tolerable egg,' and may, in certain states of the atmosphere, be perceived at some distance from the spring; and in taste it is cousin-german to a strong solution of Epsom salts and magnesia. In a short time, however, strange to say, these disagreeable properties are either not observed, or become, on the other hand, attractive. Indeed there is hardly an instance of an individual retaining his original repugnance to them longer than three or four days, and some there are who become so excessively fond of the water as to give it the preference over any other liquids. Like most of the sulphurous, this water is perfectly transparent, and deposits a whitish sediment, composed of its various saline ingredients, mingled with sulphur. It is also for the most part placid; occasionally, however, it is disturbed by a bubble of gas, which steals slowly to the surface, where it either explodes with a timid and dimpling smack, or is eagerly caught up by some careworn and almost world-weary invalid as a gem from the treasury of Hygeia."

The same pleasing medical authority recommends the use of the water in chronic affections of the brain; in chronic diseases of the bowels, kidneys, spleen and bladder; and in neuralgia, as well as in the various affections termed *nervous*, such as hypochondria, hysteria, catalepsy, chorea, etc. Dr. Mütter also found good effects from the water in constipation of the bowels, hæmorrhoids, and in irritation of the mucous membrane of the kidneys, urethra, prostate gland and bladder.

THE RED SULPHUR SPRINGS.

THE location of the Red Sulphur Springs we have already described as about forty miles from the White Sulphur. The situation is a romantic one, on Indian creek. The spring is on one side of a small, triangular plain, almost buried in mountains. The water is clear and cool—its temperature being 54° Fahrenheit—is very strongly charged with sulphuretted hydrogen gas, and contains portions of several neutral salts.

Its effects are directly sedative and indirectly tonic, alterative, diuretic and diaphoretic. It has been found efficacious or beneficial in all forms of consumption, scrofula, jaundice and other bilious affections, chronic dysentery and diarrhœa, dyspepsia, diseases of the uterus, chronic rheumatism and gout, dropsy, gravel, neuralgia, tremor, syphilis, scurvy, erysipelas, tetter, ringworm and itch; and it has long been celebrated as a vermifuge.

With reference to the value of the water as a cure for *consumption*, the reports of medical men have detracted something from the exaggerated public opinion that, many years ago, pointed out this place as a security against this fell disease, so often supposed to be put at defiance, and yet (we must sadly confess it) still unconquered by anything in the science of man or in the bounty of nature. A physician of South Carolina, who passed the summers of 1822, 1823 and part of that of 1824 at the Red Sulphur Spring, after giving a detailed report of three cases of pulmonary irritation connected with hæmoptysis that were cured by the use of this water, makes the following observations: "I do not wish to be understood as stating that the water of the Red Sulphur will cure confirmed phthisis or tuberculous consumption; but I believe we are very often mistaken in supposing a case of pulmonary irritation more desperate and hopeless than it really is; and I believe that in most cases, if this spring is resorted to early, and the clothing and diet and exercise duly attended to, its waters will be found a most powerful adjunct and assistant in the management of these hitherto unmanageable cases."

THE BLUE SULPHUR SPRINGS.

On the thoroughfare leading from the Greenbrier White Sulphur Springs to Guyandotte, twenty-two miles from the former place, and within the limits of Greenbrier county are the Blue Sulphur Springs.

The water is found to contain of *solid ingredients*—sulphate of lime; sulphate of magnesia; sulphate of soda; carbonate of lime; carbonate of magnesia; chloride of magnesium; chloride of sodium; chloride of calcium; hydro-sulphate of sodium and magnesium; oxide of iron, existing as proto-sulphate; iodine, sulphur, organic matters. *Gaseous ingredients*—sulphuretted hydrogen; carbonic acid; oxygen and nitrogen.

It is classed among the sulphuretted waters; and as a therapeutic agent it is reported to be highly valuable in chronic hepatitis, in jaundice and enlarged spleen, in chronic irritations of the kidneys and bladder, and in some diseases of the skin. There is also an establishment of baths here, medicated and vapor. The situation is one of great natural beauty, and the hotel accommodations are beyond the average of those of Virginia watering-places. The hotel is a spacious brick building, while architectural effects appear to have been studied in its composition, and in that of an imposing temple which covers the spring, and rises in the centre of an extensive and beautiful lawn.

Returning to the Greenbrier White Sulphur Springs, and looking from it in another direction, the invalid finds new resources to explore, and the tourist new beauties of country and new attractions of summer life in the mountains to enjoy. There are four famous bathing springs in Bath county (which, by the way, is therefore appropriately named), lying close together, and which, in turn, may be reached by a day's journey from the White Sulphur. There are two routes from there, each of which has its peculiar attractions. The traveler, going thence to the Hot Springs, etc., takes the Chesapeake and Ohio Railroad, moving eastward, and may leave it at Covington (eighteen miles from the White Sulphur), proceeding thence to his destination eighteen miles by stage-coaches. The turnpike is a new one, recently built. This route offers some grand and imposing mountain scenery, frequent views of Jackson's river, and passes in full view of the beautiful cataract known as "The Falling Springs," and which is mentioned among the curiosities of the State in Jefferson's "Notes on Virginia."

THE CASCADE OF THE FALLING SPRINGS.

The traveler on the route we have indicated makes a partial ascent of the Warm Springs Mountain, the road being cut and blasted on its side, about midway between its top and Jackson's river in the deep valley below. "The valley," writes an enthusiastic sight-seer, "is beautiful as that where Rasselas expected to find peace; the mountains as romantic as those of Scotland." In the fields below there are grown the blue grass and the red clover;* cattle browse lazily in the rich meadows, and great stacks of hay give promise of abundant food through the winter. The odor of thousands of walnut trees, attesting the richness of the soil, is borne to us on the breeze, while the large orchards are significant of the coming apple-brandy, which is a staple production of this country. But the great charm is the new atmosphere we have penetrated, and we already feel the exhilaration of the change. There is said to be never in the Warm Springs

---

* The red clover is said to have been introduced into Virginia by John Lewis, the progenitor of "the Lewis family," and an early founder of the white settlements in the Valley. It was currently reported by the prophets of the Indians, and believed by the savages generally, that the blood of the red men slain by the Lewises and their followers had dyed the trefoil to its sanguine hue.

Valley that alternation of a close, suffocating atmosphere with uncomfortable cold so common to the Atlantic borders. The thermometer seldom rises above 80 deg. Fahrenheit, and its usual range may be stated as 60 deg. to 75 deg.; and there is rarely a foggy morning.

At the lower end of this valley is the Falling Springs. The stream which makes the cascade rises in the Warm Springs Mountain, about fifteen miles south-west of the Hot Springs. About three-quarters of a mile from its source it falls over a rock two hundred feet into the valley below. The sheet of water is broken in its breadth in two or three places; and the projections of moss-covered rocks give it the effect of a number of beautiful falls, until at last it leaps into the chasm of the narrow valley below, the banks of which are kept perpetually verdant by the refreshing spray that breaks into numerous fanciful forms, covering every sprig of fern and grass with countless diamonds. Between the sheet of the lower fall and the rock at the bottom one may walk across dry; or standing outside, he may enjoy the better effect of seeing the cataract crowned with rainbows.

But before proceeding farther on our journey in this direction we must revert to the other route by which our destination—the Hot Springs, etc.—may be reached. The traveler will better decide on the choice of routes by a comparison *pari passu*. The *second* route, then, to the Hot Springs leaves the railroad at Millboro', twenty-nine miles east of Covington; thence by the mail-coach to the Hot Springs, twenty miles, *via* the Bath, Alum and the Warm Springs. This route, although the staging is not as good as from Covington, has the advantages of a scenery even superior to that we have described, and may be recommended to the traveler on that account.

He will have the advantage of seeing the singular "Blowing Cave," near the banks of the Cow Pasture river, and of enjoying the magnificent view from the top of the Warm Springs Mountain, which is crossed by the turnpike at an elevation of nearly fifteen hundred feet above its base, and 2250 feet above the level of the sea.

THE BLOWING CAVE.

THE cave referred to is thus described by Mr. Jefferson, who was curious about the phenomenon it exhibited: "It is in the side of a hill, is of about one hundred feet diameter, and emits constantly a current of air of such force as to keep the weeds prostrate to the distance of twenty yards before it. This current is strongest in dry, frosty weather, and in long spells of rain, weakest. Regular inspirations and expirations of air by caverns and fissures have been probably enough accounted for by supposing them combined with intermitting fountains, as they must, of course, inhale air while their reservoirs are emptying themselves, and again emit while they are filling. But a constant issue of air, only varying in its force as the weather is dryer or damper, will require a new hypothesis."

Since the date of the "Notes on Virginia" there have been some further explorations of this curiosity. A *flowing and ebbing* spring has been discovered on the same stream with the cave; and Mr. Jefferson is mistaken in supposing that the issue of air was constant, as observations have shown that at times there was no perceptible current from the cave. At other times the air comes out with great force. A traveler who, in the heat of summer, was passing in his carriage, sent a little child to the mouth of the cave, who let go before it a handkerchief, which was blown by the current of air over the horses' heads in the road, a distance of thirty or forty feet. The dimensions of the cavity, or rather its possible communications with other subterranean chambers, have not been thoroughly explored; and it is said that a small dog who entered found his way out through some unknown passage.

THE WARM SPRINGS MOUNTAIN.

AFTER refreshment in this current of air, the traveler is prepared to make the ascent of the Warm Springs Mountain, and is on his way to a view of some of the finest scenery in Virginia. The road leads up and across the mountain for five miles, and as we ascend we look down upon a succession of deep precipices and glens, environed by gloomy woods, their obscure bottoms being seen only fitfully through the foliage. On the summit of the mountain is a table, called "Flag Rock," which is frequently visited, and which affords an elevation of 2400 feet above the sea-level. There is a sublime view of parallel ridges of mountains extending for forty or fifty miles, one behind the other as far as the eye can reach, "like a dark blue sea of giant billows, instantly stricken solid by Nature's magic wand." A hundred years ago the principal route of emigration was across this mountain, and it was then practicable only for pack-horses. The emigrants came in wagons to "the camping-ground," a spot yet indicated at the eastern base of the mountain. Thence they transported to the West their baggage on pack-horses, while their wagons returned East laden with the spoils of the hunter.

THE HOT SPRINGS.

There are nine baths, each supplied with water from a separate spring, within the grounds of the Hot Springs hotel. The hottest issue from the ground with a temperature of 110° Fahrenheit.

The effects of these waters prove them to be highly medicated, and they are known to contain sulphate and carbonate of lime, sulphate of soda and magnesia, a minute portion of muriate of iron, carbonic acid gas, nitrogen gas, and a trace of sulphuretted hydrogen gas. The waters, taken internally, are anti-acid, mildly aperient, and freely diuretic and diaphoretic. But when used as a general bath their effects are great, and excel all expectation. They equalize an unbalanced circulation, and thereby restore the different important parts of the system when torpid—that natural and peculiar sensibility upon the existence of which their capacity to perform their several functions and the beneficial action of all remedies depend. They relax contracted tendons, excite the action of absorbent vessels, promote glandular secretion, exert a marked and salutary influence over the biliary and urinary systems, and often relieve, in a short time, excruciating pain caused by palpable and long-standing disease in some vital organ.

The most marked effects of these waters, and those which have most established their popularity, are in rheumatism and in cases of torpid liver. In these cases their action is almost immediate and remarkable; and it is said to be a not uncommon spectacle for those who have with difficulty traveled to the Hot Springs' baths, crippled by rheumatism of long standing, to throw away their crutches after a few days' experience of the "hot spout." In fact, the baths are recommended for almost every case of chronic disease, such as diseases of the liver, of the stomach and bowels, of the kidneys, rheumatism, gout, neuralgia, paralysis, old injuries, etc.

A writer on thermal baths thinks that their hygienical effects are not fully appreciated in this country. In the Eastern World warm and hot baths are habitually taken by persons in every class and condition of life, from the northern limits of Russia to the Tropics. The fact that they are resorted to in tropical climates as a refreshing cordial is a sufficient answer to the popular but erroneous idea that they are debilitating in their effects. The Romans, indeed, carried this luxury to such a pitch of vicious extravagance as to bring on it the title of one of the three great destroyers of human life. But this only applies to its *abuse*, and does not deny its salutary operation when properly and judiciously used. Should the warm bath ever become general in its use in this country, whether in the form of the simple plunge bath or in that of the more complex apparatus of the Russian or Turkish baths, it will probably produce a more beneficial revolution as to the health and longevity of the inhabitants than any other sanitary regulation.

It is very certain that the baths of the Hot Springs are strong stimulants, although the immediate reaction is a feeling of exhaustion and languor. After being in the bath ten minutes, the heat of the body has reached that of the water, and it then no longer feels hot. Then comes on a sensation of dreamy and languishing consciousness, halfway "betwixt sleep and wake." This continues until the bath is ended, and even through the subsequent stages of the "sweat-box." After this, most men brace themselves with a julep, and nearly all feel a strong inclination to sleep. The value of these baths is in the fact that the whole epidermis is deterged, the pores opened, the skin powerfully exercised, and the mineral qualities of the water are absorbed into the blood.

THE WARM SPRINGS.

The Warm Springs, which have given name to the entire valley and to the mountain range which forms one of its boundaries, are five miles north of the Hot Springs, at the county seat of Bath county. At this place are several fine baths, about the temperature of 98° Fahrenheit. One of these is believed to be the largest warm bath in the world, and is supplied by warm water rising from the floor of the bath with such boldness that the immense bath, an octagon of forty feet in diameter and five feet in depth, fills in less than three-quarters of an hour. It holds forty-three thousand gallons, supplied by springs pouring forth one thousand gallons per minute. The flow of water from all the springs and baths is estimated at six thousand gallons a minute, and forms a stream sufficient to drive a large mill.

The tradition respecting the discovery of the springs is, that a party of Indians hunting spent a night in the valley. One of their number, discovering the spring, bathed in it, and being much fatigued, he was induced by the delicious sensation and warmth imparted by it to remain in it some time. The next morning he was enabled to scale the mountain before his companions. As the country became settled, the fame of the waters gradually extended, and at first visitors from the low country dwelt here in rude huts. The property was patented by Governor Fauquier to the *Lewis* family in 1760. At present it is owned by a company, who have improved it by a fine hotel, with other attachments for the accommodation of visitors.

The Warm Springs water taken into the stomach is anti-acid, diuretic, diaphoretic, aperient and tonic. The bath equalizes the circulation and stimulates all the secretory organs. According to the opinion of physicians who have known the springs, and some of whom have practiced at the place for years, these waters possess great efficacy, and may be used with confidence in the following diseases: chronic and sub-acute gout and rheumatism, paralysis, dyspepsia, liver diseases, neuralgia, secondary syphilis, nephritic and calculous disorders, and some diseases peculiar to females.

The warm bath effects its purpose in an eminent degree, in most chronic cases, through its agency on the sentient extremities of the nerves distributed over the surface of the body. There is an extensive chain of sympathies established between the skin and the internal viscera, and through the medium of this channel agreeable sensations excited on the exterior are very often communicated to the *central organs and structures* themselves.

THE HEALING SPRINGS.

The Healing Springs are three miles distant from the Hot, and eight miles from the Warm Springs. The scenes around the springs invite the visitor to numerous walks and repay him with varied recreations. The valley in which they lie rises on every side amid the coolest and deepest shades, while the springs' buildings make a charming little villa shining pleasantly through the green trees. On one side, the Warm Springs Mountain pierces the sky with its long bleak boundary, and lower ledges of rock guard recesses which we shrink from exploring, but once secluded in which we find places of repose and enjoy a delightful and perfect solitude. At the end of a short walk is the cascade we have already described. In the gorge where it falls the sun in his most perpendicular glories penetrates with shorn rays and distributes a soft and shaded light. It shines, however, with full splendor on the snowy wreaths which the falling water has twined on the great rocks.

A pleasant recreation is here for the angler, who with pliant rod draws "the gamest of game fish," the speckled trout, from his native element. The sport is as much that of hunting as of fishing, as the angler has to steal upon this timid fish, disporting in the clear, crystal stream, with as silent and stealthy tread as if still-hunting for deer. He creeps softly along the stream, concealing himself behind a rock, bush or bluff, careful to throw no shadow on the water; from his cover he casts his line from a long pole; the hook is taken at once greedily, if the trout has not been alarmed; and the glittering spoil, with its purple and gold yet reeking with water, is thrown panting on the green sward. It is a fine sport, but we must avoid noise, and practice a careful step, or we spoil the catch. The mountain trout is a gem to look at, and a sweet morsel for the palate when the last offices of the kitchen have been done for him.

The waters of the Healing Springs are almost identical in their chemical analysis to the famous Schlagenbad and Ems in Germany. Dr. Burke, in a work on the mineral waters of Virginia, says: "As to the temperature of this water, it stands alone in the Springs Region, on the confines of the cold and warm. It is the most delightful

TROUT POOL.

Page 256.

bath that can be imagined. I plunged into it by way of experiment, and a greater luxury in bathing I have never enjoyed. It is the only water I have met with of a temperature that may be denominated *tepid*, and therefore possesses advantages of no ordinary character. With the least possible shock to the system it gradually abstracts from it its superabundant caloric."

The temperature of these springs is uniformly 84° Fahrenheit, and they are not subject to any variation of quantity or quality. The first employment of their water and its earliest manifestation of curative powers were in ill-conditioned ulcers and intractable affections of the skin. Dr. Hanger, a physician resident at the springs, and who has made immediate observations of the effects of the water, testifies: "There are few diseases dependent upon, or connected with, morbid secretions of the glandular structures but what are more or less modified by its use, while in others it acts as a direct curative agent. I have known it to cure some hopeless cases of scrofula, chronic thrush, obstinate cases of cutaneous disease, neuralgia, rheumatism, ulcers of the lower limbs of long standing, dyspepsia, etc."

THE BATH ALUM SPRINGS.

These springs are five miles east from the Warm Springs, and near the eastern base of the Warm Springs Mountain.

The waters issue from a slatestone cliff of twelve or fifteen feet high, and are received into small reservoirs that have been excavated near each other in the rock. These different springs, or reservoirs, differ essentially from each other. One of them is a very strong chalybeate, with but little alum; another is a milder chalybeate, with more alumina; while the others are alum of different degrees of strength, but all containing an appreciable quantity of iron.

The water is said to be of favorable effect in scrofulous, eruptive and dyspeptic affections, in old hepatic derangements, chronic diarrhœa, nervous debility, and in various uterine diseases, especially in the worst forms of mænorrhagia, and in *fluor albus*, both uterine and vaginal. The high chalybeate and aluminous impregnation manifests decided tonic and astringent powers.

There is one remarkable circumstance of the watering-places of Bath county which strikes the visitor, and which candor compels us to append. They are attractive rather as resorts for the invalid than for that other large class of summer visitors who seek to find in a "season" in the mountains rendezvous of social gayety or places of agreeable recreation. The extent of invalidism at these baths, and that, too, of the most unsightly and deformed kind, is painful to behold; and the melancholy or repulsive quality which it imparts to scenes otherwise beautiful and inspiring is quite in contrast with the gayety and *abandon* of other summer resorts in Virginia, where the votaries of pleasure outnumber the victims of disease. Thermal waters are suited only to *chronic* conditions of the system. Thus we find, at the places we have been describing, invalidism of the most depraved and despairing kind—conventicles of cripples and of indescribable specimens of effete and used-up humanity. Balls and routs are rather out of place here, although sometimes attempted. But there are milder recreations, and the invalids sometimes have their ghastly jokes with each other, from the rheumatic, who moves rustily "on his hinges," to the other cripple, whose interpretation of Virginia "hospitality" is being kept all the time in the hospital.

But the objection we are making about invalids seems unjust, and we pause. These poor afflicted ones of humanity are to be cared for somewhere, and if they offend the senses of flushed and insolent health, a more generous emotion should rebuke a feeling of superiority, which is but the accident of the animal, and, thankful that Providence has spared us like afflictions, we should rejoice that these unfortunates have found succor and solace in a kind gift of Nature, and should be really happy, in a profounder sense than that of pampering ourselves with selfish pleasures, to see them partaking of it. As a noble benefaction to humanity in the extremest distresses of disease the thermal waters of Bath county are probably without a rival in the world; and this should be boast enough for them without care for competition in any other article of attraction.

CHAPTER XIV.

FROM STAUNTON TO WEYER'S CAVE.

The Chesapeake and Ohio Railroad—Looking to the Occident—A Wilderness of Riches—THE TOWN OF STAUNTON—A Glance at its History—Views of the Surrounding Country—The Virginian "Apology" for Roads—WEYER'S CAVE—A Subterranean Diorama—"Formations" and Curiosities—Peculiarities of Subterranean Nomenclature—"Washington's Hall"—A Flight of Fancies—Dimensions of the Cave—Estimate of it as a Natural Wonder—Age of the Stalactites—The Sublimity of Nature as a Workman.

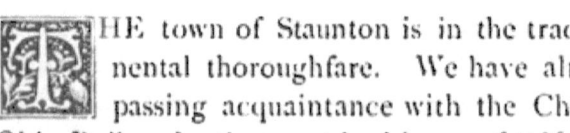HE town of Staunton is in the track of a continental thoroughfare. We have already made a passing acquaintance with the Chesapeake and Ohio Railroad—the great harbinger of "New Virginia," the herald of a vast prosperity that is to clothe the sides of her great mountains with the vivid scenes of prosperity, the colors of cultivation and the embroidery of the immigrant's home. The history of this road is not without vicissitudes, and it opens to one of the grandest visions of commercial power on which Virginia is now straining her expectations.

This line of road, which reaches unfailing navigation at Richmond, Norfolk, West Point and Washington on the Chesapeake Bay, was carried in a general western direction across the Blue Ridge, and when the war broke out was halted at Covington (two hundred and five miles), the foot of the main chain dividing the waters of the James from those of the Ohio's tributaries. The enterprise, so long cut off and set back by the cloud of war, has at last enlisted the attention of eminent New York capitalists; and it is expected that the road will be completed and equipped to the confluence of the Big Sandy and Ohio rivers in less than two years. At this latter point roads are already being built and projected to connect it with Cincinnati *via* Maysville, with Louisville *via* Lexington, with Chicago *via* Toledo and Xenia, and with Columbus *via* Portsmouth. Through these channels it will reach the whole Mississippi Valley system and the Pacific railroads. It is said the distance between Chicago and Washington by this route is no greater, and can be made in better time, than by the Pennsylvania or Baltimore and Ohio routes, while from the central tier of cities the distance is fully fifty miles shorter to tide-water, and the gradients are thirty per cent. lighter. The great feature of the business of the line will be found, however, in its touching nearly twelve thousand miles of steamboat navigation at its terminus on the Ohio river.

Beside the distant and opulent country which the connections of the Chesapeake and Ohio Railroad will reach, it is to be more immediately remembered that it will open to the tourist and immigrant a new breadth of Virginia (West Virginia), which now is not only undeveloped, but almost untrodden. Farming lands, inexhaustible minerals, lumber, etc., are to be developed and brought into market, in what is now an almost unbroken wilderness extending for some twenty-five or thirty miles on each side of the road. This breadth of land, which the railroad will command, and which is now so neglected and unconditionally surrendered to Nature, is adapted to the production of all the cereals, roots and grasses known to this latitude. The various iron ores, in the largest quantities and best qualities, will be accessible to the Chesapeake and Ohio road; the marble quarries, grind and whetstones, flag-rock and the Burr millstone are all to be found in the country just described; the coal-fields, consisting of the bituminous, splint, peacock, cannel, etc., abound for a hundred miles on each side of the road; the tan-barks, hemlock, chestnut, oak, etc., the white and yew pines, white oak, locust, black walnut, cherry, curl maple, poplar, etc., are grown throughout West Virginia, and the rivers of the region are all adapted to the transportation of lumber. The interest of the lumber is already attracting attention, and affords a new speculation to Virginians. The calculation has been made to the writer that the Greenbrier river, for eighty miles north-east of where the railroad crosses it, traverses a lumber-field; while it is said that it would take years to exhaust the country lying on the Gauley river and its tributaries of even the finest varieties of its timber.

Resources so vast, with untold prizes in the more distant Occident, are those which are now beckoning the best-managed and most sperate enterprise in Virginia. It has been calculated that the trans-Alleghany portion of Virginia alone would furnish freights enough to subsist this line of communication with the East. At present, however, the Chesapeake and Ohio Railroad is available only for the head of the Valley and the Greenbrier country. Its most important stations at this time are the White Sulphur Springs and Staunton. But these fortunately command the belt of the mountains most interesting to the tourist, and are already points of departure for a large bulk of the summer travel, which we may now hope to see each year increasing in Virginia, attracted to its springs, or scattered to explore the curiosities and beauties of the scenery which lie at convenient distances from the railroad.

THE TOWN OF STAUNTON.

STAUNTON is among the ancient towns of Virginia; it was laid off by William Beverly, Esq., and established by act of Assembly in 1761. It was once the retreat of the Virginia Legislature in the Revolutionary war, when Tarleton pursued its members to Charlottesville, and thence across the Blue Ridge. Before the recent dismemberment of the State of Virginia, and when there was a prospect of those western counties which now constitute West Virginia being filled with population, the advantage of Staunton, in central position and in security from the danger of hostile invasions, had been indicated for the seat of the State government in preference to Richmond. It was always a rendezvous for political conventions in the State, where the interests of different sections might conveniently meet and confer. It is now adorned by what are the finest monuments of the public benevolence of Virginia—an asylum for the deaf, dumb, and blind, and one for the insane, the reputation of the latter for beneficence and skill being spread over the Union. One of the best hotels south of the Potomac—the Virginia House—affords entertainment for the traveler, and a convenient pause and rest for the tourist, where he may survey the surrounding country, and decide at leisure upon the various objects of interest that beckon him in different directions. One way we look to the springs; in another direction to the scenery of the lower valley; in another to Weyer's Cave; and a few miles east, at the foot of the Blue Ridge, is the historical scene of one of the last discomfitures of the Confederacy, where a broken army took refuge in the woods, and dwindled at last to a fugitive general with two companions riding for their lives to the lines of Lee.

The country lying around Staunton is remarkable for its picturesqueness. It is just on the limits where the great Valley is determined, and the mountain and the plain debate. The railroad gives a daily liveliness to the scene. We see the hastening train puffing graceful volumes of smoke over the green fields, or scourging with its black lash the screaming side of the mountain as it emerges writhing and swift on the distant slopes of the Blue Ridge. The skill and patience of a great enterprise have at last conquered this barrier, which, hung with blue mist, was to earlier generations the very welkin of Virginia, the boundary of excursion and endeavors. The village of Waynesboro' at the western foot of the ridge is probably destined to be overgrown with machine-shops for the great railroad. It already has something of the clamor of a manufacturing town, and red eyes glow at night beneath the heavy and disturbed brow of the mountain.

On leaving any of the railroads in Virginia we are struck by one remarkable want that afflicts all parts of the State. It is the distressing uniform want of practicable country roads. While any other public work is done under the direction of skillful engineers and by competent hands, it seems that the method of building roads in Virginia is the old-time one which belonged to the exigencies of our early backwoods life, and yet survives in its grotesque absurdity. To build a road now in Virginia all the male persons living near it who can handle a hoe are drafted, and on a given day they turn out *en masse*, every delinquent being fined seventy-five cents for the benefit of the county. The work is then done after the slightest fashion: a plough runs two shallow furrows to mark out the road, the loose stones are thrown out, the scraper is used a little, and the road is declared finished. There is no surveying or grading worth talking about. Such is the average country road in Virginia, and the dirt turnpike is only a degree better.

It is curious that people, otherwise intelligent, do not understand the importance of good roads to their prosperity. It is said that our Virginia farmers spend about four times as much power to cart the same amount of produce as a New England or a Pennsylvania farmer does—all owing to bad roads; the stoutest vehicles are torn to pieces over the stumps and through the quagmires; neighborhoods are comparatively isolated from the want of roads, and all intercourse within spaces of a few miles is sometimes suspended for weeks from the effects of a freshet; and yet the Virginians of our day are satisfied to plod on in this state of things, and to use, in very sight of the steam-car, red, mangled roads for their commerce and travel—unsightly ruts which in an energetic Northern community would be condemned as eyesores and nuisances! A gentleman from New York, who recently visited Virginia to inspect her lands, remarked that there were three needs of the State: "Roads," "Roads," "Roads." He spoke truly and with a well-deserved emphasis. If the State is anxious to invite immigrants and to develop her prosperity, let her pay some attention to her country roads as the necessary complement, the feeders, of the railroads which she is now so ambitiously building in every direction. As it is, the two classes of conveyance are in the most striking contrast: the next step from where speeds the luxurious car often bringing us to the red stripe of mud or the trail through the woods, called, in amusing flattery or sometimes to our cruel deception, a "road."

These remarks apply to much of our travel in Virginia. Some of the old mountain roads, however, which were main thoroughfares before the advent of the steam-car, had to be constructed after some idea of grading, and by the regular collection of tolls upon them they are patched up and maintain some sort of decency. But the best of them are wretched by comparison with the well-surveyed and sound roads in the Northern States, required to a great extent there by the denser population, and yet, however special excuses may disguise the comparison, indicating as much as anything else a superior thrift and enterprise. From Staunton to Weyer's Cave the traveler has an old turnpike, rather better than the average country roads, yet trying and exasperating enough when we consider what little labor might have given us a really admirable road through this beautiful and picturesque country, the features of which are the wide hill, the tableland, and the thin forest in which the great clean trees stand as colonnades.

WEYER'S CAVE.

From Staunton the distance to Weyer's Cave is seventeen miles; the direction north-east, parallel to the Blue Ridge, and about two miles distant from it. The mouth of the Cave is on a hill, and has been enlarged since Bernard Weyer, some time in the year 1804, chased a deer into this retreat, the entrance of which was then masked with bushes, and scarcely admitted the body of the adventurous hunter. Now the enlarged entrance is walled; we go through a convenient doorway into what is called "the ante-chamber," and yet at the distance of a few yards we are compelled to pass through a passage contracted to the space of three or four feet square.

We are in a subterranean world—a cosmos of scenes, cities, monuments, tribunals beneath the ground. The golden day is left behind us; it struggles, dying in the narrow passage through which we entered; our tapers stab the mysterious darkness, which retreats with the reluctance of an evil thing, and at the slightest effort of our voices a growl of distrust and anger is heard from chambers into which we are entering. Our imagination is wrought upon at once by images of the world overhead. Passing through chambers and galleries of infinite variety, we are struck by beholding in a dark recess on one side of the cave a very natural representation of the moon, as she might be imagined in her last quarter, rising in the morning. In another part, emerging from what is called "the Wilderness," a rough passageway not more than ten feet wide, but towering to the height of ninety or one hundred feet, we see a surface of rock on which colors and shades are so disposed as to represent a foaming cataract, recalling the weird, poetic image of the giant Water,

> " as seized at once
> By sudden frost, with all his hoary locks
> Stood still."

But a few steps away we have passed a group of beautiful white stalagmites, which the fancy has designated as "Bonaparte with his body-guard crossing the Alps." The journey (our own, not Bonaparte's) so far is toilsome, uneven, and we are often required to stop and to practice ungraceful postures. The visitor, resolved on a thorough exploration, must not expect to stroll through "rooms and galleries" as in an "Arabian Nights" entertainment. We are often on our knees, often defiled with mud, often wounding our hands on the sharp rock. The way is studded with all the minor curiosities of "formations," and we are constantly plucking grotesque bunches and stems of rock, until our hands are full of them. But the spoils of visitors are not only in stalactites and stalagmites. In the deepest apartment, to which the visitor hesitates to penetrate, affected by its name, "the Infernal Regions," there is a mass, not exactly of precious stones, but of the most brilliant white crystals; the floor of this sunken and dismal room being composed mostly of layers of these crystals, in some instances three feet deep. A person who had made a choice collection of these stones was offered a hundred dollars for them, which he refused.

A strange and vicious jumble of nomenclature describes the wonderful and intricate scenes through which we pass. In some instances the names have originated in such low imaginations that we cannot transcribe them; and it is infamous that the grandest and most beautiful mysteries of nature should be degraded and insulted, as they often are, by unclean human wretches, viler than the worm that turns from the leaf of the rose to moil in the filth that manures it. But even in the admissible titles the most absurd anachronisms and follies are perpetrated, though the contrasts are sometimes not a little amusing. From "the Dragon's Room," through "the Devil's Gallery," we pass into "Solomon's Temple." Next we are pointed to "Solomon's Meat-house." "The Radish Room" is so named because of the form of stalactites resembling this vegetable. "Ajax's Shield" and "the Devil's Bake-oven" are adjacent curiosities. "Congress

Hall" and "the Tan-yard" are in close proximity. Near "Jacob's Ladder" are "Jacob's Tea-table" and "Jacob's Ice-house." "The Infernal Regions" and "the Ball-room" are separated by a very thin partition, through which are transmitted the least sounds from one to the other. The "Rock of Gibraltar" stands close by "the Pyramids of Egypt." From "the Garden of Eden" we go into "the Fly-trap." The "Church" and "the Lawyer's Office" are in friendly neighborhood. The "Tower of Babel," an immense mass of solid stalagmite, thirty-five feet long, thirty broad and thirty high, arrests the eye, and just by it is "Bonaparte crossing the Alps!"

The most magnificent apartment in the whole cave is undoubtedly "Washington's Hall." It is worthy of the grand associations of its name, which is singularly appropriate from a calcareous formation that stands near the centre of the room, rising to the height of six or seven feet, and bearing a striking resemblance to a statue in classic drapery. A sheet of rock-work runs through the room, but the fine arch expands high over the head, untouched. The dimensions of the apartment are, 257 feet in length; breadth, from 10 to 20 feet; height, 33 feet. It is said that before the war there had been annual illuminations on the 4th of July of "Washington's Hall;" but the lights by which we saw it, though less than on these occasions, we are inclined to think, were just about sufficient to produce the best effects. The perspective of the room is very fine; the tapers which burn near us are encumbered by dark shadows, and a dim religious light falls upon what is about four times the length of an ordinary church. The roof is vaulted and amazing. The lights which stream below strike with uncertainty upon the carved and knotted surface which they barely reach. The shadows that have flitted upon the walls hesitate in groups, and rally in the distance like reassured ghosts. And amid these uncompleted resemblances the imagination constructs worlds of its own: the distant tapers checking like stars the darkness—the maimed and uncertain shadows that walk and stumble by our side—the assassin that stands or shifts or cowers behind the white throne, in front of which the lights dance—the saffron knotted arm of the giant grown out of the shapeless rock—the drip that is ceaseless in our ears, the water-clock that measures the weird time, ever and ever,—all impress us that we are withdrawn from the living world, and put us under the spell of a strange and illimitable enchantment.

In these abodes of darkness, never penetrated by light except what is artificial, but few creatures are known to inhabit. There is no standing water in all the cave. A limpid spring, covered over with a thin pellicle of stalagmite, flows near the "Fly-trap" and appears to be the source of a subterranean stream; and if there are finny inhabitants in these measureless caverns, they are beyond the reach of our observation. The floor of the cave is generally a stiff clay. We were told that bats were sometimes found to harbor here in winter, their habit being to form clusters pendent from the ceiling after the fashion of bees, and that when the taper, out of cruel curiosity or barbarous sport, was applied to them or near them, they would set up a strangely human cry, most pitiful, but would never let go the hold by which they clung to each other. The artificial door which opens into the "Ante-chamber" excludes wild beasts; but no doubt they once had here their refuges and lairs, and fierce eyes might have looked from the terrible darkness at the adventurous intruder.

The "main path" by which the visitor traverses the apartments and galleries of the cave is sixteen hundred and fifty feet in length. By the more winding paths the length is quite double this. At all times the air of the cave is damp, and some precautions should be taken before entering it, especially to preserve an equilibrium of temperatures. In all seasons the temperature of the cave is about 56°, and it is important that the visitor in summer should become cool before he enters, else he is likely to be chilled by the sudden loss in the atmosphere of thirty or more degrees of heat. In winter, of course, we feel this subterranean air to be warm and comfortable. In the spring and autumn the atmosphere without and that within are more nearly equal in temperature; and those visiting the cave at other seasons should be careful to defend themselves by change of clothing, or otherwise, against the very marked differences they must experience in degrees both of heat and moisture.

On the whole, Weyer's Cave is one of the greatest sights in Virginia, and is eminent in its own class of wonders. The emotions it excites are of the most various description, and though many a single object of sublimity may produce a stronger impression, it would be difficult to imagine a combination of objects more rich and powerful in an æsthetic sense, in which curiosity, delight, apprehension, awe, admiration, by turns or together possess the mind, and in which at the climax Sublimity reigns, having her residence and domain in darkness, silence and depths profound. There is no toyish effect, as one might suppose, in its slightest curiosities; everything looks weird, and the taper-lights which exhibit them allow only that indistinct vision which suggests images to the fancy, and leaves them unfinished.

The feeble and broken light secures the best effects. The hollow reverberations of the lofty arches alarm us; the fanastic shapes keep the imagination in constant exercise; and a thought of greatest sublimity possesses us as we contemplate this ceaseless workshop of silent forces, going on in grim, straightforward energy, never looking to right or left upon their visitors as they build their curious world. The human workman looks sometimes away from his work; he eats, he sleeps, he rests, he observes the spectator. But Nature, here and everywhere—in its subterranean forge, or in the ripening field, or in the decaying wood—is incessant; and this grand thought comes to us in this underground workshop with a peculiar and mysterious force. It is the Sphynx, living rather than monumental. We stand by the patient endeavor that rears these forms; we confront in unutterable mystery the stony-eyed persistence of the secret force that answers no question, that never glances from a perpetual task, that heeds no watcher or intruder, doing its work deep down in earth, while overhead the same law of the unceasing goes on, and Nature continues

> "Her old quiet toil in the heart of green
> Summer silence, preparing new buds for new blossoms,
> And stealing a finger of change o'er the bosom
> Of the unconscious woodlands."

How sublimely does Nature work! Day and night—when the golden sun swings in the open spaces, and when the glittering chains of stars have riveted the darkness on the sky—unceasingly, from a time no man knows to an end unimaginable, have been wrought the wonders that we look upon with strained eyes and amazed hearts among these subterranean monuments of the ages. The stalactite upon which our hand rests has been building from a time long before man made the first letter of history or planted the first seed of his empire—before, as Professor Rogers has calculated, man was known to exist in the Biblical chronology. It had commenced to form before a single tower of man's greatness or of his folly was raised toward the sky; it will continue to increase, the water will percolate and drop, as long as the scroll of the upper world endures, and while a thousand histories have been written and consumed upon it. The crowd upon the imagination becomes painful in the darkened chamber in which we stand; it is the sublime carried to the last point of endurance; and yet the lesson we take away is sweet and powerful, for it is the lesson that Nature perpetually teaches of patience and persistence, when she shows us every achievement of Time and Labor identified, the grand, unimpeachable economies of her universe.

8

PRACTICAL HINTS TO THE VIRGINIA TOURIST.

THE route which we would recommend to the Virginia tourist is, with some exceptions, that which runs through the preceding pages, serving as a thread of narrative to hold them together. The exceptions are those which are suggested for the mere topical convenience of the traveler.

First to Lynchburg. The Natural Bridge and the Peaks of Otter may be taken as outlying attractions, each reached in a day's journey.

Thence to the Alleghany Springs, doubly attractive for their medicinal water and scenery; in the latter catalogue, Puncheon Run Falls and Fisher's View. The Montgomery White Sulphur Springs and the Yellow Sulphur Springs are near by, and may be compassed in a ride of a few hours.

Farther to the south-west are three ranges for the tourist, which may be taken in order. From Bristol to the Natural Tunnel (undoubtedly the greatest wonder of Virginia). From Glade Springs Station into and through Tazewell county, an excursion into the Alps of Virginia. From Christiansburg into Giles county, taking in the scenery of New river, Salt Pond, Stony creek and Bald

Knob. All these three ranges are transverse to the Virginia and Tennessee Railroad, the points of departure occurring in the order named: Bristol, Glade Springs and Christiansburg. We may substitute for the two latter, Wytheville and Montgomery White Sulphur Springs.

Returning to the rail, leave it at Coyner's Springs; thence to Lexington, Rockbridge Baths, Rockbridge Alum Springs, etc. We are now in the Valley of Virginia, and the Chesapeake and Ohio Railroad and stage-lines branching from it give access in every direction.

No summer traveler in Virginia will omit the Greenbrier White Sulphur Springs.

Thence, at the end of a day's journey and in the four quarters of the compass, are spas in three counties: Monroe, Greenbrier and Bath. Return east by the thermal waters of Bath.

From Staunton go to Weyer's Cave. Thence back to Staunton and the Chesapeake and Ohio Railroad, striking the avenue of *continental* travel at Charlottesville, from which we may go north, south, east or west to our homes.

The route described is, to some extent, on three sides of a triangle, making its apex at Charlottesville. Beyond this triangular plot there is, to be sure, much in the State to attract the tourist; but he may content himself that within the boundaries described he has compassed what is most interesting in Virginia in the measure of its twin attractions—natural scenery and mineral springs.

Such a tour as we have described may be done in twenty days if sight-seeing is only concerned, and for an expense of about one hundred and twenty-five to one hundred and fifty dollars, considering the traveler in motion, or as stopping only single days at the places named.

The charges at the Virginia watering-places are uniformly three dollars per day and seventy dollars for the month, but with one exception of excess, and that is the Greenbrier White Sulphur Springs, where the rates are four dollars for the day, and for the month in proportion.

Horses may be hired in the country for a dollar and a half a day. At Bristol and at Liberty we got good mounts at that rate. At the springs the charges for horses and vehicles are higher, but very moderate in comparison with the liveries of the North. There was a stud of very stylish horses at the Alleghany Springs, which were hired for the saddle at one dollar for the first hour and fifty cents for the succeeding hours, or three dollars for the whole day. Excellent carriages, seating four, were hired at five dollars a day.

Let the tourist bring his fishing-rods, and a gun to shoot deer. A common fault at the springs, and which is perhaps prevalent at all watering-places, is the idle and dawdling life; but the spas of Virginia have this great and peculiar advantage—that instead of the visitor being compelled to walk or ride on a dusty thoroughfare or hunt a paltry stroll on the beach, he may lose himself in a few moments in the neighboring forest, where recreation may be sweetened with perfect solitude, or exercise freshened with the mental excitement that makes it alike pleasant and profitable.

One word to visitors from the North. So far from apprehending any unpleasantness or any coldness of reception in the summer resorts of Virginia, they may be assured of a welcome much more lively than what pecuniary interest habitually extends to its customers. The writer noticed at all the Virginia springs which he visited, that wherever a guest hailed from the North there was a special and sedulous effort on the part of the company, so far as it might be done without officiousness, to pay such stranger extraordinary attention, and to reassure his or her doubts of the hospitality and social generosity of the South. Such efforts were made in excellent taste, quite removed from vulgar importunities, and with a purpose that merits hearty commendation; and, indeed, we have witnessed no happier occasions of re-establishing the social reunion of the two sections than at these rendezvous of pleasure in Virginia, where the inspirations of Nature dispose the mind to forget alike its griefs and passions, and where invariably attend some of the most genial and cultivated people of the South. Those persons in the North who may be induced to turn away from the worn resorts of the tourist and the invalid in their own section, to try, if only for novelty, a season in the Virginia mountains, will be received there with the most cordial welcome, will enjoy the advantages of marked efforts to please them, and will have the satisfaction of assisting in a social "reconstruction," in which the people of the South are prepared to meet them with gracious readiness and with grateful alacrity. "Let us have peace" is at least written on every signboard that displays to the Virginia tourist a fountain of health or an appointment of pleasure.

To the peaceful and richly-endowed spaces of her springs and mountains and scenery the State invites all comers; and what Nature has bestowed, a generosity that does not encumber with its obligations, and a hospitality that never wearies of its offices, unite to dispense.

COYNER'S
WHITE AND BLACK SULPHUR SPRINGS.

THIS WELL-KNOWN WATERING-PLACE,

Situated in Botetourt county, Virginia, on the line, and in full view, of the Virginia & Tenn. Railroad, is

OPEN FOR THE RECEPTION OF VISITORS.

Persons leaving BALTIMORE, WASHINGTON, RICHMOND, NORFOLK and PETERSBURG will arrive the same evening at the Springs; those coming from the South and West reach the Springs in about ten hours from Bristol.

Visitors desiring to stop, by informing the Conductor, when they strike the Virginia & Tennessee Railroad, of the fact, will be landed at the platform IMMEDIATELY OPPOSITE TO THE SPRINGS.

NO STAGING.

The **HOTEL** being only about two hundred yards from the platform, makes it a very desirable **RESTING-PLACE** for persons from the South going North or returning home at any season of the year.

The undersigned (formerly of Richmond) takes pleasure in informing his friends and the public generally that he has removed to this place with the intention of making it his permanent residence, and will spare neither trouble nor expense to render it PLEASANT AND AGREEABLE TO HIS GUESTS. There are

FIVE SULPHUR SPRINGS,

the medicinal qualities of which are so generally and favorably known that it is deemed unnecessary to speak of their virtues.

☞ **A Fine Band of Music will be in attendance during the season.**

BOARD per Day $3.00
  " *per Week* 16.00
  " *per Month (of four weeks)* 60.00

For a longer period than one month special arrangements will be made.

WM. H. FRY, Proprietor.

☞ POST-OFFICE, BONSACK'S, ROANOKE CO., VA.

CONGRESS SPRING, SARATOGA, N.Y.

CONGRESS SPRING, the most famous of the medicinal springs of Saratoga, was discovered in 1792. It has been successively owned by the LIVINGSTONS (who obtained the property under an early grant or purchase); GIDEON PUTNAM, one of the founders of the village of Saratoga; Dr. JOHN CLARKE, who was the first, in 1830, to bottle the water for exportation and sale; LYNCH & CLARKE, CLARKE & WHITE, and the CONGRESS AND EMPIRE SPRING COMPANY, who are the present proprietors, and by whom the waters are now sent to all parts of the civilized world.

CONGRESS WATER is a purely natural mineral water, cathartic, alterative, and slightly stimulating and tonic in its effects, without producing the debility that usually attends a course of medicines. It is used with marked success in affections of the Liver and Kidneys; and for Dyspepsia, Gout, Chronic Constipation and Cutaneous Diseases it is unrivaled. It is especially beneficial as a general preservative of the tone of the stomach and the purity of the blood, and a powerful preventive of Fevers and Bilious Complaints.

The same company are also proprietors of the COLUMBIAN, a Chalybeate Mineral Spring, situated near the Congress; and also of the famous EMPIRE SPRING, whose waters, being similar to the Congress, are extensively used, with very beneficial effects, as a remedy for a great variety of bilious disorders, rheumatic and scrofulous affections, etc.

During the many years in which these waters have been before the public they have enjoyed a steadily increasing popularity, and they remain at the present day

PURE, UNCHANGED, UNFAILING!

BUY ONLY THE BOTTLED WATERS. NONE GENUINE SOLD ON DRAUGHT.

FOR SALE BY DRUGGISTS THROUGHOUT THE COUNTRY.

Every Genuine bottle of Congress Water has a large "C" raised upon the glass.

Purchasers will find a full supply of these Waters, fresh from the Springs, in the hands of the following agents: BULLOCK & CRENSHAW, 528 Arch St. & 531 North St., Phila., Pa.; HURLBUT & EDSALL, 32 Lake St., Chicago, Ill.; F. E. SUIRE & CO., cor. of 4th and Vine Sts., Cincinnati, Ohio; A. A. MELLIER, 600 Main St., cor. Washington Avenue, St. Louis, Mo.; E. J. HART & CO., 73, 75 & 77 Tchoupitoulas St., New Orleans, La.

Orders addressed to us by mail will receive prompt attention.

THE CONGRESS AND EMPIRE SPRING CO.,

Saratoga Springs, N.Y., or 94 Chambers St., New York City.

VIRGINIA HOTEL,
STAUNTON, VA.

WM. FRAZIER, *Late Proprietor Rockbridge Alum Springs.*
CAPT. WM. H. SALE, *Late Supt. Rockbridge Alum Springs.*

The new proprietors of this LEADING AND POPULAR HOTEL beg to announce that the same has been remodeled, newly painted and refitted throughout with NEW FURNITURE AND BEDS, of best quality and at heavy cost. HOT, WARM AND COLD BATHS; BILLIARDS! (Being the only Hotel in Staunton with Bathing Rooms and Billiard Saloon.)

The Bar is stocked with as PURE WINES AND LIQUORS as can be found in this country. An extensive Livery Stable connected with the House.

Springs visitors and tourists in Virginia will find this an attractive point for spending a few days or weeks. The great State Institutions established here, the flourishing Seminaries, male and female, the various Churches, the notable healthfulness of this "City of the Hills," and the picturesque scenery of the great Valley of the Shenandoah, have long made STAUNTON a favorite Summer Resort, and the "VIRGINIA" the leading Hotel of the place.

From this point parties visit the famous "*Weyer's Cave*," the "*Cave of Fountains*," the "*Natural Chimneys*" or "*Cyclopean Towers*," and "*Elliott's Knob*," the loftiest mountain peak in Virginia.

☞ *Omnibus to and from Railroad Depôt free.*
Stage Office, to all points, is kept in the house.

FRAZIER & SALE.

A BOOK FOR EUROPEAN TOURISTS.

HINTS FOR SIX MONTHS IN EUROPE:
BEING THE
Programme of a Tour through Parts of France, Italy, Austria, Saxony, Prussia, the Tyrol, Switzerland, Holland, Belgium, England and Scotland.

BY JOHN H. B. LATROBE.
16mo. Toned paper. Extra Cloth. $1.50.

"A volume most delightful and entertaining, as well for the general reader as for one who, about to embark upon a half year's travel, needs an intelligent view of a pleasant route to be taken, and of annoyances to be avoided. Mr. Latrobe's book will be highly appreciated wherever read."—*Baltimore Statesman.*

"It is a genuine treasure-book for every new European traveler. . . . And if this programme should be carefully studied by one about to start on a summer tour in Europe, and be substantially followed by the tourist, he would secure for himself manifold more enjoyment, and save himself from countless disappointments and vexations which he would be sure otherwise to experience."—*Boston Evening Traveler.*

"The result is a highly satisfactory volume, which we commend and recommend to travelers, whether they go abroad or stay at home."—*The Philadelphia Press.*

For sale by all Booksellers, or will be sent by mail, postage free, on receipt of price.

Published by J. B. LIPPINCOTT & CO.,
715 and 717 Market St., Philadelphia.

LIST OF PUBLICATIONS

OF

J. B. LIPPINCOTT & CO.

PHILADELPHIA.

Will be sent by mail, post paid, on receipt of the price.

The Albert N'Yanza. Great Basin of the Nile, and Explorations of the Nile Sources. By SIR SAMUEL WHITE BAKER, M. A., F. R. G. S., &c. With Maps and numerous Illustrations, from sketches by Mr. Baker. New edition. Crown 8vo. Extra cloth, $3.

"It is one of the most interesting and instructive books of travel ever issued; and this edition, at a reduced price, will bring it within the reach of many who have not before seen it."—*Boston Journal.*

"One of the most fascinating, and certainly not the least important, books of travel published during the century."—*Boston Eve. Transcript.*

The Nile Tributaries of Abyssinia, and the Sword-Hunters of the Hamran Arabs. By SIR SAMUEL WHITE BAKER, M. A., F. R. G. S., &c. With Maps and numerous Illustrations, from original sketches by the Author. New edition. Crown 8vo. Extra cloth, $2.75.

"We have rarely met with a descriptive work so well conceived and so attractively written as Baker's Abyssinia, and we cordially recommend it to public patronage. . . . It is beautifully illustrated."—*N. O. Times.*

Eight Years' Wandering in Ceylon. By Sir SAMUEL WHITE BAKER, M. A., F. R. G. S., &c. With Illustrations. 16mo. Extra cloth, $1.50.

"Mr. Baker's description of life in Ceylon, of sport, of the cultivation of the soil, of its birds and beasts and insects and reptiles, of its wild forests and dense jungles, of its palm trees and its betel nuts and intoxicating drugs, will be found very interesting. The book is well written and beautifully printed."—*Balt. Gazette.*

"Notwithstanding the volume abounds with sporting accounts, the natural history of Ceylon is well and carefully described, and the curiosities of the famed island are not neglected. It is a valuable addition to the works on the East Indies."—*Phila. Lutheran Observer.*

Tricotrin. The Story of a Waif and Stray. By
OUIDA, author of "Under Two Flags," &c. With Portrait of the Author from an Engraving on Steel. 12mo. Cloth, $2.

"The story is full of vivacity and of thrilling interest."—*Pittsburg Gazette.*
"Tricotrin is a work of absolute power, some truth and deep interest."—*N. Y. Day Book.*

"The book abounds in beautiful sentiments, expressed in a concentrated, compact style which cannot fail to be attractive, and will be read with pleasure in every household."—*San Francisco Times.*

Granville de Vigne; or, Held in Bondage. A
Tale of the Day. By OUIDA, author of "Idalia," "Tricotrin," &c. 12mo. Cloth, $2.

"This is one of the most powerful and spicy works of fiction which the present century, so prolific in light literature, has produced."

Strathmore; or, Wrought by His Own Hand. A
Novel. By OUIDA, author of "Granville de Vigne," &c. 12mo. Cloth, $2.

"It is romance of the intense school, but it is written with more power, fluency and brilliancy than the works of Miss Braddon and Mrs. Wood, while its scenes and characters are taken from high life."—*Boston Transcript.*

Chandos. A Novel. By Ouida, author of "Strath-
more," "Idalia," &c. 12mo. Cloth, $2.

"Those who have read these two last-named brilliant works of fiction (Granville de Vigne and Strathmore) will be sure to read *Chandos.* It is characterized by the same gorgeous coloring of style and some what exaggerated portraiture of scenes and characters, but it is a story of surpassing power and interest."—*Pittsburg Evening Chronicle.*

Idalia. A Novel. By Ouida, author of "Strath-
more," "Tricotrin," &c. 12mo. Cloth, $2.

"It is a story of love and hatred, of affection and jealousy, of intrigue and devotion.... We think this novel will attain a wide popularity, especially among those whose refined taste enables them to appreciate and enjoy what is truly beautiful in literature."—*Albany Evening Journal.*

Under Two Flags. A Story of the Household
and the Desert. By OUIDA, author of "Tricotrin," "Granville de Vigne," &c. 12mo. Cloth, $2.

"No one will be able to resist its fascination who once begins its perusal."—*Philada. Evening Bulletin.*
"This is probably the most popular work of Ouida. It is enough of itself to establish her fame as one of the most eloquent and graphic writers of fiction now living."—*Chicago Journal of Commerce.*

Ouida's Novelettes. First Series, Cecil Castle-
maine's Gage. *Second Series,* Randolph Gordon. *Third Series* Beatrice Boville. Each of these volumes contains a selection of "OUIDA'S" Popular Tales and Stories. 12mo. Cloth, each $1.75.

"The many works already in print by this versatile authoress have established her reputation as a novelist, and these short stories contribute largely to the stock of pleasing narratives and adventures alive to the memory of all who are given to romance and fiction."—*N. Haven Jour.*

PUBLICATIONS OF J. B. LIPPINCOTT & CO.

The Old Mam'selle's Secret. After the German
of E. Marlitt, author of "Gold Elsie," "Countess Gisela," &c. By Mrs. A. L. Wister. Sixth edition. 12mo. Cloth, $1.75.

"A more charming story, and one which, having once commenced, it seemed more difficult to leave, we have not met with for many a day."—*The Round Table.*

"Is one of the most intense, concentrated, compact novels of the day. . . . And the work has the minute fidelity of the author of 'The Initials,' the dramatic unity of Reade, and the graphic power of George Elliot."—*Columbus (O.) Journal.*

"Appears to be one of the most interesting stories that we have had from Europe for many a day."—*Boston Traveler.*

Gold Elsie. From the German of E. Marlitt,
author of the "Old Mam'selle's Secret," "Countess Gisela," &c. By Mrs. A. L. Wister. Fifth edition. 12mo. Cloth, $1.75.

"A charming book. It absorbs your attention from the title-page to the end."—*The Home Circle.*

"A charming story charmingly told."—*Baltimore Gazette.*

Countess Gisela. From the German of E. Marlitt, author of "The Old Mam'selle's Secret," "Gold Elsie," "Over Yonder," &c. By Mrs. A. L. Wister. Third Edition. 12mo. Cloth, $1.75.

"There is more dramatic power in this than in any of the stories by the same author that we have read."—*N. O. Times.*

"It is a story that arouses the interest of the reader from the outset."—*Pittsburg Gazette.*

"The best work by this author."—*Philada. Telegraph.*

Over Yonder. From the German of E. Marlitt, author of "Countess Gisela," "Gold Elsie," &c. Third edition. With a full-page Illustration. 8vo. Paper cover, 30 cts.

"'Over Yonder' is a charming novelette. The admirers of 'Old Mam'selle's Secret' will give it a glad reception, while those who are ignorant of the merits of this author will find in it a pleasant introduction to the works of a gifted writer."—*Daily Sentinel.*

Three Thousand Miles through the Rocky Mountains. By A. K. McClure. Illustrated. 12mo. Tinted paper. Extra cloth, $2.

"Those wishing to post themselves on the subject of that magnificent and extraordinary Rocky Mountain dominion should read the Colonel's book."—*New York Times.*

"The work makes one of the most satisfactory itineraries that has been given to us from this region, and must be read with both pleasure and profit."—*Philada. North American.*

"We have never seen a book of Western travels which so thoroughly and completely satisfied us as this, nor one written in such agreeable and charming style."—*Bradford Reporter.*

"The letters contain many incidents of Indian life and adventures of travel which impart novel charms to them."—*Chicago Evening Journal.*

"The book is full of useful information."—*New York Independent.*

"Let him who would have some proper conception of the limitless material richness of the Rocky Mountain region, read this book."—*Charleston (S. C.) Courier.*

Our Own Birds of the United States. A Familiar
Natural History of the Birds of the United States. By WILLIAM L. BAILY. Revised and Edited by Edward D. Cope, Member of the Academy of Natural Sciences. With numerous Illustrations. 16mo. Toned paper. Extra cloth, $1.50.

"The text is all the more acceptable to the general reader because the birds are called by their popular names, and not by the scientific titles of the cyclopædias, and we know them at once as old friends and companions. We commend this unpretending little book to the public as possessing an interest wider in its range but similar in kind to that which belongs to Gilbert White's Natural History of Selborne."—*N. Y. Even. Post.*

"The whole book is attractive, supplying much pleasantly-conveyed information for young readers, and embodying an arrangement and system that will often make it a helpful work of reference for older naturalists."—*Philada. Even. Bulletin.*

"To the youthful, 'Our Own Birds' is likely to prove a bountiful source of pleasure, and cannot fail to make them thoroughly acquainted with the birds of the United States. As a science there is none more agreeable to study than ornithology. We therefore feel no hesitation in commending this book to the public. It is neatly printed and bound, and is profusely illustrated."—*New York Herald.*

A Few Friends, and How They Amused Themselves.
A Tale in Nine Chapters, containing descriptions of Twenty Pastimes and Games, and a Fancy-Dress Party. By M. E. DODGE, author of "Hans Brinker," &c. 12mo. Toned paper. Extra cloth, $1.25.

"This convenient little encyclopædia strikes the proper moment most fitly. The evenings have lengthened, and until they again become short parties will be gathered everywhere and social intercourse will be general. But though it is comparatively easy to assemble those who would be amused, the amusement is sometimes replaced by its opposite, and more resembles a religious meeting than the juicy entertainment intended. The 'Few Friends' describes some twenty pastimes, all more or less intellectual, all provident of mirth, requiring no preparation, and capable of enlisting the largest or passing off with the smallest numbers. The description is conveyed by examples that are themselves 'as good as a play.' The book deserves a wide circulation, as it is the missionary of much social pleasure, and demands no more costly apparatus than ready wit and genial disposition."—*Philada. North American.*

Cameos from English History. By the author of
"The Heir of Redclyffe," &c. With marginal Index. 12mo. Tinted paper. Cloth, $1.25; extra cloth, $1.75.

"History is presented in a very attractive and interesting form for young folks in this work."—*Pittsburg Gazette.*

"An excellent design happily executed."—*N. Y. Times.*

The Diamond Edition of the Poetical Works of
Robert Burns. Edited by REV. R. A. WILLMOTT. New edition. With numerous additions. 18mo. Tinted paper. Fine cloth, $1.

"This small, square, compact volume is printed in clear type, and contains, in three hundred pages, the whole of Burns' poems, with a glossary and index. It is cheap, elegant and convenient, bringing the works of one of the most popular of British poets within the means of every reader."—*Boston Even. Transcript.*

J. B. Lippincott & Co.'s Magazines.

Messrs. J. B. LIPPINCOTT & Co. have now the pleasure of offering to the reading public a series of monthly Periodicals distinguished alike for the excellence and variety of their matter and for the number and beauty of their illustrations. Subscriptions may begin with any number.

LIPPINCOTT'S MAGAZINE.
An Illustrated Monthly of Literature, Science and Education.
YEARLY SUBSCRIPTION, $4.

LIPPINCOTT'S MAGAZINE has already secured for itself the highest literary reputation, and since its commencement has steadily gained in public favor. The object of the publishers will continue to be, to present to the American public a magazine of the highest class; and they will avail themselves of every means to render it still more valuable, attractive and entertaining.

THE SUNDAY MAGAZINE.
Profusely Illustrated. Edited by THOMAS GUTHRIE, D.D.
YEARLY SUBSCRIPTION, $3.50.

The SUNDAY MAGAZINE will continue to be instructive on religious subjects, stimulating by its stories of the lives of the wise and good, and so interesting in its tales and sketches of life and character as to render it attractive in the homes of tens of thousands; to be read by people of all Christian denominations; to be of no class, of no sect, of no party, but belonging to all, and profitable to all.

GOOD WORDS.
Profusely Illustrated. Edited by NORMAN MACLEOD, D.D.
YEARLY SUBSCRIPTION, $2.75.

GOOD WORDS is in every respect a first-class monthly, its contributions being from the pens of the most able writers of England. It is now by far the most popular magazine issued in that country, and is already favorably known here. Its contents embrace Novels, Tales, Sketches of Travel, Papers on Science and Art, Essays on Popular Subjects, Poems, etc., by well-known authors.

GOOD WORDS FOR THE YOUNG.
Profusely Illustrated. Edited by GEORGE MACDONALD, LL.D.
YEARLY SUBSCRIPTION, $2.50.

GOOD WORDS FOR THE YOUNG is a beautifully illustrated Magazine for young people, containing Stories, Sketches, Poems, etc., adapted to the comprehension of young readers. In the words of the *Baltimore Statesman*, "We pronounce it unhesitatingly the first of juvenile periodicals. We have seen nothing of its class that can compare with it in the beauty, variety, and good taste of the reading matter, nor that approaches it in the number and excellence of the illustrations."

☞ FOR SALE AT ALL THE BOOK AND NEWS STORES.

The FOUR MAGAZINES, to one address, $10.25 per annum. SPECIMEN NUMBER of any one of above mailed on receipt of 25 cents; or one of each for 75 cts. A FULL PROSPECTUS of the above, with CLUB RATES and PREMIUM LISTS, mailed on application to

J. B. LIPPINCOTT & CO., Publishers,
715 and 717 Market St., Philadelphia.

WASHINGTON HOUSE,

Cor. EIGHTH AND CHURCH STS.,

LYNCHBURG, VIRGINIA.

T. C. S. FURGUSON, Proprietor.

Offers Accommodations to the Traveling Public

Unsurpassed by any Hotel in Virginia.

Low Charges, Good Fare and Careful Attention.

☞ OMNIBUS FREE. ☜

THE ORANGE, ALEXANDRIA AND MANASSAS RAILROAD.

Passing out of Washington City, the main line of this road extends through Piedmont Virginia, celebrated for fertile soil and unsurpassed climate—a district made famous by events of the recent war—Manassas, the Rappahannock, Culpeper, the Rapidan, Orange, Gordonsville, Charlottesville, and the University of Virginia, and to Lynchburg, connecting there to all the South-west.

At Gordonsville, going south, and at Charlottesville, northbound, connection is made with the Chesapeake and Ohio R. R. to *Richmond*, and all points in the Atlantic States south, and westward to Staunton, Lexington, National Bridge, and all the notable Virginia Springs. The Greenbrier White Sulphur is reached by continuous rail in twenty-four hours from New York City.

At Manassas, a branch makes off over a beautiful and fertile country through a gap of the Blue Ridge, and sixty-eight miles up the Valley of Virginia to Harrisonburg, one hundred and forty-five miles from Washington, passing the best farming and grass lands of the State.

The comfort and safety of the trains on this road are well known and appreciated by the traveling public.

May, 1870.   I. M. BROADUS, *G. T. A.*

ANNOUNCEMENT.

The undersigned, Lessees of the

WHITE SULPHUR SPRINGS,

announce that these celebrated Springs, so long and favorably known for their valuable ALTERATIVE WATERS, their charming summer climate, and the large and fashionable crowds that annually resort to them, will be opened for the season of 1870 on the

FIFTEENTH DAY OF MAY.

The location is 2000 feet above the level of the sea, affording entire relief from summer prostrating heats.

Their capacity for accommodation is from 1500 to 2000 persons.

☞ Prof. Rosenberger's Celebrated BAND will be in attendance to enliven the *Lawns* and *Ball-rooms*.

☞ *Masquerade* and *Fancy Balls* will be given as usual through the season.

☞ An extensive LIVERY will be kept on the premises. **HOT AND WARM SULPHUR BATHS,** so efficacious in many cases, always at the command of the visitor.

Neither effort nor expense will be spared to make these Springs merit a patronage as liberal as they have heretofore so constantly received.

☞ The *Chesapeake and Ohio Railroad* is now completed and running to the Springs, so that travelers from every section of the Union can now reach them by continuous railroad lines.

☞ A *Telegraphic* line is in operation to the Springs.

CHARGES FOR THE SEASON.

Board per week $25
    " *month of 30 days* 90
Children and Colored Servants, half price.
White Servants, according to the accommodations furnished.

PEYTONS & CO.

WHITE SULPHUR SPRINGS, W. VA., May 5, 1870.

www.ingramcontent.com/pod-product-compliance
Lightning Source LLC
Chambersburg PA
CBHW022027240426
43667CB00042B/1209